EXPLORING

THE WORLD OF
MATHEMATICS

JOHN HUDSON TINER

EXPLORING
THE WORLD OF MATHEMATICS

First printing: June 2004
Seventh printing: August 2021

Master Books* is a division of the New Leaf Publishing Group, Inc.

ISBN13: 978-0-89051-412-2
ISBN13: 978-1-61458-155-0 (digital)
Library of Congress Number: 2003116034

Interior Design and Layout: Carol and Eric Sawyer of Rose Design, Greenfield Center, NY 12833

Please consider requesting that a copy of this volume be purchased by your local library system.

Printed in the United States of America

Please visit our website for other great titles:
www.masterbooks.com

For information regarding author interviews, please contact the publicity department at (870) 438-5288.

Master Books®
A Division of New Leaf Publishing Group
www.masterbooks.com

Dedication

To Paul Conner Stephens, again.

SURVEY OF SCIENCE HISTORY & CONCEPTS
GRADE 9-12 [1 YEAR / 1 CREDIT]

Students will study four areas of mathematics, physics, biology, and chemistry, gaining an appreciation for how each subject has affected our lives, and the people God revealed wisdom to as they sought to understand Creation.

Exploring the World of Biology

Exploring the World of Mathematics

Exploring the World of Physics

Exploring the World of Chemistry

Table of Contents

Counting the Years

People have been numbering and counting since ancient times. Counting days is mentioned in the first chapter of Genesis: "And there was evening, and there was morning — the first day." The seven days of the creation week are counted in Genesis 1:5–2:2.

For measuring time, people in the ancient world needed an event that repeated itself exactly. It also had to be clearly visible. The sun made a perfect choice for measuring time. Its motion followed a regular path in the sky that anyone could track. The sun rose, wheeled across the sky, and set. Then after a period of darkness it rose again. The time from sunrise to sunrise made one day.

Although people followed the sun to count days, the motion of the sun that they saw was actually due to the earth spinning on its axis. The sun did not go around the

PROBLEMS

1. How can time be measured without a clock or calendar?

2. How did farmers know the best time to plant and harvest crops?

3. How did 11 days vanish?

Can You Propose Solutions?

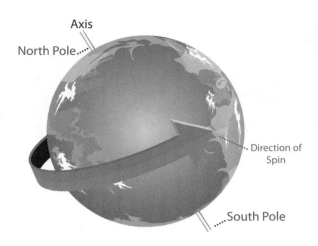

The earth spins on its axis; each complete rotation takes one day.

earth. Instead, the earth rotated on its axis like a top. The sun appeared to move. The time for the earth to make a complete spin gave the sun the apparent motion that marked the passage of one day.

Keeping track of time by days can become cumbersome. Except for small babies, listing a person's age in days gives rise to large numbers. How old is a student who is 4,380 days old? A year is 365 days (for simplification, don't include leap years), so divide 4,380 days by 365 days per year to change days to years. A student who is 4,380 days old is 12 years old: 4,380 days ÷ 365 days per year = 12 years. A person who has lived to be 72 years old would be 26,280 days old: 72 years x 365 days per year = 26,280 days.

Ancient people quickly saw that the moon could be a celestial timekeeper. The moon passed from a particular phase, such as full moon, back to the same phase in about 29.5 days. The word month comes from the word moon.

A month was convenient for measuring longer periods of time. The United States and Canada have four distinct seasons: winter, spring, summer, and autumn. The time from one season to the next was about three moons, or three months. People could also plan events for those nights when the moon was full. The harvest moon was the full moon falling closest to the first day of autumn (about September 21). It gave farmers light to gather crops at night.

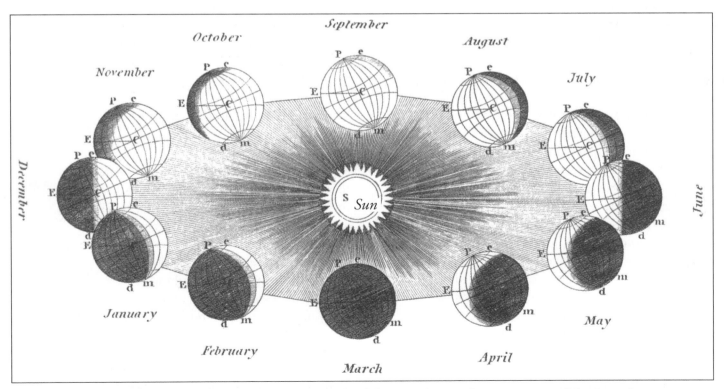

The earth's orbit around the sun and the tilt of the axis create the seasons and the imaginary lines of the equator and the tropics. Each complete revolution takes one year.

(From George Adams Astronomical and Geographical Essays, London 1795)

A lunar calendar is based upon the phases of the moon.

Keeping track of seasons was not an idle pastime for ancient people. Sailors needed to winter in ports to avoid seasonal storms. The Romans sailed the Mediterranean Sea. It was known for stormy weather in the winter. The New Testament describes how a storm destroyed a ship carrying Paul to Rome for trial. The ship's master had refused to stay in the safe harbor for the winter. (Read Acts 27:12–44.)

The seasons are actually caused by the tilt of the earth's axis and its motion around the sun. The tilt makes days and nights of different lengths. During summer, the sun's rays strike the Northern Hemisphere more directly. The length of daylight is longer and the weather is warmer. During winter, the sun is more to the south and its rays strike the Northern Hemispheres at an angle and give less light. The start of winter is the shortest day of the year.

On the first day of summer in the Northern Hemisphere, the sun is at its highest at noon. Shadows of buildings are at their shortest. Ancient people measured a year from the first day of summer to the next.

A year is actually due to the motion of the earth. During a year, the earth makes a complete trip around the sun. A person who is 12 years old has gone around the sun 12 times. A person with an average life expectancy will travel around the sun 72 times in his or her lifetime.

The motions of the earth and moon in relation to the sun give the three easiest ways of measuring time: day, month, and year. A day is the time it takes for the earth to spin once on its axis. The month is the time for the moon to go once around the earth. A year is the time for the earth to go once around the sun.

But all of these measures do not come out evenly when compared with one another. A lunar month is not a whole number of days. It is about 29.5 days long. A solar year is not a whole number of days, either. It is about 365.25 days. Nor is it a whole number of lunar months. Twelve months of 29.5 days gives a year of 354 days: 12 months x 29.5 days per month = 354 days. A lunar year of 12 months is 11 days short of a solar year: 365 days - 354 days = 11 days.

Suppose a farmer enjoyed a bountiful harvest by planting crops on a certain day one year. The farmer would want to repeat the success from one year to the next. He needed a calendar that kept itself in step with the seasons. A calendar that gave the wrong date for the start of spring could lead to disaster. Crops planted too early or too late would die. The farmer's family would face starvation.

A lunar calendar with 12 months of 29.5 days quickly got out of step with the seasons. After one year, it was off by 11 days. After three years, farmers would be planting a month too soon. Over the years, a date in spring would slowly drift into winter. One solution was to insert an extra month about every three years into the calendar.

The Jewish calendar had months based on the moon, but years based on the sun. To keep them in step with one another, they put in an extra month seven times in 19 years.

Some countries ignored the problem entirely. The Babylonians lived along the Tigris and Euphrates Rivers in what is now

Iraq. The Old Testament mentions Babylon. Daniel, for instance, served in the palace of the king of Babylon (Daniel 1:1–7). The Babylonians used 30 days rather than 29.5 days for a month. Their calendar had 12 months of 30 days to give a year of 360 days: 12 months x 30 days per month = 360 days.

All three ways of measuring time — day, month, and year — came out even in the Babylonian calendar. Even parts of years came out as whole number days. A half of a year was 180 days: 360 days per year ÷ 2 = 180 days. A fourth of a year was 90 days: 360 days per year ÷ 4 = 90 days. A sixth of a year was 60 days: 360 days per year ÷ 6 = 60 days. A twelfth of a year was 30 days: 360 days per year ÷ 12 = 30 days.

The Babylonian calendar missed the right time to plant crops by five days every year: 365 days - 360 days = 5 days. Within six years, the calendar slipped when compared to the seasons by a full month. However, the Babylonians were mainly shepherds and people who gathered crops that grew wild. They did not view with alarm the difference between the calendar and the seasons.

Their neighbors, the Egyptians, planted crops. The Egyptians required a calendar that matched the seasons. Farmers in Egypt planted crops right after the Nile River flooded. The flood was very dependable. The river left a rich layer of soil on the farmland after it returned to its banks.

Egyptians predicted the Nile flood by watching the stars. The brightest star in the sky was Sirius, also known as the Dog Star. When it appeared in the east just as the sun was setting in the west, then the flooding of the Nile could be expected. Egyptian astronomers carefully

Living along the Nile River, the Egyptians needed an accurate calendar to predict the time of spring floods.

Why Is a Leap Year So Named?

A year with an extra day is called a leap year. Here's why.

A week has seven days. A year of 365 days has 52 full weeks and one day left over: 365 days ÷ 7 days per week = 52 weeks with a remainder of 1 day.

Because of the remainder of one day, a month that starts on one day of the week this year, will start one day later the next year. For instance, March 1, 2009, is a Sunday; March 1, 2010, is a Monday; March 1, 2011, is a Tuesday, and so on.

Or rather it would be "and so on" if it were not for the extra day in February. The year 2012 is a leap year. Rather than 52 full weeks and one extra day, the leap year has 52 weeks and two extra days: 366 days ÷ 7 days per week = 52 weeks with a remainder of 2 days.

Rather than March 1, 2012, falling on Wednesday, the extra day on February 29 causes March 1, 2012, to fall on Thursday. It skips or leaps over Wednesday. Hence, the name "leap year."

measured the time from the appearing of Sirius to the next appearance of Sirius. They realized that a calendar should have 365 days in a year.

The Egyptians retained the Babylonian calendar of 360 days. To make up for the five lost days, they added five extra days at the end of the year. It was a five-day holiday.

However, the Egyptian calendar had an error that slowly threw the calendar off. A solar year — the time for the earth to go around the sun — is actually 365 days, 5 hours, 48 minutes, 46 seconds. So the Egyptian calendar had a year that was too short by almost six hours, or about ¼ of a day. In four years, the Egyptian calendar would be off by one full day: 4 years x ¼ lost day per year = 1 lost day. In 120 years, the calendar would slip behind the seasons by a full month. It lost a day every four years, and four divided into 120 years gives 30 days: 120 years ÷ 4 years per lost day = 30 lost days.

The Roman calendar was based on the Egyptian calendar, so it lost days against the seasons. When Julius Caesar (100 B.C.–44 B.C.) came into power, the Roman calendar was 80 days behind the seasons. The winter months were falling in the autumn, the autumn months were in the summer and so on. It was a mess. Julius Caesar's astronomers suggested that he remake the calendar. He agreed.

First, he decreed that the next year (what we call 46 B.C.) would be 445 days long to make up the 80 days that the calendar was behind the seasons: 365 days + 80 days = 445 days. It was the longest year in civilized history. After that, years would follow a new calendar.

He set the start of the year as January 1. Before then, different countries started the year at the beginning of different months.

Rather than having five extra days at the end of the year, he spread them throughout the year. The next Roman leader, Augustus Caesar (63 B.C.–B.C. 14), made a few other changes. The final result was seven months with 31 days each, four months with 30 days each. The Romans considered February an unlucky month for some reason. Days were taken away from it so the unlucky month would be only

Names for Months from the Roman Calendar

Most names for months in our calendar are from the Roman calendar. The ancient Roman calendar originally had only 10 months and 304 days. The year began with the month of March. Later, the months of January and February were inserted before March, and the new year began with January.

January was named for Janus. In Roman mythology, he was the keeper of doorways. January was the entrance to the new year. February was from a Roman word meaning "festival." March was named after Mars, the Roman god of war. April came from a Roman word meaning "to open," probably because buds opened in April. May was named after Maia, the mother of Mercury. June was named for Juno, the queen of the gods in Roman mythology. She was portrayed as the protector of women.

In the Roman calendar, months after June had names based on their positions in the original calendar before January and February were inserted: Quintilis (quin, "fifth"), Sextilis (sex, "sixth"), September (sep, "seventh"), October (oct, "eighth"), November (non, "ninth"), and December (dec, "tenth").

Julius Caesar took the month Quintilis and named it July after himself. The next Roman ruler, Augustus Caesar, took the month Sextilis and named it August after himself.

August had only 30 days but July had 31 days.

Augustus took another day from February and added it to August so his month would be as long as the one for Julius Caesar. This left February with 28 days. (Augustus Caesar was the Roman Emperor who decreed that a tax should be taken at the time Jesus was born [Luke 2:1].)

Because of changes made to the calendar, the prefixes of months after August are off by two. September is the 9th month, not the 7th, October is the 10th month, not the 8th, and so on.

Julius Caesar — July is named for him.
(courtesy of Justin D. Paola)

Augustus Caesar — August is named for him.
(courtesy of Justin D. Paola)

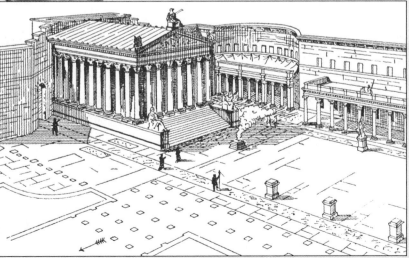

Forum of Augustus

28 days long. This gave a year of 365 days.

Most important of all, Julius Caesar found a way to take care of the annoying ¼ of a day. He decreed that February would have an extra day every four years. It would have 29 days rather than 28 days. This gave the year an average length of 365¼ days. Written as a decimal, ¼ = 0.25. So the year by the new calendar had an average of 365.25 days.

The calendar with the extra day every four years became known as the Julian Calendar. Many countries began using it. The extra day was called a leap day, and the year with the longer February was called a leap year.

A person born on February 29 has an interesting problem when it comes to celebrating a birthday — the birthday comes but once every four years. One day out of every 1,461 days is a leap day: 365 days + 365 days + 365 days + 366 days = 1,461 days. So about one person out of every 1,461 will have a birthday on February 29. A town of 5,000 people is likely to have three or four people with birthdays on a leap day: 5,000 ÷ 1,461 = 3.4.

The Julian calendar did a good job of keeping the seasons and calendar together. However, it still had a slight error. The Julian year was 365¼ days. One-fourth of a day is six hours: 24 hours ÷ 4 = 6 hours. However, the earth takes 365 days, 5 hours, 48 minutes,

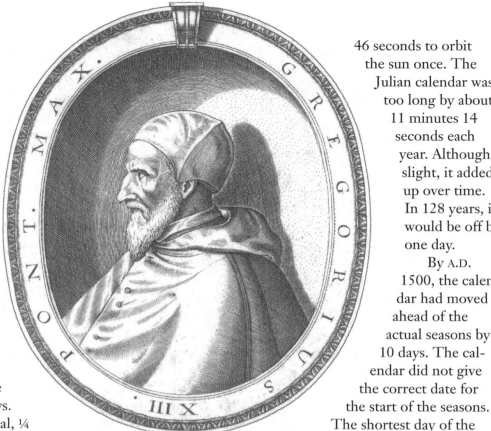

Pope Gregory XIII
(Courtesy of the Smithsonian)

46 seconds to orbit the sun once. The Julian calendar was too long by about 11 minutes 14 seconds each year. Although slight, it added up over time. In 128 years, it would be off by one day.

By A.D. 1500, the calendar had moved ahead of the actual seasons by 10 days. The calendar did not give the correct date for the start of the seasons. The shortest day of the year, the official start of winter, fell on the calendar's date of December 12. The shortest day of the year should fall on December 21. Christmas, according to the calendar, actually fell before the seasonal start of winter. If something wasn't done, Christmas would slowly gain until it occurred in summer.

A new calendar was designed to remove the error. The new calendar was named the "Gregorian calendar" after Pope Gregory XIII. He approved the changes for use by the Catholic Church in 1582.

First, the calendar had to be put back in step with the seasons. Thursday, October 4 on the new Gregorian calendar was immediately followed by Friday, October 15. The calendar skipped the days from October 5 through October 14. Ten whole days vanished.

Next, the Julian calendar had put in too many leap days. Every year evenly divisible by four received a leap day. The Julian calendar had 100 leap days every 400 years. The new Gregorian calendar removed three of those leap days. The year 1600 had a leap day. But the new calendar removed leap days from the years 1700, 1800 and 1900.

In other words, the Gregorian calendar had a leap day every four years, except every 100 years it took one out, but every 400 years it put one back in. The years 2000 and 2100 are both evenly divisible by four. The year 2000 had a leap day, but 2100 will not have the extra day.

Protestant countries delayed changing to the Gregorian calendar. But in 1752, Great Britain and most of the English-speaking countries switched over to the Gregorian calendar. Because of the delay, the error had grown to 11 days. England matched the seasons with the calendar by skipping 11 days from September 3 through 13. The day after September 2 became September 14.

People who went to sleep on the evening of September 2, 1752, woke up on the morning of September 14. Many people became upset because 11 days had disappeared overnight. It did cause confusion. Some people had reason to complain. Landlords demanded to be paid a month's rent during September although it had only 20 days. Workers, in turn, demanded that their employers pay wages for the days that had disappeared.

It caused confusion in other ways, too. How should birthdays be celebrated? George Washington was born on February 11 in 1732

HEBREW/JEWISH CALENDAR OF THE OLD TESTAMENT				
Hebrew Month	Our Month	Farm Season	Climate	Festivals
Nisan	March/April	Barley Harvest	Latter Rains	Religious New Year Passover First Fruits
Iyyar	April/May	General Harvest	Latter Rains	
Sivan	May/June	Wheat Harvest Vine Dressing	Dry Season	Pentecost
Tammuz	June/July	Early Grape Harvest	Dry Season	
Ab	July/August	Harvest: Grapes, Figs, Olives	Dry Season	
Elul	August/Sept	Summer Fruit	Dry Season	
Tishri	Sept/October	Plowing, Olive Harvest		Civil New Year Day of Atonement Tabernacles
Marchesvan	Oct/Nov	Olive Harvest, Grain Planting	Early Rains	
Chislev	Nov/Dec	Grain Planting	Early Rains	Dedication of Temple
Tebeth	Dec/January	Late Planting, Spring Growth	Rainy Season	
Shebat	January/Feb	Late Planting, Winter Figs	Rainy Season	
Adar	Feb/March	Pulling Flax, Almonds Bloom	Rainy Season	
Adar Sheni (Second Adar)	This additional month was added to the end of the year 7 times every 19 years to to keep in step with calendars based on the sun.			

A solar year is 365.2422 days or 365 days, 5 hours, 48 minutes, 46 seconds in length.

Type	Average Length	Approximate Error
Babylonian	360 days	5.25 days too short every year
Egyptian	365 days	1 day too short every 4 years
Julian	365.25 days	3 days too long every 400 years
Gregorian	365.2425 days	1 day too long every 3,323 years

under the Julian calendar. The British colonies in America switched to the new calendar in 1752. Washington changed his birthday to February 22. This matched his true age of 20 years. For a time, people gave dates on both calendars. For instance, Washington listed his birthday as February 11 Old Style and February 22 New Style.

Some religious groups chose to observe religious events on the old calendar. The Greek Orthodox Church (also known as the Eastern Orthodox Church) continues to use the Julian calendar. They observe Christmas on December 25 of their calendar, although it is January 6 by the Gregorian calendar. The Jewish religion continues to follow a lunar calendar in which an extra month is added about every three years.

However, countries around the world use the Gregorian calendar for most commercial activities. It is the one used in the United States.

It is very exact, but not perfect. It, too, is slightly too long. Every 400 years it has 303 regular years with a total of 110,595 days (303 years x 365 days per year = 110,595 days) and 97 leap years with a total of 35,502 days (97 years x 366 days per year = 35,502 days). In 400 years it has 146,097 days: 110,595 days + 35,502 days = 146,097 days. Dividing the total days, 146,097, by the total years, 400, gives the average number of days per year: 146,097 days ÷ 400 years = 365.2425 days per year.

The Gregorian year of 365.2425 days works out to be 365 days, 5 hours, 49 minutes, 12 seconds. But the year measured by how long the earth takes to orbit the sun is 365.2422 days or 365 days, 5 hours, 48 minutes, 46 seconds. The Gregorian calendar is still too long by 26 seconds per year.

How long will it take for the 26 seconds to make a difference? In about 3,323 years, the Gregorian calendar will have run ahead of the seasons by a full day. Around the year A.D. 5329 something will need to be done to correct the Gregorian calendar.

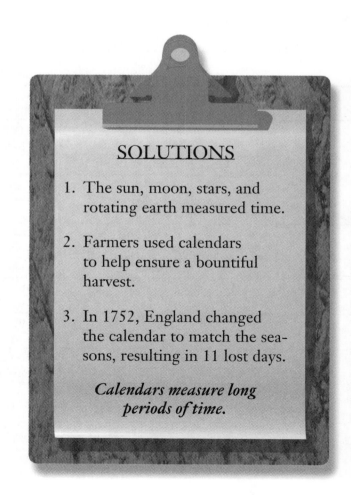

SOLUTIONS

1. The sun, moon, stars, and rotating earth measured time.

2. Farmers used calendars to help ensure a bountiful harvest.

3. In 1752, England changed the calendar to match the seasons, resulting in 11 lost days.

Calendars measure long periods of time.

T F   1. The extra day, or leap day, every four years was put in the calendar to honor Augustus Caesar.

T F   2. The Gregorian calendar has 100 leap days every 400 years.

       3. What is the main reason to have leap days?

A B C D   4. The first calendar with a leap day every four years was the one (A. authorized by Julius Caesar   B. used by the American colonies after 1752   C. used by the Babylonians   D. used by the Egyptians).

Matching

5. _____ day   a. due to the tilt of the earth's axis, equal to three months

6. _____ week   b. earth revolves around the sun once

7. _____ month   c. earth rotates on its axis once

8. _____ season   d. moon revolves around the earth once

9. _____ year   e. seven days

Try Your Math

10. The Bible says that Methuselah died at age 969 years (Gen. 5:27). What would be that age in days? (Ignore leap years.)

11. Using the Babylonian calendar of 360 days in a year, how many days are in one-third of a year; one-fifth of a year; one-twentieth of a year; one-sixtieth of a year?

12. Find the population of your city and calculate how many people are likely to have a birthday on February 29.

$$\tan\phi = \frac{X_C}{R}$$

$$E = \Delta mc^2$$

$$\sqrt{a^2 + b^2}$$

Counting the Hours

Megan's ride home on the bus took 25 minutes. The second she stepped off, snow began falling. Spring would arrive in only two weeks, but winter continued to hang on. The night promised to be cold. Megan lived in a big house that had been built more than a century ago. Its furnace — two decades old — threatened to quit at any moment. She looked at her watch. It showed 4:15 p.m. In an hour, her friend Juliann would be over to spend the weekend.

Notice the number of words that refer to time in the paragraph above: minutes, second, spring, weeks, winter, night, century, decades, moment, p.m., hour, and weekend.

Today, our lives are marked off in seconds, minutes, and hours. Clocks, watches, and electronic gadgets constantly remind us of the time. School bells dismiss students from class. Stores

PROBLEMS

1. How can the sun measure hours?

2. How can sand measure time?

3. How can extremely short periods of time be measured?

Can You Propose Solutions?

open for their customers at a set time. Many games give players only a limited amount of time to score.

But for most of history, people seldom needed short divisions of time. The majority of people lived in the country. They measured time by days, weeks, months, or years. Farm families worked from early morning to late evening. They estimated the time of day by the sun.

Farmers needed an accurate calendar far more than they needed an accurate clock. A calendar told them when to plant their crops. It helped them keep track of market days and other special events. Astronomers and mathematicians made calendars by watching events that could be readily seen from earth.

The shortest naturally occurring period of time was the day, which could be measured from sunrise on one day to sunrise on the next. The apparent motion of the sun was caused by the rotation of the earth on its axis.

But no natural events marked off periods of time shorter than a day. Humans invented hours, minutes, and seconds and the timepieces to measure them.

The ancient Egyptians invented the hour. They thought of the lighted part of the day as having 12 divisions, or hours. They used a sundial to measure daylight hours. At first, the sundial was merely a pole set up in the ground so that it would cast a shadow. Later, they built it with a raised crosspiece at one end of a long base. It looked like a T standing at one end of a flat board. The sun cast a shadow of the crosspiece on the base. The shadow moved along the base because of the daily passage

Roman officer and an hourglass

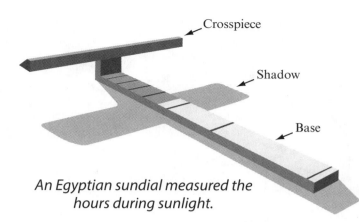

An Egyptian sundial measured the hours during sunlight.

of the sun. Lines marked on the base showed the hours.

The Egyptian sundial did not keep good time. The shadow moved more rapidly in early morning and late evening than at midday. In addition, summer days had more daylight than winter days. An hour in summer was longer than an hour in winter. The sundial only worked when exposed to sunlight. It could not be used indoors, on cloudy days, or at night. The Egyptians ignored keeping time at night. Only later did people begin thinking of the night as also having 12 hours.

The military knew that soldiers could not remain alert all night. They arranged for soldiers to stand guard only a few hours at a time. They called these duty times watches. Most watches lasted for three or four hours. In Roman times, a watch began at sunset. The second and third watches fell in the middle of the night. Soldiers found it difficult to stay awake.

The Bible mentions the fact that late-night watches could be difficult. For instance, Jesus says, "It will be good for those servants whose master finds them ready, even if he comes in the second or third watch of the night" (Luke 12:38).

For measuring time at night, the Romans used a variety of devices to measure time, including the hourglass. It kept time indoors or outdoors, day or night. The Romans made an hourglass with two narrow-mouth bottles. They filled one of the bottles with pure, dry sand. Then they placed the bottles together so they touched at the mouth. A wooden frame tied with cords held the bottles against one another. When upended, the sand trickled

Clockmaker's shop in the 1600s

from the top bottle through the narrow opening into the bottom bottle.

Putting in the right amount of sand caused the top bottle to empty in exactly an hour. The Roman government used an hourglass to time how long a senator could speak.

Despite its name, an hourglass could be modified to measure other intervals of time. The British Navy designed hourglasses that marked half-hours. A young sailor had the job of watching the hourglass. When time ran out, he would turn it over and then ring a bell. The ringing of the bell every thirty minutes helped lookouts know how long they had been on duty.

The British Navy had watches four hours long. The first watch began at midnight. Suppose a sailor reported for the midnight watch. After thirty minutes he would hear the first bell and know that he had been on duty for one-half hour. Two bells marked the end of the first hour. Finally, after four hours — eight bells — his watch ended. Another sailor came on duty to take the second watch. A new series of bells began. Suppose a sailor on the second watch sighted a ship at three bells. What time would it be? The second watch began at 4:00 a.m. Three bells was 1½ hours, so he saw the ship at 5:30 a.m.

Hourglasses continued to be used into modern times. For instance, in the 1800s, Queen Victoria of England believed a sermon should last no more than 30 minutes. She had a 30-minute hourglass made. During chapel service on Sunday, the preacher turned it over to start the sand falling. He had to finish his sermon before all of the sand had fallen to the bottom.

Even today, some games have sandglasses that time how long a player has to make a move or answer a question.

In the Middle Ages (about 475 to 1450), most villages had a church with a bell tower and steeple. The bell rang to call people to the church service. It also rang to mark the passing hours. The villagers used the sound of the bell as their clock. The word clock is from a Dutch word meaning bell.

Starting in the 1300s, craftsmen built the first mechanical clocks. A falling weight attached to a cord turned a drum. A series of large, wooden gears transferred the motion of the rotating drum to the clock face. Clocks were installed in towers at city halls and in the bell towers at churches.

Mechanical clocks with falling weights had a special part called an escapement. It kept the weight from falling faster and faster. The escapement rocked back and forth. First, it rocked one way to release the gear attached to the weight. The weight fell. Then the escapement rocked the other way and stopped the weight.

A clock measures time by counting regularly occurring events. The first clocks had nothing to keep the escapements rocking at set rates. They kept faulty time. Even the best clocks gained or lost as much as one hour each day. Their builders equipped them only with hour hands.

The Italian scientist Galileo discovered that a swinging pendulum had a regular back and forth motion. A simple pendulum had a weight tied to a string. A string exactly 39.14 inches long gave the pendulum a period of one second. The weight took exactly one second to make a swing from one side to another. Dutch scientist Christian Huygens discovered how a pendulum could keep an escapement working regularly. He built the first pendulum clock in 1658. His clock measured hours, minutes, and seconds.

Of course, time can be measured informally. A person may say "it happened in a heartbeat." This means a very short period of time, or about a second. Measuring time by counting heartbeats is not very accurate. The heart rate can change as one becomes active. A person doing brisk exercise may double his or her heart rate.

Not only does the heart rate change as a person exercises, but it also differs from one person to the next. A healthy body has a slower heart rate. Astronauts and athletes are in tiptop condition. They may have heart rates of about 52 beats per minute when they are at rest. Average people have heart rates of about 70 times a minute.

Animals have heart rates that vary even more. The shrew is a small, highly active animal about the size of a mouse. Its heart beats 700 times a minute. It is interesting to calculate how many times a person's heart beats in a lifetime and compare it to the number of heartbeats of animals.

	beats per min	maximum lifetime in years	approximate beats per lifetime
shrew	700	1.5	552,258,000
cat	130	20	1,367,000,000
horse	25	40	525,960,000
elephant	30	75	1,104,516,000
human	70	115	4,233,978,000

The beats are calculated by simple multiplication. For the shrew, 700 beats per min x 60 min per hr x 24 hr per day x 365.25 days per yr x 1.5 yr = 552,258,000 beats per lifetime. The other beats per lifetime are found in the same way. A shrew's heart beats about ½ billion times, as does the heart of a horse. The cat and elephant have hearts that beat between 1 and 1½ billion times.

According to medical records, the oldest living humans usually reach a maximum age of 115 years. In 115 years, a human heart beats 4,233,978,000 times, or about 4¼ billion times. Even for a lifetime of 72 years (which is more common), the human heart beats more than 2½ billion times. That is twice as many beats as the hearts of any other mammal.

At first, clock faces had three separate dials. One showed hours and had the numerals 1 through 12. Another dial showed the minutes and was marked from 1 through 60. A third dial, also marked 1 through 60, showed the seconds.

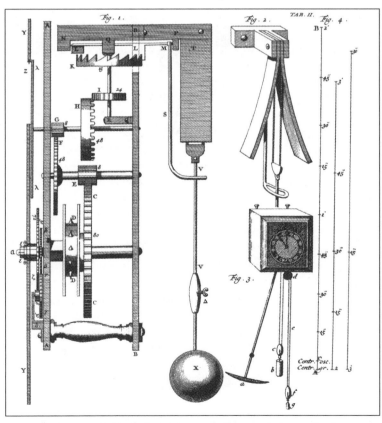

Diagram of Christian Huygens's pendulum clock, the first accurate clock

Soon, however, clockmakers learned how to combine all three hands on one dial. (Sometimes they put the display for seconds on a smaller dial. It was usually above the six at the bottom of the clock face.)

A young child who learned to tell time from the clock face could claim a real accomplishment. Numbers around the edge of the clock face (1 through 12) gave the hour by the hour hand. They also showed the minutes by the minute hand. An hour hand pointing to three meant three hours, but the minute hand pointing to three meant 15 minutes.

Suppose the hour hand was between 3 and 4 and the minute hand at 7. To fully read the time, a person had to quickly figure out that the time was 35 minutes past 3 o'clock. The word o'clock is a shortened form of the phrase "of the clock." Learning to tell time by a clock face was complicated by the use of phrases such as "half past three" (three thirty, 3:30), "five 'til six" (five fifty-five, 5:55), or "a quarter after six" (six fifteen, or 6:15.)

Today, clocks and watches are of two types: analog and digital. A clock that shows time with hour and minute hands moving around a dial is an analog clock. An analog device uses moving parts that continuously show information. A second hand sweeping around a clock face is a good example of analog movement.

A clock that shows time by changing numerals is a digital clock. A digital device shows information in steps. A display constantly changing numbers to show seconds on a digital clock is a good example of a digital display. It jumps forward a second at a time.

Digital clocks became popular after the invention of microchips in the 1950s. Digital clocks display time directly in numerals that specify hours, minutes, and sometimes seconds.

Reading time on a digital clock is far easier than reading an analog clock. In addition, digital clocks eliminate phrases such as "half past," "quarter 'til," and "minutes 'til." A digital

Minutes and Seconds

A second is slightly less than the time between average heartbeats. However, the second was probably not based on the human heartbeat. The idea of 60 seconds in a minute and 60 minutes in an hour came from Egyptian astronomer Ptolemy. He lived more than 2,000 years ago. Still earlier, the Babylonians had divided a circle into 360 equal parts called degrees. Angles are measured in degrees. The angle from the horizon to directly overhead is 90 degrees. A complete circle has 360 degrees.

Ptolemy divided each degree into 60 smaller parts. Latin was the language spoken by the ancient Romans. They called these 60 divisions *pars minutae primae,* which means "first small parts." The word *minutae* was shortened to "minute," mean-

ing small. Ptolemy also divided each minute into 60 *pars minutae secundae,* meaning "second small parts." The word *secundae* became our word second.

Ptolemy divided a circle into degrees, minutes, and seconds. Sixty minutes made a degree, and 60 seconds made a minute. The number 60 found ready use in the ancient world. The number systems they used could not handle fractions very well. But 60 could be divided by many other numbers without a remainder: 2, 3, 4, 5, 6, 10, 12, 15, 20, 30, and 60. This reduced the need for fractions. When shorter divisions of the time were needed, it was natural to also divide the hour into minutes and seconds.

display showing 5:35 is usually read as "five thirty-five" and not "twenty-five 'til six."

Even with digital displays, keeping track of the right time has pitfalls. In the United States, 12 hours are used to display time although there are 24 hours in a day. An expression such as "meet me tomorrow at 8 o'clock" can be misunderstood. The time could be 8:00 in the morning or 8:00 at night.

In the United States, the day begins at midnight. To avoid confusion, the 12 hours from midnight to noon are labeled a.m. The 12 hours from noon to midnight are labeled p.m. The abbreviations a.m. and p.m. stand for ante meridiem and post meridiem.

Meridians are imaginary lines on the earth's surface that pass through the North and South Poles. As the earth rotates, the sun crosses each meridian. In any particular location, when the sun passes directly over the meridian, then the time is twelve noon. Before that, the sun is in the morning sky and has not yet passed over the meridian. It is ante meridiem, or a.m. Ante means before and meridiem is an older form of the word meridian. When the sun passes across the meridian, then the time is post meridiem (post means after), or p.m.

The day starts at midnight, so 12:00 a.m. is midnight. The afternoon hours start at noon, so 12:00 p.m. is noon. However, not everyone knows these facts. A time of 12:00 a.m. could be confused for noon when it actually means midnight. Most people say 12 noon rather than 12:00 p.m. to avoid confusion. Midnight is given as 12 midnight rather than 12:00 a.m.

Once the industrial revolution began in the late 1700s, the clock began to govern people's daily work schedules. David Livingstone (1813–1873) was a doctor, explorer, and missionary to Africa. He grew up in Scotland at a time when children often worked in factories. At age ten, he began working in a mill that wove cotton thread into fabric. His day at the mill began at 6 a.m. and ended at 8 p.m. The mill gave thirty minutes off for breakfast and

The Royal Observatory at Greenwich is the prime meridian of the world, the line of zero longitude.

an hour break for lunch. How many hours did he work each day?

One way to solve the problem is to remember that from 6 a.m. to 6 p.m. is 12 hours. By staying on the job until 8 p.m., he would have worked another two hours. His day lasted 14 hours. He was released from work for 1½ hours for meals. Subtracting 1½ hours from 14 hours gives 12½ hours. He worked 12½ hours a day. (After that, he also attended two hours of school.)

An easier way to work the problem is to use military time, also known as 24-hour time. The military uses a 24-hour day. Five thirty in the morning, 5:30 a.m., is 0530 hours. Five thirty in the afternoon, 5:30 p.m., is 1730 hours. Any p.m. time is changed to military time by adding 1200 to it. For instance, 8:00 p.m. is 2000 hours: 1200 + 800 = 2000. David Livingstone's day began at 0600 and ended at 2000.

Standard time zones were another improvement in keeping time. Many cities had a large clock on the courthouse tower. This clock was adjusted to local time at noon. People would set their clocks and watches by the official time of the courthouse clock.

As the apparent motion carried the sun across the United States, each town had a different local time. Noon for a town 15 miles to the west would occur one minute later.

Some towns were off even more because they did not use any official time. Instead of using the sun, some people set their watches at

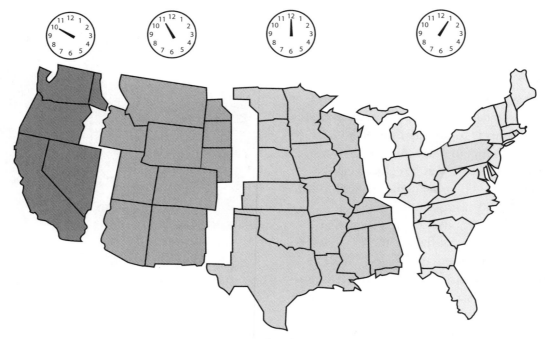

Time zones in the United States

the sounding of the noon whistle at the local factory. The person blowing the noon whistle used his own watch that often did not keep good time.

Towns only a few miles apart could have clocks that differed by 10 minutes or more. Differences in local time did not matter when people traveled by horses or riverboats. Travel between towns took so long that clocks a few minutes in error with one another would not be noticed.

In the 1800s, railroads began running between cities. Passengers found it difficult to meet train schedules. Also, trains shared the same track. Keeping clocks on the same time over a wide area became important to avoid accidents.

In 1883, the United States and Canada adopted a system for standard time. Instead of using a different meridian for each city, they divided the continent into four time zones. All cities in the same time zones set their clocks to noon based on the central meridian. Rather than watching the sun or listening for the noon whistle, official time was kept by the Naval Observatory in Washington, D.C. They flashed a signal of the correct time across the nation by telegraph. Clocks inside the same time zone read the same time.

The lines between time zones were not straight. They zigzagged to avoid running through large cities. Otherwise, people living in the same city would have a major problem keeping time straight — friends on the other side of the city would have time that differed by an hour.

The continental United States has four standard time zones: Eastern (EST), Central (CST), Mountain (MST), and Pacific (PST). The rotation of the earth makes the sun appear to rise in the east. An event broadcast by television that starts at 6:00 a.m. EST would be seen at 5:00 a.m. CST.

Other countries also began using standard time zones. Today, the world is divided into 24 time zones. Each one is 15 degrees of longitude wide, or $\frac{1}{24}$ of the distance around the earth. The actual boundaries vary considerably so entire countries can be in the same time zone. For instance, the Central Time Zone of the United States is also used by most of Mexico and the seven countries in Central America.

Crossing a time zone line going west gives a time one hour earlier. If the time is 12:00 noon on the east side of the time zone line, then the time is 11:00 a.m. on the west side. People traveling west set their watches back so they say they have gained an hour. Crossing a time zone line going east gives a time one hour later. A watch set at 12:00 noon is changed to 1:00 p.m. People say they have lost an hour.

Imagine a fast jet that can travel at 1,000 miles per hour. It leaves the East Coast at 12:00 noon on Tuesday and flies west across the United States. The jet crosses a time zone every hour, so it is 12:00 noon all the way across the nation. An aircraft that continues to fly west will leave North America and fly over the Pacific Ocean. The time will still be 12:00 noon.

If the jet continued to stay even with the sun, then it would be noon all along its flight. But it would not forever stay 12:00 noon on Tuesday. When the jet crossed the International Date Line, the day would change to Wednesday. The International Date Line is an imaginary north-south line that runs through the Pacific Ocean. Rather than changing an hour from one side to the other, an entire day is gained or lost.

The use of standards is important in making measurement. A standard is an agreed-on quantity that does not change. For instance, until the 1900s, the day served as the standard for time. A day was defined as the average time for the earth to rotate on its axis once in relation to the sun. All other measures of time derived from it. An hour was 1/24 of a day. The minute and second were derived from the day, too.

Scientists, however, were not certain that the earth's rotation could be trusted not to change. They knew that tides acted against the rotation of the earth. The heaps of water pulled up by the gravitation of the moon and sun struck the shoreline. The tides acted as a brake to slow the earth.

Highly accurate clocks showed that the earth's rotation was not uniform. The discrepancy was small, however. Although it averages out over time, the rotation of the earth can change by as much as four to five thousandths of a second every day. For ordinary affairs, that would not matter, but for scientists, it posed a serious problem. They had defined the second and other measures of time with the day as a

Atomic Clocks

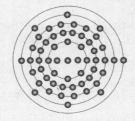

Diagram of a cesium atom

By the 1950s, it became possible to build clocks accurate enough to measure the small irregularities in the earth's rotation. The key to making an accurate clock was to regulate it with precisely regular events. Most modern watches used quartz crystals to control their movements. An electric spark that passed through the quartz crystal caused the crystal to expand and contract. The expansion and contraction, or vibration, was very regular. When put in an electronic circuit, the quartz crystal vibrated about 100,000 times a second. Clocks and watches with a quartz timer were first made in the 1940s. They were extremely accurate. They had an error of about one second every 10 years.

In 1959, scientists at Harvard University built the first atomic clock. It proved to be remarkably accurate. It used the vibration of a cesium atom to mark time. During one second, the cesium atom vibrated 9,192,631,770 times; that is, 9 billion, 192 million, 631 thousand, 770 times. The latest cesium clocks can keep time accurate to billionths of a second. They have an error of about one second every million years.

standard. But the day had proved to be unacceptable as a time standard.

In 1967, scientists from 40 nations met in Paris. They decided to use the second as the time standard. They defined the second as

The starting point for years

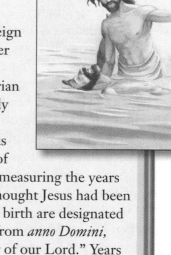

A time measuring system has to have a starting point. The day is measured from midnight. Years are measured from midnight on January 1. Longer periods of time are given as A.D. or B.C. These are references to the birth of Jesus Christ.

Until about the 1500s, people counted years based on the king who ruled at the time: For instance, the Bible, in the Gospel of Luke, describes the year John the Baptist began preaching as "the fifteenth year of the reign of Tiberius Caesar" (Luke 3:1).

Counting years by different kings can be confusing. The 15th year of the reign of the king of one country might be entirely different from the reign of the king of another country.

The new Gregorian calendar also officially changed how years were numbered. Jesus was called the King of kings. People began measuring the years from the date they thought Jesus had been born. Years after His birth are designated A.D. The letters are from *anno Domini,* meaning "in the year of our Lord." Years before His birth are given the letters B.C., which mean "before Christ."

measured by 9,192,631,770 ticks of the cesium clock. Other units of time were defined from the second. A day was defined as 86,400 seconds: 60 sec/min x 60 min/hr x 24 hr/day = 86,400 seconds. (The slash mark, /, is read as "per." 60 sec/min is read "60 seconds per minute.")

People do need to measure intervals of time less than a second and greater than a year. For instance, when scientists averaged the earth's rotation over several years, they found that it was slowing by 16 milliseconds per millennium. A millisecond ($\frac{1}{1000}$ second) is a very short period of time, while a millennium (1,000 years) is a very long period of time.

Time shorter than a second is given by decimal fractions. High school track events are usually timed to tenths of a second, while Olympic events are measured in hundredths of seconds. For instance, at the start of the year 2000, the record time for the 100-meter dash was 9.79 seconds.

Scientists use even smaller measures of time. A millisecond is one thousandth of a second, 0.001 second. A microsecond is one millionth of a second, 0.000001 second. A nanosecond is one billionth of a second, 0.000000001 second.

For longer periods, years are grouped by powers of ten. A decade is 10 years. The American census, or numbering of the people, takes place every 10 years. Ten decades (100 years) is a century. Because of better health care more and more people are living to be 100 years old. A person that old is called a centenarian. Ten centuries (1,000 years) is a millennium. The prefix *milli* actually means one-thousandth, but it is used to mean 1,000 in this case.

SOLUTIONS

1. Sundials measure time by the shadow cast by the sun.

2. Hourglasses measure short periods of time by falling sand.

3. Clocks with vibrating crystals or atoms measure fractions of seconds.

Timepieces measure time shorter than a day.

A B C D   1.   The shortest naturally occurring period of time that ancient people could observe was the (A. day   B. hour   C. week   D. year).

T F   2.   The Egyptians divided daylight into 8 to 12 hours depending on whether it was winter or summer.

A B C D   3.   The inventors of the hourglass were the (A. Babylonians B. British Navy   C. Egyptians   D. Romans).

A B   4.   A watch with a sweep second hand is known as (A. an analog B. a digital) watch.

T F   5.   Meridians are imaginary lines going around the earth parallel to the equator.

A B C D   6.   Military time has hours numbered from 0000 to (A. 0400   B. 1200 C. 2400   D. 3600).

A B C D   7.   Time zones were introduced when it became common to travel by (A. airplanes   B. ox carts   C. ships   D. trains).

A B   8.   The International date line is in the (A. Atlantic   B. Pacific) ocean.

A B   9.   Atomic clocks proved that the earth's rotation (A. is   B. is not) uniform.

A B C   10.   The United States became an independent nation in 1776. In 1976, the country celebrated the fact that the United States was two (A. decades   B. centuries   C. millenniums) old.

Try Your Math

11.   Assume that the first four-hour watch began at midnight. What time would it be at five bells on the second watch?

12.   Feel your pulse at the wrist and count the number of beats in a minute. Calculate the number of times your heart beats in a day.

13.   An office job is often described as working from 9 to 5. This means 9:00 a.m. to 5:00 p.m. How many hours is this?

14.   At 4:00 p.m., a family on vacation drives from Mountain Standard Time into Central Standard Time. Should their watches be set one hour earlier to 3:00 p.m. or one hour later to 5:00 p.m.?

$$\tan\phi = \frac{X_C}{R}$$

$$E = \Delta mc^2$$

$$L = 2\pi f L$$

$$\sqrt{a^2 + b^2}$$

23

Muddled Measuring

Which weighs more: a pound of gold or a pound of feathers? This riddle is a trick question. Gold weighs far more than an equal volume of feathers. But the question refers to equal weights — a pound of gold and a pound of feathers. The correct answer is that they both weigh the same.

But even that answer needs an explanation. To understand why, think about the system of weights and measures used in the United States. The weights of common things such as meat, potatoes, and gumdrops are measured in ounces, pounds, and tons. These weights are part of the avoirdupois (AV-er-de-POIZ) system of weights, also called the Customary System. An avoirdupois or Customary pound has 16 ounces.

However, not all things are measured in the Customary System. Jewelers use a system of weights known as the troy

PROBLEMS

1. Why did the Mars Climate Orbiter crash into Mars?

2. Why are standards important for commerce between nations?

3. What do the span, hand, and fathom have in common?

Can You Propose Solutions?

Artist's conception of the Mars Climate Orbiter

system. A troy pound contains only 12 troy ounces.

A pound of feathers measured in the Customary System weighs 16 ounces. A pound of gold measured in the troy system weighs 12 ounces. An avoirdupois pound of feathers is heavier than a troy pound of gold!

A mile is 5,280 feet — usually. But the Customary System has two types of miles, one for land and one for sea. The land mile, officially known as a statute mile, is 5,280 feet. The sea mile, known as a nautical mile, is 6,076 feet. An ocean voyage of 3,000 nautical miles covers more distance than a road trip of 3,000 statue miles.

How about capacity? Which is more: a quart of strawberries or a quart of milk? A dry quart for measuring strawberries is about 16 percent bigger than a liquid quart for measuring milk. England also has a liquid quart, and it is 20 percent bigger than the United States liquid quart. A liquid pint contains 16 liquid ounces. If you buy a bottle of ketchup marked 16 ounces, then is this 16 ounces by weight or 16 ounces by capacity? They aren't the same.

Agreeing on the same system of measurement is important. For instance, in 1998, NASA (National Aeronautics and Space Administration) launched the Mars Climate Orbiter to photograph the clouds, dust storms, and atmosphere of Mars. The unmanned spacecraft appeared to be following the right course. It reached the planet in September 1999. Instead of going into orbit around Mars, the Climate Orbiter burned up in the Martian atmosphere. An investigation showed the disturbing reason.

Engineers on earth radioed messages to the ship to control its rocket engines. They programmed thrust in newtons, a unit of force in the metric system. But a different group of scientists calculated the force needed. They sent their answer to the flight engineers in English pounds. The difference sent the spacecraft 60 miles off course by the time it reached Mars. The heat of friction from striking the Martian atmosphere destroyed the multi-million dollar spacecraft. The engineers and scientists had used different units of measure.

Standards for weights and measures arose as a practical matter for buying and selling

Merchants used balance scales to sell their products by weight.

a pound of beans, the shopkeeper put a pound weight on one pan. Then the shopkeeper poured beans into the pan on the other side until they balanced. A pound weight kept by one shopkeeper might be different from the pound weight kept by another shopkeeper. Variation of measurements from city to city and from country to country led to arguments and confusion.

People from neighboring cities who needed to weigh items had to agree on a standard. They agreed to use the weight of a barley grain. This standard weight was called, reasonably enough, a grain. A barley grain was tiny, and it did not weigh much.

People measured the weight of expensive items such as perfume, spices, or gemstones with grains. They placed the item to be weighed in one pan and added barley grains to the other until the pans balanced.

Troyes, a city in France, had a large trade fair each year. People traveled to Troyes from all over Europe to buy and sell goods. Merchants at Troyes used the grain as a standard unit of measure. They defined a troy ounce as 480 grains. The troy ounce became the first standard for weight. It was named for Troyes, France. Twelve troy ounces made a troy pound.

products. Shopkeepers kept a balance scale to measure weight. It worked like a teeter-totter. A pan hung from either side of a rod that pivoted in the middle. When a customer ordered

Standards are Important

Standard weights make it easier for people from different countries to trade goods with one another. Governments have a role in promoting business by passing laws requiring merchants to use standard weights and to be honest with their customers.

Ancient Israel had laws governing standards of measure. "Do not have two differing weights in your bag — one heavy, one light. Do not have two differing measures in your house — one large, one small. You must have accurate and honest weights and measures, so that you may live long in the land the LORD your God is giving you" (Deuteronomy 25:13–15; NIV). And in Proverbs 20:10, Solomon wrote, "Differing weights and differing measures — the LORD detests them both."

Merchants made exact duplicates of the official troy standard ounce and carried them throughout Europe. Europeans settled all over the world and brought the troy system with them. After America became independent, the United States Mint stamped out silver dollars that contained a troy ounce of silver.

Druggists who prepared and sold drugs used the troy grain, ounce, and pound. For smaller measures, they also used drams (60 grains) and scruples (20 grains.) By law, official troy standard weights had to exactly match the one kept in a vault in France. Making the weights was expensive. Druggists with a full set of weights were considered particularly honest. But those without the weights were described as "having no scruples." The word unscrupulous is still used today to describe a dishonest person.

Poor shopkeepers could not afford to equip their scales with official troy standard weights. A more rough and ready system arose among farmers and shopkeepers who bought and sold less expensive goods. They needed to weigh common, heavier items such as grain, flour, potatoes, or coal. The system they used became known as the avoirdupois system. Avoirdupois is from a French word meaning "weighty things." A weight marked as a pound might be slightly more or less than a pound. But most customers did not mind because they bought large amounts of inexpensive goods. The slight variation made no big difference, especially if the shopkeeper gave them a fair price.

Over time, then, three different systems came into common use. Jewelers used the troy system. Druggists used the apothecary (uh-poth-uh-KA-ree) system, which was based on the troy system. Apothecary is an older name for druggist. The word means storeroom clerk. Ordinary merchants used the avoirdupois, or Customary System. Imagine the confusion that the different weights could have. A jeweler, druggist, and merchant could weigh the same item, and each one could give an answer in different units.

Diamonds, Gold, and the Carat

People from the Arab world who traded in gems and precious metals introduced the carat as a standard of weight. The carat may have been the weight of a particular type of bean. However, the troy system set it equal to 24 grains. A common gold coin in use at that time weighed 24 grains. But gold was a soft metal. It wore away easily. People who minted gold coins mixed in copper to make the coins harder. A gold coin that weighed 24 grains might contain only 14 grains of gold. Goldsmiths labeled the gold content as 14-carat gold. Today, the carat is used to describe the ratio of gold to a cheaper metal. Pure gold is 24-carat gold. A 12-carat gold chain is only one-half gold by weight: 12/24 = 1/2.

Dealers in gemstones also used the carat to measure the weight of diamonds and other gems. A 142-carat diamond weighed a Customary ounce. When people speak of ounces or pounds without saying the system, it is understood that they mean the avoirdupois or Customary system — the one used in the United States.

The largest diamond ever uncovered came from a mine in South Africa. Known as the Cullinan diamond, it weighed 3,106 carats, or about 1⅓ pounds. It was cut into smaller stones. The largest, named the Star of Africa, weighed 530 carats. It now sits atop the British royal scepter.

Star of Africa

Goods were often shipped in barrels
because they could be rolled aboard ships and wagons.

Even more confusing was the fact that both the troy and Customary System began with the grain. A grain in either system weighed the same. The Customary ounce was lighter than a troy ounce because the Customary ounce had fewer grains. But a Customary pound was heavier than a troy pound because the Customary pound had 16 ounces, but the troy pound had only 12 ounces.

Table of Weights

(Do not confuse the grain with the metric gram)

Troy System
1 ounce = 480 grains
1 pound = 12 ounces = 5,760 grains

Avoirdupois (Customary) System
1 ounce = 437.5 grains
1 pound = 16 ounces = 7,000 grains

For heavier items, the pound alone was not large enough. In the United States, a hundredweight was used to measure things that weighed, 100 pounds. Twenty hundredweights made a ton, or 2,000 pounds: 20 hundredweights x 100 pounds per hundredweight = 2,000 pounds.

The United States Customary System and the British Imperial System began in agreement. The American states were originally British colonies. But in the 1800s, the British changed several of their standards and the United States did not follow their lead. For that reason, the British Imperial System and the United States Customary System do not always agree.

The British had a weight called a stone. It weighed 14 pounds. Some people in England still give their weight in stones. It sounds better to weigh 15 stones than 210 pounds: 15 stones x 14 pounds per stone = 210 pounds.

The British defined a hundredweight as 8 stones, or 112 pounds: 8 stones x 14 pounds per stone = 112 pounds. In the British system, a hundredweight did not weigh 100 pounds. Instead, it weighed 112 pounds. A British ton was 20 hundredweights or 2,240 pounds: 20 hundredweights x 112 pounds per hundredweight = 2,240 pounds. The British ton (2,240 pounds) and the United States ton (2,000 pounds) did not weigh the same.

A sailing ship might leave a United States port with a cargo of 28 tons of coal. But weighing the coal at a British port showed it had only 25 tons of coal. Leaving port, the coal was measured at 2,000 pounds per ton. Arriving, it was measured at 2,240 pounds per ton. To help keep it straight, some people spelled ton differently: *ton* in American English, but *tonne* in British English. Others referred to a short ton for the American ton and the long ton for the British ton.

The Customary System was put together by combining features from several different countries and different commercial activities without any overall plan behind the selections. For instance, the Customary System had two different kinds of tons, a long ton and a short ton, three different kinds of ounces (troy, Customary, and liquid), and two different kinds of quarts (liquid and dry.)

Years ago, schools expected students to memorize all of these different units of measure and convert between them. As you can imagine, they sank into a quicksand of grains, scruples, drams, troy ounces, Customary ounces, pounds, stones, hundredweights (two sizes), and short and long tons. It was difficult to keep all the measures straight. And that is merely weight. Units of measure for length and capacity could be just as confusing.

Commerce between nations depended upon a system by which repeated measurements of the same quantity by different individuals (buyer and seller, for example) agreed. Some things were sold by weight, others by capacity, and still others by length: 60 pounds (weight), one gallon (capacity), a quarter of a mile (length.)

Length was one of the most common quantities that early people measured. Merchants sold silk thread, ribbon, rope, and fabric by length. The first measurements for length used

Cubit in the Bible

In the Bible, Moses was given directions in cubits for building the tabernacle of God (Exod. 25:10).

The cubit was a measure of length and could vary from about 17 to 22 inches. The fact that cubits had different lengths is shown by 2 Chronicles 3:3. The verse states, "The foundation Solomon laid for building the temple of God was sixty cubits long and twenty cubits wide (using the cubit of the old standard)."

One common value for the cubit was 18 inches. In Genesis 6:15, the King James Version of the Bible says that God told Noah to fashion the ark 300 cubits long, 50 cubits wide, and 30 cubits high. The New International Version gives the dimensions as 450 feet long, 75 feet wide, and 45 feet high. The length of the ark in both NIV and KJV are equal but are given in different units.

The NIV used 18 inches for the cubit. To see why this is so, first change 450 feet into: 450 ft x 12 in/ft = 5,400 in. Next, divide 5,400 inches (the NIV length of the ark) by 300 cubits (the KJV length of the ark): 5,400 in ÷ 300 cubit = 18 in/cubit.

the human body as a standard. For instance, the Bible tells of a distance called the cubit. It was roughly the distance from the tip of the outstretched middle finger to the elbow.

Most of the early units of length were rough and ready measures. Like the cubit, they changed from time to time, too, depending on the location and the person doing the measuring.

Shopkeepers measured fabric with their outstretched arm. From their thumb and forefinger of the outstretched arm to the tip of their nose became a common unit of measure. Customers complained that the length depended on the shopkeeper. King Henry I ruled England from 1100 to 1135. He declared the standard yard as the distance from his forefinger to his nose. Shopkeepers used sticks measured from his standard yard. The word yard comes from an Old English word for stick.

Later, in 1845, the British filed two marks exactly one yard apart on a metal bar. The scratches on the metal bar became the standard. Yardsticks were measured from it.

At first, a foot was the length of a human foot. Obviously, the foot could vary from one individual to another. According to legend, the first official foot was measured with the foot of Charlemagne. He was a ruler who lived about A.D. 800. If he did serve as the model of the foot, then he had big feet. Later, the size of the foot was changed so that exactly three of them made a yard.

An inch is almost exactly the width of the thumb of an adult man, or from the knuckle to the end of the thumb of an adult woman. However, the inch was defined in terms of seeds, perhaps because of using the barley grain for measuring weight. King Edward II of England, who ruled from 1307 to 1327, decreed that an inch was the length of three barley grains laid end to end. Later, the length of the inch was adjusted so 12 of them made a foot. The word inch is from a Latin word meaning one-twelfth.

Several other measures based on the human body were in common usage until recently.

Mark Twain

During the early days of steamship travel on American rivers, steamboat crews measured river depth in fathoms. Most riverboats needed 12 feet of water, or two fathoms, to navigate safely. Otherwise, they would run aground. A crewmember would tie a weight to a rope and throw it overboard. The rope had knots one fathom apart. The crewmember counted the knots that passed through his hand before the weight struck bottom. The call of "mark twain" meant all was well. The word twain meant two, so the river was two fathoms deep.

Samuel L. Clemens piloted a riverboat on the Mississippi River. Later, he wrote about Huckleberry Finn, Tom Sawyer, and his experiences on the river in the book *Life on the Mississippi*. Clemens is better known as Mark Twain. He took his pen name from the riverboat call of "mark twain," meaning the channel was at least two fathoms deep.

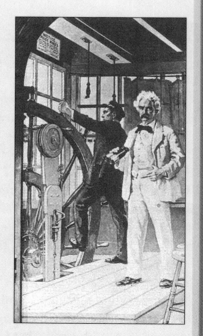

One was the span. Hold out your hand. Spread your fingers apart from one another as far as you can. A span is the distance from the tip of the thumb, across the palm, to the tip of the little finger. A span of an adult is about nine inches.

covered 21,660 minutes of arc (360 degrees x 60 minutes per degree = 21,660 minutes.) A nautical mile is one minute of arc, or about 6,076 feet. The word nautical is from a Greek word meaning ship.

A ship's speed is determined by knots and not miles.

The Bible describes the giant Goliath as being six cubits and a span tall (1 Samuel 17:4; KJV.) If the cubit was 18 inches, and the span was nine inches, then he was 117 inches tall, or 9 feet 9 inches.

A hand is another unit of measure. A hand is the width of the back of the hand across the knuckles. In an adult, it is about four inches. This term is still used today among people who raise horses. The height of a horse from the ground to the top of the shoulders is given in hands. An average horse is about 14 to 16 hands tall.

Spread out both arms as wide as you can. The distance from the tip of one index finger across your body to the tip of the finger of the other hand is a fathom. It was officially set equal to six feet.

Seamen use the nautical mile to measure distance. Distance on the sea was measured by latitude and longitude in degrees of arc. A trip around the world covered 360 degrees and each degree had 60 minutes of arc, so the entire trip

Seamen using a knotted rope to measure the ship's speed

To measure the speed of the ship, seamen used a knotted rope. They threw a log tied to a rope overboard. The log floated on the water as the ship left it behind. The cabin boy would start timing with a 30-second sandglass. A sailor would count knots in the rope as they passed through his hands. When the 30 seconds had passed, the cabin boy called a stop to counting. Given the time, the distance between knots, and the number of knots that passed through the sailor's hands, the captain could calculate the speed of the ship. The speed was given in nautical miles per hour, which became known as "knots."

The captain recorded the information given by the rope and floating log in his log book. A knot measured speed, not distance. One knot was a speed of one nautical mile per hour, about 6,076 feet per hour.

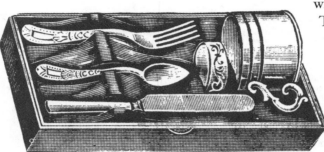

A set of tableware used by wealthy people, containing a teaspoon and cup, which were used to measure capacity

A knot is still used today for the speed of ships. Sailors know that knot includes the phrase "per hour." Suppose a ship is sailing at 12 nautical miles per hour. Sailors say the speed is 12 knots. If a person says "12 knots per hour" the sailors know the speaker is a landlubber who is unfamiliar with proper seamanship terms.

Airplane pilots also measure distance in nautical miles and speed in knots.

The mile is the most common English measurement for distance greater than a yard. Romans invented the mile. The ancient Romans conquered most of Europe including England. They built well-constructed roads throughout the Empire. To mark the distance, they placed a stone post known as a milepost at every mile along the way. Many of the roads, and some of the mileposts, still exist today.

Roman soldiers were trained to march with the same stride. A pace was the distance from where the right foot came down to the next place the right foot came down. A Roman pace was about five feet.

A distance of 1,000 Roman paces gave the name to the mile. The ancient Romans spoke Latin, and the Latin word for 1,000 is *milli*. When soldiers had walked 1,000 paces, they had gone a milli. The word became "mile." The Roman mile was equal to about 5,000 feet.

A distance of 5,000 feet is not a whole number of yards. It is 1,666 yards 2 feet: 5,000 ft ÷ 3 ft per yard = 1,666 yards with 2 feet remainder, which could also be written as 1,666 ⅔ yards. The British wanted the mile to come out as a whole number of yards. They didn't want fractions. They defined a mile as 1,760 yards, or 5,280 feet: 1,760 yards x 3 ft per yard = 5,280 ft. Today, the old Roman mileposts are too close together to mark off British and American miles.

Distance in the Customary System

1 foot = 12 inches
1 yard = 3 feet = 36 inches
1 mile = 1,760 yards = 5,280 feet

Business and commerce needed three basic measurements for goods that were bought and sold: length, weight, and capacity. Capacity is a measure of volume.

Cooks probably were the first to use capacity measurements. Some ingredients could be used without much concern about the amount. A pinch of salt, a shake of spices, a handful of flour, a cup of water, more or less. However, some recipes needed the ingredients measured exactly. Baking of bread, for instance, is a chemical reaction in which the sugar, flour, and yeast must be measured carefully.

To measure ingredients more exactly, cooks used spoons and cups. The ancient Romans used knives, forks, and spoons. But during the Middle Ages, after the fall of Rome, the knife was the only tableware in common use. People ate by dipping food with bread, or they used their fingers. Starting in the 1500s, spoons again appeared on the dinner table.

Rich families used tableware made of expensive metals such as silver. Poor people used spoons carved of wood. The word spoon is from an Old English word meaning chip of wood. The teaspoon was the smallest spoon. A tablespoon was larger. The word table is from an Old English word meaning board. A

of Jesus with a pound of costly ointment. The New International Version says that she used a pint of ointment. Read John 12:3.

Two pints make a quart, and four quarts make a gallon. The word quart is from a Latin

2 pints   1 quart

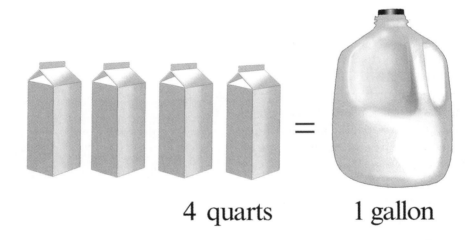

4 quarts   1 gallon

"board" spoon was larger than a "chip of wood" spoon. Today, a tablespoon is defined as having a capacity of three teaspoons.

A fluid ounce is equal to two tablespoons. A fluid ounce is a unit of volume, not weight. Liquids such as soda and juice are often sold by the fluid ounce. Eight fluid ounces make a cup, and two cups or 16 fluid ounces make a pint.

The pint was originally chosen because a pint of water weighed a pound. Children memorized the catchy phrase, "A pint is a pound the world around." It is only true for water, but many other liquids have a weight that is similar to water. For instance, the King James Version of the Bible says that Mary anointed the feet

word, *quarto,* meaning one-fourth. When you cut something into quarters, you cut it into four equal pieces. A quart is one-fourth of a gallon.

A gallon of water weighs eight pounds. Equal volumes of water, milk, and human flesh weigh about the same. Suppose a person goes on a diet and manages to lose 16 pounds. The person could say, "I have lost two gallons." Pick up two gallons of milk. You can see that two gallons of excess weight to carry around is a heavy load.

The Customary System measures capacity by teaspoons, tablespoons, fluid ounces, cups, pints, quarts, gallons, and barrels. Most of these units are for liquid measure. Gasoline is sold by the gallon. Milk is sold by the gallon, quart, or pint. Crude oil is priced by the barrel.

A barrel was a convenient way of shipping goods before the invention of equipment that ran by steam engines or gasoline motors. The muscles of animals or humans did heavy lifting. They could roll a barrel up a ramp easier than lift a crate the same distance. For that reason, many different items were shipped in barrels, both liquid and dry. Olive oil, crackers, dried fruit, and even meat were shipped in barrels. The size of a barrel varied widely. They could hold anywhere from 31 to 55 gallons. Today, crude oil is priced by a 42-gallon barrel.

Liquid Capacity Measure

1 tablespoon = 3 teaspoons
1 fluid ounce = 2 tablespoons
1 cup = 8 fl oz
1 pint = 16 fl oz = 2 cups
1 quart = 32 fl oz = 2 pints
1 gallon = 128 fl oz = 4 quarts

For dry measure, the Customary System uses dry pints, dry quarts, pecks, and bushels. Potatoes and grains such as wheat and rice are sold by bushels. Berries, such as strawberries, are sold by dry quarts. The pint and quart used in dry measure are not the same size as the pint and quart used in liquid measure. The dry measures are larger than the liquid measures. A dry quart is about 1.164 times the size of a liquid quart. The British have an Imperial quart. It is larger still, about 1.2 times the size of the American liquid quart.

Dry Capacity Measure

1 quart = 2 pints
1 peck = 8 quarts
1 bushel = 4 pecks

Changing from one measure to another is made easier by two simple steps. First, find the conversion factor. Then decide whether you need to multiply or divide. The conversion factor is the number that relates one measure to another. For instance, the conversion factor for feet and inches is 12.

But do you multiply by 12 or divide by 12? Thinking helps. A foot is longer than an inch. Changing feet into inches gives a larger number. If a measure is in feet and you want inches, then multiply feet by 12 to give inches. For a measure in inches that needs to be converted to feet, then divide by 12.

For instance, one of the wettest spots in the world is on the island of Kauai, Hawaii, where 460 inches of rain falls each year. How many feet is this? Dividing 460 inches by 12 gives the answer: 460 in ÷ 12 in per ft = 38 ft 4 in or 38.33 ft. The remainder of 4 can be expressed as 4 inches or 0.33 feet.

This two-step process of finding the conversion factor and then deciding whether to multiply or divide works for other units of measure, too.

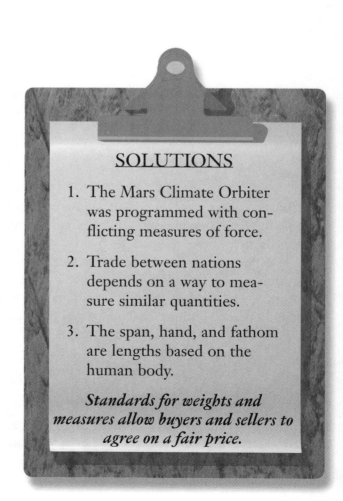

SOLUTIONS

1. The Mars Climate Orbiter was programmed with conflicting measures of force.

2. Trade between nations depends on a way to measure similar quantities.

3. The span, hand, and fathom are lengths based on the human body.

Standards for weights and measures allow buyers and sellers to agree on a fair price.

A B C D   1.   NASA's Climate Obiter to Mars failed because (A. American and French engineers did not communicate with one another B. engineers used two different measures of force C. fuel had been measured improperly D. the spacecraft weighed too much).

A B   2.   A troy ounce was used to measure (A. small and expensive B. large and inexpensive) items.

A B C D   3.   A scruple was a standard of weight for measuring (A. barley B. diamonds C. drugs D. potatoes).

A B C D   4.   At first, the United States Customary system agreed with that of (A. Britain B. France C. Morocco D. Spain).

T F   5.   The American ton and the British tonne are identical in weight.

A B C D   6.   Most early measures of distance were based on (A. animal strides B. human body C. parts of ships D. Roman military terms).

   7.   The length of a mile in feet is _____.

   8.   "A pint is a _____ the world around."

Choose the larger:

A B   9.   A. foot B. yard

A B   10.   A. fathom B. yard

A B   11.   A. nautical mile B. statute mile

A B   12.   A. cup B. quart

A B   13.   A. bushel B. peck

Try Your Math

  14.   Recall that a hand is four inches. How tall is a horse in inches that is 15 hands tall? How tall in feet?

  15.   Change your weight from pounds to ounces.

  16.   The tallest mountain on earth is Mt. Everest. Its summit is 29,035 feet above sea level. How high is the mountain in miles?

$\tan\phi = \dfrac{X_C}{R}$

$E = \Delta mc^2$

$\sqrt{a^2 + b^2}$

$L = 2\pi f L$

Measuring by Metric

In the late 1700s, France was the leading country in Europe. Following a civil war known as the Revolution of 1789, France began a process of rebuilding. The country's business was in chaos. No one could agree on standards for measuring goods. The leaders of France decided the country needed a uniform system of standard weights and measures. In 1791, they gave the job of designing the system to the French Academy of Sciences. The academy was a group of scientists.

Members of the academy set three simple rules before they began. First, except for time, the system would be based on 10. The United States had shown the advantage of decimals with its monetary system. The word decimal means tenth part. At Thomas Jefferson's suggestion, the United States became the first country in the world to set up

PROBLEMS

1. What country's monetary system showed the advantage of using base 10?

2. What official measure was based on an arc surveyed along the earth's surface?

3. Why can water be used to mark a temperature scale on a thermometer?

Can You Propose Solutions?

Louis XIV and his minister Jean Baptiste Colbert visit the French Academy of Sciences.

its money based on 10. The dime was a tenth part of a dollar and the penny was the tenth part of a dime. Before then, the United States had used the British monetary system. Twelve pence made a shilling and 20 shillings made a British pound.

Going up and down by multiplying and dividing by 10 was far easier than memorizing the odd conversions such as 2 pints make a quart, but four quarts make a gallon, or 12 inches make a foot, three feet make a yard, and 1,780 yards make a mile.

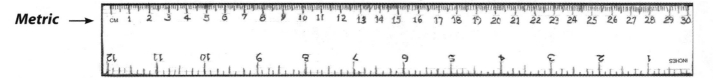

Metric measurements can be found on most rulers.

The second ground rule for the French system stated that prefixes for the main measure would describe larger and smaller quantities. Whether distance, weight, capacity, or any other unit of measure, simple prefixes would describe sizes. The three most common prefixes were kilo for 1,000, centi for 1/100 and milli for 1/1,000. A kilo-unit (regardless of what the unit measured) would be 1,000 times bigger than the main, or base, unit. A centi-unit (regardless of what the unit measured) would be 1/100 as small as the base unit.

The third ground rule required that the units be selected so everyone — bankers, business people, farmers, merchants, and scientists — could use them. No longer would there be separate weights and measures used by druggists, jewelers, and merchants. The motto of the new system was "for all people."

As a first step, the scientists decided to tackle the problem of finding a unit for length. They tossed out the idea of using the length of a person's foot as a standard. The 1700s had been an era of great exploration in which most of the earth's oceans had been crossed and the continents mapped. Scientists worked toward a precise value for the size of the earth.

The committee decided to define the new unit of length as 1/10,000,000 (one ten-millionth) of the distance from the equator to the North Pole along a line passing through Paris, France. But what was that distance?

Surveyors would not have to measure the entire distance from equator to North Pole. Instead, a smaller arc would serve. They could calculate the rest of the distance from the smaller arc. Surveyors took six years to accurately measure the distance from Barcelona, Spain, to Dunkirk, France. In 1799, they announced the total distance and calculated the length of the new unit for distance. They called it a meter, from *metron*, a Greek word meaning measure. The meter was 39.37 inches.

To have the meter as a ready reference, they marked the distance with two lines a meter apart on a metal bar. At that time, France supplied copies of the metal bar to other countries.

Later, scientists more accurately measured the distance from the equator to the North Pole. Rather than 10,000,000 meters, it was actually 10,002,288 meters as defined by the marks on the metal rod. The improved distance would change the length of the meter. Rather than doing that, the committee decided the distance marked on the bar — and not the distance on the earth — would be the standard.

The meter became an international standard of length. The French system of measure became known as the metric system. Other countries accepted the meter and the metric system as their standard. The United States Congress approved the metric system in 1866, but did not require people to use it. Many people were reluctant to abandon the measures they already knew. Even residents of France took about 40 years before they completely switched to the new system.

Using two fine scratches on a metal bar for defining length did present problems. Warmer temperature caused the metal bar to expand. The marks got farther apart. Cooler temperature caused the metal bar to contract. The marks got closer together. In 1875, French officials made the bar of an alloy of platinum and iridium. The alloy resisted changes in length because of temperature changes.

The metal bar as a standard length still was not satisfactory. The single bar served as a pattern for making secondary bars to be used elsewhere. The slightest error could cause the pattern to vary from the original.

Scientists found a better way to measure the meter. They used light itself. Light has a wave motion like waves of water on a lake. The waves are extremely tiny. Krypton gas is in the same family as helium, argon, and neon. Like neon, krypton glows when electricity flows through it. Krypton emits light with a very precise wavelength. In 1960, a conference of scientists agreed to ignore the metal bar. Instead, they defined the meter as 1,640,763.73 wavelengths of the reddish-orange light emitted by krypton gas.

But even that standard did not last. For the fourth time, scientists made another change. By 1983, the second had been precisely defined, and light was known to travel at a set speed in a vacuum. Scientists agreed to change the definition (but not the actual length) of a meter. They set it equal to the distance that light traveled in a vacuum during $\frac{1}{299,792,458}$ of a second.

The meter is the standard for length. Even the Customary System yard is measured from it. A yard is $^{36.00}\!/_{39.37}$ of a meter. The other Customary units for length such as the inch, foot, and mile are measured from the yard, so they too depend on the meter.

Like the Customary System with its shorter units of length (inch, foot) and longer units of length (mile), the metric system also needed units shorter and longer than the meter.

A centimeter is $\frac{1}{100}$ of a meter. The prefix centi means $\frac{1}{100}$. A centimeter is about the width of a person's little finger. It takes 2.54 centimeters to make an inch. A millimeter is $\frac{1}{1000}$ of a meter. The prefix milli means $\frac{1}{1,000}$. It takes 25.4 millimeters to make an inch.

A kilometer is 1,000 meters. The prefix kilo means 1,000. Although some people pronounce kilometer as KIL-uh-mee-tur, most people say kuh-LOM-uh-tur. The longer length of kilometer describes distances between cities. A meter is a little over three feet (3.28 feet), and 1,000 meters (a kilometer) is a little over 3,000 feet (3,281 feet.) The kilometer is considerably smaller than a mile (5,280 feet.) Two cities 62 miles apart are about 100 kilometers from one another.

The scientists who designed the metric system defined only a few basic units and then

Mass and Weight

Scientists have learned that mass and weight are not the same quantity. Isaac Newton showed that mass is a measure of the amount of matter in an object. Weight is how strongly a body is pulled upon by gravity. The force of gravity grows weaker as one moves farther from the center of the earth. A person on top of a tall building weighs slightly less than the same person down on the street.

The spin of the earth causes it to bulge at the equator. Quito, Ecuador, is nearly on the equator. A person there is about 26 miles farther from the center of the earth than at the North Pole. A person who weighs 140 pounds at the North Pole would weight about 138 pounds at Quito, Ecuador. The two pounds of reduced weight are a result of the weaker force of gravity.

Because weight can change from one place to another, scientists prefer to speak of mass. The metric unit of kilogram measures mass. However, if two objects are weighed in the same location and are found to have the same weight, then they have the same mass, too. Most people use mass and weight as if they were the same. Even scientists say they are weighing an object. They do not say they are massing it.

Motorcycle engines are sized in cubic centimeters — a metric measurement.

derived others from them. Capacity or volume is one example. They made the unit for capacity from the meter. Imagine a container shaped like a cube that is 1/10 of a meter in length, width, and height. The metric committee said that such a container held one liter. A tenth of a meter is 10 centimeters — about four inches. A container 10 centimeters on a side holds a liter. It is slightly larger than a United States liquid quart.

In the metric system, both liquid and dry capacities are measured in liters. For smaller measures, a milliliter is used. A milliliter is equal to 1/1,000 of a liter. It is equal to the volume of a cube one-centimeter on a side. A cubic centimeter, abbreviated cc, and a millimeter, abbreviated ml, measure equal volumes.

The size of a motorcycle engine is described by the amount of space inside the cylinder. The size is measured in cubic centimeters. A small motorcycle engine may have a single cylinder with a total size of about 50 cc. A large motorcycle may have as many as four larger cylinders. The total size may be about 1,500 cc.

How big is 1,500 cc in liters? A cubic centimeter is equal to a milliliter, and 1,500 cc is equal to 1,500 ml. It takes 1,000 ml to make a liter, so 1,500 ml equals 1.5 liters: 1,500 ml ÷ 1,000 ml per liter = 1.5 liters.

With a liter defined, the metric committee had an opportunity to relate mass to length and capacity. They chose to define mass by setting one kilogram equal to the weight of a liter of water.

Measuring the weight (mass) of one liter of pure water proved difficult to repeat time and again. Scientists could not produce water of the same purity each time. Also, they had to measure the water at the same temperature. Otherwise, its volume would change. Like other substances, water expands and contracts with temperature changes. Using a liter of water to measure one kilogram of mass proved difficult.

The French made a platinum cylinder with the exact weight (exact mass) of a liter of pure water. Scientists set a kilogram equal to the mass of the platinum cylinder. This meant that with improved measurements, the liter no longer held exactly a kilogram of water. But the difference was so slight it could be ignored for everyday purposes.

Today, the platinum cylinder in the vault at Sèvres, France, is still the standard kilogram. It is about the size of a small orange juice can. Mass is the only metric quantity measured against a physical object. All other units are defined by scientific constants such as the speed of light and events that take place inside atoms.

A kilogram is 2.2 pounds. For many purposes, a kilogram is too large, so the gram is used instead. It takes 454 grams to make a pound, and about 28 grams make an ounce. A still smaller measure is the milligram. It is very tiny indeed. The smallest unit of measure in the Customary System is the grain. But it takes 65 milligrams to be one grain. As another example, a one-carat diamond weighs 200 milligrams.

For larger quantities, 1,000 kilograms are used. The prefix kilo means 1,000. The

Common Metric Prefixes			
Value	**Power of 10**	**Prefix**	**Examples**
billion	1,000,000,000	giga	gigabyte, computer memory
million	1,000,000	mega	megawatt, electric power
thousand	1,000	kilo	kilohertz, frequency
hundred	100	hecto	hectare, area
one	1	(unit)	meter, gram, liter, etc.
hundredth	0.01	centi	centimeter, distance
thousandth	0.001	milli	milliliter, capacity
millionth	0.000001	micro	microcurie, radioactivity
billionth	0.000000001	nano	nanosecond, time

expression 1,000 kilograms is equal to 1,000 x 1,000 grams, or one million grams. The prefix for one million in the metric system is *mega*. A mass of 1,000 kilograms is one megagram. However, a megagram is called a metric ton. A metric ton, 1,000 kilograms, is about 2,200 pounds. This gives three different types of tons in common use: Customary ton (2,000 pounds), British ton (2,240 pounds), and metric ton (2,200 pounds.)

The table of common metric prefixes above shows the prefixes that can be put together with any of the metric units to show a larger or smaller quantity.

From the very beginning of history, people used time, length, weight, and capacity in everyday life. They needed these units to conduct business. However, they seldom needed a precise measure of temperature. The first accurate thermometer was not invented until 1709. Daniel Gabriel Fahrenheit (FAH-ren-hite) made it. He was a German scientist who lived in Holland. He made weather instruments.

Daniel Gabriel Fahrenheit

Fahrenheit's thermometer became a popular instrument to own. People mounted thermometers outside their windows. The temperature readings helped them decide whether to wear heavy coats or light wraps when they left their homes.

Fahrenheit built his thermometers for the study of weather. He wanted the coldest reading to be well below the freezing point of water. Otherwise, negative numbers would be common during winter. He experimented with an ice and salt-water mixture. He set the lowest temperature he could produce in this way equal to zero.

While experimenting with his thermometer, Gabriel Fahrenheit made a remarkable discovery. He heated water. The temperature of the water rose until the water came to a boil. Once water started boiling, it did not get any hotter. More heat merely made it boil faster. The temperature stayed constant until all the water boiled away. On Fahrenheit's thermometer, water boiled at 212 degrees.

Derived Units

The metric system has but seven basic units. Two are seldom used outside of science: the candela for measuring the

brightness of light and mole for measuring large numbers of very small particles such as atoms and molecules. The other five, however, are in daily use: ampere (electricity), second (time), meter (distance), kilogram (mass), and kelvin degree (temperature).

Other units of measure can be built by referring to standards that have already been set. For example, speed measures how quickly an object moves. In the English system, speed is given in miles per hour or feet per second. In the metric system, speed is given in kilometers per hour or meters per second. Each quantity is distance (miles, feet, kilometer, or meter) divided by time (hour or second.)

Because both second and meter have been defined, a separate unit for speed is not needed. Speed is a derived quantity.

Acceleration, force, energy, and other units used in the metric system are derived from the seven basic units.

Water also has a fixed freezing temperature. Water gets colder and colder until ice starts to form. The temperature hovers at the same reading until all of the water turns to ice. The freezing point of water is 32 degrees on Fahrenheit's temperature scale. The number of degrees from the freezing temperature of water to its boiling temperature is 180 Fahrenheit degrees: 212 - 32 = 180.

Most people liked the Fahrenheit scale because throughout most days the temperatures stayed between 0°F and 100°F.

Scientists, however, were not as enthusiastic. They could not repeat Fahrenheit's starting point of 0°F. Ice, water, and salt did not always give a temperature of exactly 0°F.

In 1742, Swedish astronomer Anders Celsius (SEL-see-us) proposed a different scale. His design assigned the value 0°C to the freezing point of water and 100°C to the boiling point of water. He made 100 equal divisions between the two marks.

Scientists could easily mark a scale on a Celsius thermometer. They placed the new thermometer in pure water and let it cool to the freezing point. They marked the mercury level as 0°C. Next, they put the thermometer in boiling water. They marked that point as 100°C.

Anders Celsius called his invention the centigrade scale. The prefix centi means 100 and grade means mark. However, in 1948, scientists agreed to honor Celsius by calling his invention the Celsius scale. People in most of the countries of the world use it.

Converting between Celsius and Fahrenheit temperature scales is not straightforward. They have different starting points and the degrees are different sizes. It is like a race between two runners in which one gets a head start and takes bigger steps. The Fahrenheit starting point of 0°F is colder than the Celsius starting point of 0°C.

The Celsius degrees are bigger than Fahrenheit degrees. A temperature rise of one degree Celsius is a greater temperature change than a temperature rise of one degree Fahrenheit. Between the freezing and boiling points of water, the Celsius temperature scale has 100 degrees but the Fahrenheit temperature scale has 180 degrees.

Most people use one or the other, so converting between them is not needed. It is convenient, however, to know a few key temperatures.

Fahrenheit and Celsius Temperatures

Freezing temperature of water	32°F = 0°C
Room temperature	72°F = 22°C
Normal body temperature	98.6°F = 37°C
Boiling temperature of water	212°F = 100°C

In the 1850s, William Thomson investigated heat. He knew that when a substance cools, its atoms move more slowly. William Thomson asked himself, "How cold must a substance be for its atoms to stop moving?"

He imagined a temperature so cold all motion ceased. This would be the coldest temperature possible. An object at that temperature could not be cooled any further because its atoms would have lost all motion. William Thomson called this temperature absolute zero. Scientists have since learned that the atoms do keep a small amount of motion that cannot be removed.

His calculations showed that -273°C (-459°F) was the coldest possible temperature. William Thomson called -273°C absolute zero. He suggested that scientists use a temperature scale that began at this temperature. Scientists agreed because many of the laws of nature could be more easily expressed if temperature was measured from absolute zero.

In later life, William Thomson became a British nobleman. He chose the name of Kelvin after the Kelvin River that flowed near Glasgow University, Scotland, where he taught science for more than 50 years. He became well known as Lord Kelvin. Scientists named the absolute temperature scale in his honor — the Kelvin scale. The freezing point of water is 273 degrees kelvin (273°K).

The Celsius degree and the kelvin degree are the same size. If an object becomes warmer

Boiling Temperature and Air Pressure

The boiling temperature of 212°F for water is only true at sea level and when the air pressure is normal. Changes in the weather can change atmospheric pressure.

Thinner air found higher on the slopes of a mountain changes atmospheric pressure and the boiling temperature of water. The top of Mount Everest is 29,035 feet (8,850 m) above sea level. At its summit, water boils at only 160°F. The city of Denver, Colorado, is a mile above sea level. There the boiling point is 203°F, not 212°F. Cooks have to consider this. At sea level, an egg is hard after being boiled for three minutes. But in Denver, it would be soft boiled. It must be boiled for five minutes.

The Dead Sea is below sea level. The thicker air along its shores keeps water from boiling until the temperature reaches 214°F.

William Thomson, Lord Kelvin
(Courtesy of the Smithsonian)

world, and nearly all scientists including druggists and physicians, used the metric system.

The United States passed a law in 1866 that permitted the use of the metric system but did not require its use. The United States has been slowly changing over to the metric system, but many older Customary units are still in everyday use. However, people effortlessly switch from one system to the other. They buy milk by the gallon but soft drinks in two-liter bottles. They use cameras that take 35-mm film but have four-by-six-inch prints made from the exposed film. They purchase meat by the pound but read the label to see how many grams of fat are in a serving.

by 1°C it has also become warmer by 1°K. The only difference is that the Kelvin temperature scale starts at absolute zero while the Celsius temperature scale starts at the freezing temperature of water. On the Kelvin scale, there are no negative readings. Every temperature is a positive one. Converting from Celsius to Kelvin is especially easy. Merely add 273 degrees to the Celsius temperature to get Kelvin temperature.

Countries that use the metric system give temperatures in weather forecasts in Celsius degrees. Often, the Celsius and not the Kelvin scale is referred to as the metric temperature scale.

People are often slow to accept new ideas. Most of the English-speaking countries continued using measures first introduced by the British. However, by the middle of the 1900s, most people in the

SOLUTIONS

1. The United States based its money on powers of 10.

2. The meter was based on a fraction of the distance from the equator to the North Pole.

3. The freezing and boiling temperatures of water are constant.

Almost all scientists and most nations use the metric system.

A B   1.   The metric system began in (A. Britain   B. France).

A B C   2.   The metric system is based on powers of (A. 2   B. 10   C. 12).

T F   3.   The metric system was designed specifically to meet the needs of merchants.

A B C D   4.   Currently, the meter is defined as (A. 1,640,763.73 wavelengths of krypton gas   B. $\frac{1}{10,000,000}$ of the distance from the equator to the North Pole   C. the distance between two scratch marks on a metal rod   D. the distance light travels in $\frac{1}{299,792,458}$ of a second).

T F   5.   Volume (capacity) is a derived unit because it is based on a container that is $\frac{1}{10}$ of a meter on each side.

A B C   6.   One meter is slightly longer than one (A. inch   B. yard   C. mile).

A B C   7.   One liter is slightly larger than one (A. pint   B. quart   C. gallon).

A B C   8.   One kilogram is about 2.2 times as much as (A. one ounce   B. one pound   C. one ton).

A B   9.   A standard kilogram is defined by (A. the mass of a platinum cylinder   B. the wavelength of krypton gas).

A B C D   10.   Daniel Fahrenheit set the boiling temperature of water on his thermometer at (A. 0   B. 32   C. 100   D. 212) degrees.

A B C D   11.   Most people liked Fahrenheit thermometers because (A. they were free   B. they were accurate   C. Fahrenheit was an Englishman   D. daytime temperatures stayed between 0 and 100 degree).

T F   12.   The metric system is illegal to use in the United States.

A B C   13.   The (A. Celsius   B. Fahrenheit   C. Kelvin) temperature scale starts at absolute zero.

$$\tan\phi = \frac{X_C}{R}$$

$$E = \Delta mc^2$$

$$\sqrt{a^2 + b^2}$$

$$L = 2\pi fL$$

Practical Mathematics

Ancient Egyptians farmed the rich flood plains of the Nile River. Each year the rainy season caused the Nile to spill over its banks. The Nile River was 4,000 miles long. It flowed from the central highlands of Africa. The water rushed to the sea and gathered rich soil all along its route. The current slowed when it reached the flat plains of the Nile valley in Egypt. The river left its burden of new soil behind after a flood receded.

Crops grew well in the fertile soil on either side of the Nile. Egypt prospered. Deserts surrounded Egypt. The harsh conditions prevented invading armies from destroying the Egyptian civilization. But the deserts also kept Egyptians close to the river. The Nile became their lifeline. Boats transported goods up and down the river. Hand dug canals carried water to fields. Great cities — Cairo, Memphis, Thebes — grew up along

PROBLEMS

1. How did a river promote the use of geometry?

2. Can a knotted rope form a perfect 90-degree angle?

3. If you were 50 feet tall, how high could you jump?

Can You Propose Solutions?

The Nile River and the pyramids of Giza

its banks. The country became known as "the gift of the Nile."

In ancient times, some groups of people lived in cities, while others lived a more simple life. They raised livestock and gathered food that grew wild. They lived in tents so they could move with the seasons to graze their animals. Their lives were simple, so they had little reason to develop mathematics.

Other groups, such as the Egyptians, stayed in one place to tend their crops. They measured out fields, built homes and larger structures, and dug canals. These activities required cooperation. The larger structures cost money, too, which the government collected as taxes.

The Egyptians developed mathematics and geometry to design buildings, measure fields, plan watercourses, and calculate taxes.

The annual flood of the Nile contributed to the development of geometry. The action of the water erased property lines and farm boundaries. Farmers built stone markers that withstood the flood. They measured the location and size of their fields from the stone markers. For this task, they needed an understanding of geometry. The word geometry is from Greek words *geo* meaning earth and *metry* meaning to measure. Geometry means "to measure the earth."

The geometry of figures on flat surfaces is plane geometry. The word plane means flat. The earth's surface is not flat, but the Egyptians farmed level land and their fields were small. The fact that the earth's surface is part of a sphere did not hinder their calculations.

The Egyptians learned the basic geometric properties of triangles, rectangles, squares, and circles. They laid out fields, set foundations of buildings, and built silos to store grain. They figured the surface area of fields and the amount of grain stored in their silos. They also built pyramids and monuments as burial sites for their rulers, the pharaohs.

The ancient Egyptians built the largest and most imposing pyramid, the Great Pyramid of Giza. The Great Pyramid sloped up from a square base with the sides running along north-south and east-west lines. Each side was about 746 feet long. When first constructed, it rose 481.4 feet, although erosion and vandals carried away some of its outer material.

The age of the Great Pyramid is difficult to imagine. A Roman who lived at the time of Jesus would view the pyramids as extremely ancient — more than 2,500 years old. They were older in his day than the ancient Romans are to us.

The Great Pyramid became one of the seven wonders of the ancient world. It alone, of the seven wonders, still survives today. The engineering feat of building the pyramids clearly showed that the Egyptians had mastered practical geometry.

Egyptian builders used a triangle to set the corners of their buildings at a right angle. A right angle is 90 degrees. It is the angle formed where the walls of a room meet. The hands of a clock that show three o'clock form a right angle. The hour hand is at 3 and the minute hand is at 12. The angle between the hands is 90 degrees.

The Egyptians discovered a simple way to ensure that the walls met at exactly 90 degrees. They took a rope and tied 12 equally spaced knots in it. Then they held the rope in the form of a triangle. They staked out the triangle so that one side of the triangle had five knots, one side had four knots, and one side had three knots. The angle opposite the long side — the side with five knots — formed a perfect right angle. They did not know why this worked. They merely knew that it gave them the right angle that they desired.

The two short sides of a right triangle — the ones with three knots and four knots — were called the legs. They built the walls in line with the legs. The side opposite the right angle — the side with five knots — was the hypotenuse (hye-POT-uhn-ooss.)

A triangle is the simplest example of a polygon. A polygon is any closed plane figure with straight sides. A plane figure must be flat and have the two dimensions of length and width but not height. The word polygon is from two Greek words, *poly* meaning many and *gon* meaning angles.

The first few polygons are given special names using the prefixes tri (3), quad (4), penta (5), hexa (6), octa (8) and deca (10). For

Ancient Egyptian Thinkers

Very little is known about ancient Egyptian scientists. Only two scientists are known by name. One is Imhotep (im-HOH-tep). He is credited with building one of the first pyramids.

Another scientist known by name was an Egyptian scribe, Ahmes (AH-mes), who lived about 1650 B.C. He signed his name to a papyrus scroll that listed mathematical problems and their solutions. He explained, for instance, how to divide loaves of bread among several people so each one would get an equal share. He also included geometry problems about simple figures such as triangles, rectangles, squares, and circles.

IMHOTEP

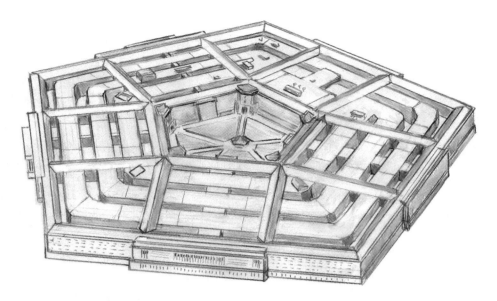

The Pentagon, used by the United States Department of Defense, is a five-sided polygon.

example, a triangle has three sides and three angles. A pentagon is a five-sided polygon. The most famous pentagon is the Pentagon in Washington, D.C., where the United States Department of Defense is located. An octagon has eight sides. Stop signs are octagons.

A polygon always has as many corners, or angles, as it has sides. A quadrilateral has four straight sides. The word lateral comes from a Latin word meaning side. A quadrilateral will also have four corners, or angles. A quadrilateral can also be called a quadrangle, meaning four angles.

A rectangle is a special type of quadrilateral. All of its angles are right angles and the opposite sides are of equal length. The longer side is its length and the shorter side is its width.

Egyptians measured the perimeter, or distance around, their fields and buildings. The word perimeter is from *peri* meaning around and *meter* meaning to measure. Perimeter means to measure around. For any quadrilateral, the distance around is equal to the sum of the lengths of the four sides. The perimeter of a rectangle can be found by doubling the length and width and adding them together. This can be written as a formula: $P = 2L + 2W$.

A formula is a shorthand mathematical expression for finding an answer. In the formula $P = 2L + 2W$, the P stands for perimeter, L for length, and W for width. In an equation

or formula, when two items are pushed together (such as the 2 and the L, or the 2 and the W in this case), it means to multiply them ($2 \times L$, $2 \times W$). The formula could also be written as $P = 2 \times L + 2 \times W$.

A square is a special type of rectangle. All four of its sides are of equal length. To find the perimeter of a square, the Egyptians measured one side and multiplied by four ($P = 4S$). This formula says that the perimeter of a square is equal to four times the length of one side.

A sheet of paper is about 8.5 inches by 11 inches. If you traced all the way around the very edge of the paper, how far would your pencil travel? Answer: $P = 2L + 2W = 2 \times 8.5$ inches + 2×11 inches = 17 inches + 22 inches = 39 inches.

A square field is 0.5 miles on a side. A rancher plans to enclose the field with three strands of barbed wire. How much wire will he need? Answer: $P = 4S = 4 \times 0.5$ miles = 2.0 miles; but he needs to go around it three times, so the answer is 6.0 miles of barbed wire.

In everyday life, Egyptians were also interested in the surface area covered by rectangles and squares. Their fields, the size of their rooms, and pieces of carpet were usually rectangles or squares. For a rectangle, they learned that the area (the total size of the interior) could be measured by multiplying length by width: $A = L \times W$.

A square's area could also be found in the same way, but length and width of a square are

Acre

For areas larger than a room, the most common unit for measuring surface area is the acre. The word acre comes from a Latin word meaning pastureland. The acre was an area that a yoke of oxen could plow in one morning. Of course, the actual surface area plowed depended on the strength of the oxen, the skill of the ox driver, the type of soil, and so on. To give a standard to the acre, the English set an acre equal to a square field that was about 209 feet on a side.

Many homes in the United States are built on 1/4-acre lots. The house and yard have a total area equal to a square about 105 feet on a side, (105 ft)^2 or 11,025 square feet. The home itself may be 1,500 to 2,000 square feet.

In the 1800s, the United States government encouraged people to move west

and settle land. The government gave the homesteaders a plot of land measuring one-quarter mile on a side. A field this size contains 40 acres. A square measuring one mile on each side has 640 acres, 1 square mile = 640 acres.

---

always the same. The area of a square is equal to the length of one side times itself: A = S x S = S^2. The small 2 is an exponent. The expression S^2 is read "S squared" and it means to multiply the side of the square by itself.

An area measurement has length and width. The answer is always stated in some measure of length times itself — square inches, square feet, or square meters.

In the United States, one common way of measuring small areas is by square feet. If a room is 12 feet by 14 feet, then the surface area is 168 square feet: 12 x 14 = 168, and ft x ft = ft^2 = 168 ft^2 or 168 square feet.

Surface area is measured in two dimensions, length and width. Volume is measured in three dimensions, length, width, and height. The volume, or capacity, of a room is given by the area of the floor times the height of the walls: V = Ah, with V the volume, A the area,

and h the height. If the room has a rectangular floor, then the area of the floor is length times width, A = LW. The volume is the product of the three dimensions, V = Ah = LWh.

The area and height have to be based on the same measure — feet, inches, meters, etc. If the area is in square feet, then the height of the room must also be in feet. In addition, the walls must be straight and not slope in or out. If a storage bin were smaller at the top than at the bottom, then the formula V = Ah would not give the right answer for volume.

Suppose a storage bin were 12 feet wide, 14 feet long, and 10 feet high. How much would it hold? Answer: V = Ah = 12 ft x 14 ft x 10 ft = 1680 ft^3. The exponent 3 shows that feet is multiplied times itself three times (cubed). The expression ft^3 can be read as cubic feet.

If the room is a cube, then it has a square base and a height equal to the sides of the square. In other words, length, width, and height are the same. For such a figure, the volume is equal to one side cubed: $V = S^3$. The exponent 3 means that the length of the side is multiplied by itself three times.

Volume goes up quickly with increasing size. For instance, a cube measuring 1 foot on a side holds 1 cubic foot. But a cube measuring 2 feet on a side holds 8 cubic feet: $V = S^3 = (2 \text{ ft})^3 = 2 \text{ ft} \times 2 \text{ ft} \times 2 \text{ ft} = 8 \text{ ft}^3$. Doubling each dimension of a box increases its capacity by 8 times: $2^3 = 8$.

Anytime a number greater than 1 is squared or cubed, the result quickly becomes larger than the original number. For example, a cube 1 foot (12 inches) on a side holds 1,728 boxes that are 1 inch on a side: $V = 12 \text{ in} \times 12 \text{ in} \times 12 \text{ in} = 1,728 \text{ in}^3$.

One of the problems in Ahmes's papyrus scroll was how to measure the area of a circle. The Egyptians built some silos with circular bases. They rose like tall cylinders. The volume of a cylinder is also given by the formula $V = Ah$. Multiply the area of the circular base by the height of the silo. However, finding the area of a circle is not as easy as calculating the area of a rectangle or square. A circle is a curve in which each point on the curve is the same distance from the center of the circle. A circle does not have straight sides, so it is not a polygon.

The radius is the distance from the center of the circle to any point on the circle. The word radius is from a Latin word meaning ray. The radius radiates out from the center to the circle. The diameter of a circle is any straight line that goes from one side of the circle to the other side and passes through the center. A diameter cuts the circle in half. The word diameter means to measure through.

The perimeter of a circle is the distance around the circle. However, people use the word circumference, rather than perimeter, to describe the distance around the circle. The word circumference means to carry around.

The Egyptians and early mathematicians made a remarkable discovery that related the circumference and diameter of a circle. The circumference (distance around) of a circle was

The Problem of Size

The multiplying effect of increased volume has profound effects in nature. For instance, a small insect such as a grasshopper can jump several times its own length. It can support its weight with tiny feet. Enlarge the grasshopper to the size of an elephant and its feet would not be able to support the body. The grasshopper would be unable to jump at all.

Why? The strength of muscles goes up by the square of the size, but the weight of an animal goes up by the cube of its size. So if the grasshopper were made 50 times larger, its muscles would be 2,500 times stronger ($50^2 = 50 \times 50 = 2,500$), but its volume and weight would be 125,000 times greater ($50^3 = 50 \times 50 \times 50 = 125,000$). The size of its muscles does not get larger by the same ratio as its weight.

An elephant is 50 times bigger than a grasshopper in every direction. It has huge pillar-like legs and broad, flat feet. An elephant cannot jump.

equal to a little more than three times the diameter (distance through) of the circle. This was true for any circle regardless of its size. For instance, if a wheel were four feet across and it turned once, then the wagon would go a little more than 12 feet. If a tree were one foot thick, then a tape measure wrapped around the tree would show the tree to be a little more than three feet around.

Many of the ancient people did not have a good way to write numbers. The Egyptians, Hebrews, and Greeks used letters of the alphabet. The Greek letter delta, Δ, represented 10. One hundred was shown by the Greek letter H, and 1,000 by the Greek letter chi, Χ. This was a clumsy system and one that was difficult to use.

Showing fractions was even more difficult. Often, ancient mathematicians used ratios instead. Rather than saying one number was one-third of another number, they would say that the ratio of the numbers was one to three. In other words, the second number was three times as large as the first one.

The ratio of the circumference to the diameter of a circle is roughly equal to the ratio of 22 to 7. If they had used fractions, they would have written the ratio of 22 to 7 as $\frac{22}{7}$, or $3\frac{1}{7}$. Today, mathematicians give the name pi, π, to the ratio of circumference of a circle to its diameter. As a decimal fraction, pi is about 3.14.

More about pi later, but for now it can be used to find how much grain a silo can hold.

The area of a circle is equal to π times the radius squared: $A = \pi r^2$. Or, if 3.14 is used for pi, the area is 3.14 times the radius squared, or as an equation: $A = 3.14 \times r^2$. Multiplying A by the height of the cylinder gives the volume: $V = Ah$.

Suppose the inside dimensions of a silo are 10 feet for the radius and 20 feet for the height. What is the volume or capacity? Answer: $V = Ah = (\pi \times r^2 \times h = 3.14 \times (10 \text{ ft})^2 \times 20 \text{ ft} = 3.14 \times 100 \text{ ft}^2 \times 20 \text{ ft} = 6,280 \text{ ft}^3$.

Think first

Sometimes people can become so bogged down by formulas that they miss simple solutions to math problems. For instance, the American inventor Thomas Edison gave an odd-shaped glass bulb to an assistant. He instructed the assistant to find the volume of the bulb. The assistant spent hours carefully measuring the size and shape of the different figures that made the bulb. He tried to calculate the volume. But he could not arrive at a satisfactory answer.

Edison came in, took the glass bulb, filled it with water, and poured the water into a measuring cup. He had the answer without resorting to complicated formulas. Thinking is always a useful first step in doing math.

SOLUTIONS

1. The annual flood of the Nile River erased property lines.

2. A rope with 12 equally spaced knots can form a right angle.

3. You would not be able to jump at all.

Geometry is useful to farmers, scientists, and people of all professions.

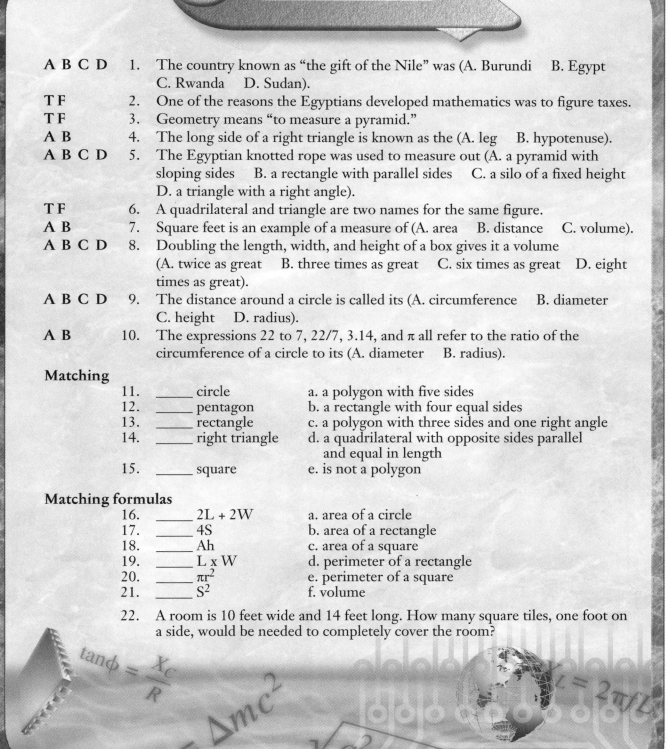

Questions

A B C D   1.   The country known as "the gift of the Nile" was (A. Burundi   B. Egypt   C. Rwanda   D. Sudan).

T F   2.   One of the reasons the Egyptians developed mathematics was to figure taxes.

T F   3.   Geometry means "to measure a pyramid."

A B   4.   The long side of a right triangle is known as the (A. leg   B. hypotenuse).

A B C D   5.   The Egyptian knotted rope was used to measure out (A. a pyramid with sloping sides   B. a rectangle with parallel sides   C. a silo of a fixed height   D. a triangle with a right angle).

T F   6.   A quadrilateral and triangle are two names for the same figure.

A B   7.   Square feet is an example of a measure of (A. area   B. distance   C. volume).

A B C D   8.   Doubling the length, width, and height of a box gives it a volume (A. twice as great   B. three times as great   C. six times as great   D. eight times as great).

A B C D   9.   The distance around a circle is called its (A. circumference   B. diameter   C. height   D. radius).

A B   10.   The expressions 22 to 7, 22/7, 3.14, and π all refer to the ratio of the circumference of a circle to its (A. diameter   B. radius).

Matching

11. _____ circle   a. a polygon with five sides
12. _____ pentagon   b. a rectangle with four equal sides
13. _____ rectangle   c. a polygon with three sides and one right angle
14. _____ right triangle   d. a quadrilateral with opposite sides parallel and equal in length
15. _____ square   e. is not a polygon

Matching formulas

16. _____ 2L + 2W   a. area of a circle
17. _____ 4S   b. area of a rectangle
18. _____ Ah   c. area of a square
19. _____ L x W   d. perimeter of a rectangle
20. _____ πr^2 e. perimeter of a square
21. _____ S^2 f. volume

22.   A room is 10 feet wide and 14 feet long. How many square tiles, one foot on a side, would be needed to completely cover the room?

$\tan\phi = \dfrac{X_C}{R}$ $E = \Delta mc^2$ $\sqrt{a^2 + b^2}$ $X_L = 2\pi f L$

The Greek Way with Math

The Egyptians followed a practical approach to solving math problems. They were content to use the 3-4-5 knotted rope to make a right angle without thinking about how it worked. Many other ancient people had learned this simple rule. It helped them lay out their buildings with square corners. The use of the knotted rope was a successful rule of thumb that they discovered by trial and error.

The ancient Greeks investigated further. They strived to understand the basic principles of geometry. Thales (THAY-leez) was the first of the great Greek scientists. He was born about 600 B.C. in Miletus, a city in what is now Turkey. Thales studied static electricity, magnetism, and astronomy. A year before it happened, he succeeded in predicting that an eclipse of the sun would take place on May 28, 585 B.C.

Thales also worked with ratios of numbers and

PROBLEMS

1. What do a credit card and a driver's license have in common?

2. Who wrote the most widely read textbook of all time?

3. How can 1,000,000 be expressed by using only one zero?

Can You Propose Solutions?

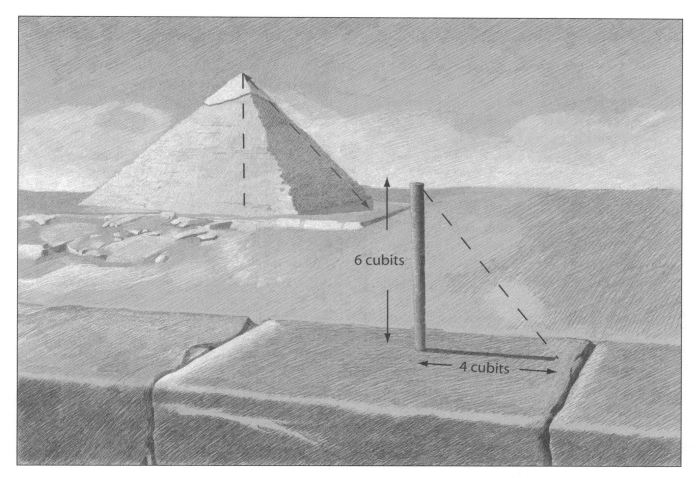

Thales measured the height of the Great Pyramid using a stick, a shadow, and simple geometry.

showed a simple way to measure the height of tall buildings. He set a stick vertically in the ground. He measured the height of the stick and the length of its shadow. Then he compared the length of its shadow to the length of the shadow of a building. The ratio of one to the other gave the unknown height.

Thales measured the height of the pyramids in this way. The length of the shadow of the Great Pyramid of Giza was 214 cubits long. A measuring rod six cubits high cast a shadow of four cubits. The ratio of rod height (6 cubits) to the length of the rod's shadow (4 cubits) is one and a half: 6 cubits / 4 cubits = 1.5. Multiplying the length of the pyramid's shadow by 1.5 gives the pyramid's height: 214 cubits x 1.5 = 321 cubits, or about 481 feet high.

Pythagoras (pih-THAG-oh-rus) was another Greek mathematician. He lived about 500 B.C.; that is, about 2,500 years ago.

Pythagoras was born on the island of Samos in the Aegean Sea. He traveled with his father who bought and sold grain. Pythagoras learned how to convert weights and measures from one system to another, exchange money in different countries, calculate taxes, and figure profit. He may have attended a school begun by Thales. His travels gave Pythagoras an unusually broad education.

Pythagoras began applying numbers to other areas of science. He investigated music made by stringed instruments such as the lyre and harp. He found that the most pleasing tones came from strings with lengths in simple ratios of whole numbers: one to two, three to four, and so on. His theories about the sounds of music have proven to be correct, and are still studied today.

Pythagoras discovered that the three angles of any triangle, regardless of its shape, always added together to give 180 degrees, and it does not have to be a right triangle.

If you know any two angles of a triangle, you can find the third one by subtracting their sum from 180. A right triangle has one angle of 90 degrees. If another one is 30 degrees, then the remaining angle will be 60 degrees: 180 - (90 + 30) = 180 - 120 = 60. The parentheses show that you should add the 90 and 30 together first and then subtract from 180.

Pythagoras saw a difference between trial and error and a true scientific proof. Pythagoras proved that the knotted rope trick the Egyptians used did in fact give a right angle. His proof is known as the Pythagorean theorem: The sum of the squares of the legs of a right triangle is equal to the square of the hypotenuse. In symbols, this could be written as $a^2 + b^2 = c^2$, with a and b the length of the legs of the triangle and c the length of the hypotenuse. The Pythagorean theorem is the best-known mathematical discovery of the ancient world.

The Greeks used letters of their alphabet to stand for numbers. Showing addition and subtraction was difficult, and multiplication and division were nearly impossible. Instead, Pythagoras proved the Pythagorean theorem with geometric figures. He constructed a square on each side of the triangle. He proved that the sum of the areas of the squares on the legs was equal to the area of the square on the hypotenuse.

Any triangle is a right triangle provided the sum of the squares of the lengths of the legs equals the square of the length of the hypotenuse. A triangle with sides of three, four, and five gives a right triangle because three squared plus four squared equals five squared:

$$a^2 + b^2 = c^2$$
$$3^2 + 4^2 = 5^2$$
$$9 + 16 = 25.$$

The Pythagorean theorem revealed that other numbers would give a right angle, too. For instance, a rope pegged out in a triangle with 5, 12, and 13 equally spaced knots along the sides would also give a right triangle:

$$5^2 + 12^2 = 13^2$$
$$25 + 144 = 169.$$

One number that came up time and again in Greek mathematics was the golden ratio. This number is equal to about 1.618. It is an unusual number. If you divide 1.0 by 1.618, the result, rounded off, is 0.618. The digits after the decimal point are identical in both. Another curious fact is that 1.618 squared is equal to 1.618 plus one: $(1.618)^2 = 1.618 + 1$.

The Greeks did not work with decimal fractions — they had not yet been invented. They instead used line segments to describe the golden ratio. Take a line segment and cut it into a long and short segment. Two ratios can be formed from the different segments. One ratio is the length of the short part to the length of the long part. The other ratio is length of the long part to the length of the entire line segment. A cut about 61.8 percent of the way along the line gives equal ratios. The first ratio (short part to long part) will be about 1.618 and so will the second ratio (long part to entire line).

A golden rectangle can be of any size provided the ratio of length to width is 1.618. A golden rectangle with a width of 1 foot will have a length of 1.618 feet.

Because it is pleasing visually, the golden ratio is found in many paintings. For instance,

The golden ratio: A/B = (A + B)/A. The length of A divided by B is equal to the length of A + B divided by A. The ratio is about 1.618.

The golden rectangle: The length and width are equal to the golden ratio: length/width = 1.618

width

length

More Examples of the Golden Ratio

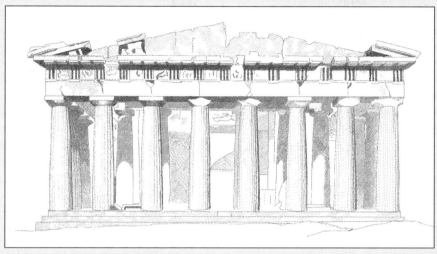

The Parthenon's size is less than one percent different than the golden ratio.

Many people think a golden rectangle is visually appealing. The Greeks used it in the design of the Parthenon, built about 440 B.C. on a hill called the Acropolis in Athens, Greece. The Parthenon is partially in ruins today, but still attracts worldwide attention because of its architecture. It is 101 feet wide and 62 feet high. The ratio of 101 to 62 is 1.63, which is less than one percent different than the golden ratio.

Any figure with measurements in the ratio near 1.618 will have a pleasing proportion. In the Bible, God gave the size for Moses to make the ark of the covenant to hold the Ten Commandments. "Have them make a chest of acacia wood — two and a half cubits long, a cubit and a half wide, and a cubit and a half high" (Exodus 25:10). The ratio of length to width is 1.67: 2.5/1.5 = 1.67. The golden mean is so close to this number that any difference would not be visible to the unaided eye.

Earlier, God told Noah to build an ark 450 feet long, 75 feet wide, and 45 feet high (Genesis 6:15). The ratio of width to height is 75 to 45 is 1.67, which is the same ratio as the ark of the covenant, and very close to the golden ratio.

the Italian artist Leonardo da Vinci (1452–1519) used the ratio in his painting of *The Last Supper. The Last Supper* portrays Jesus with his apostles on the night He was betrayed.

In the 1600s, the golden ratio became known as the divine ratio, meaning supremely beautiful. In modern times, driver licenses, playing cards, and credit cards have the shape of a golden rectangle. A credit card has dimensions of 84 millimeters by 52 millimeters.

Dividing 84 by 52 gives 1.62, which is the same as the golden ratio when it is rounded.

The number 1.618 is only an approximation to the actual value of the golden ratio. Michael Maestlin, a German mathematician who lived about 400 years ago, was the first person to show its approximate value as a decimal. However, the decimal goes on forever and never repeats: 1.6180339887498948482. . . . The number never ends.

Using the same amount of fence (100 feet), the circle encloses more space.

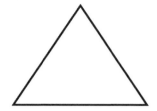

Equilateral Triangle
480 square feet

Square
625 square feet

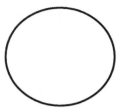

Circle
796 square feet

One of the problems the Greeks tackled was to find the best way to enclose the most space. Suppose a figure has a perimeter of 100 feet. What shape would give the greatest area?

The area changes depending on the type of polygon and its shape. A long, skinny rectangle with length of 40 feet and width of 10 feet has a perimeter of 100 feet: $P = 2W + 2L = 2 \times 10 + 2 \times 40 = 20 + 80 = 100$ feet. It has an area of 400 square feet: $A = LW = 40 \text{ ft} \times 10 \text{ ft} = 400 \text{ ft}^2$. The same amount of fence will enclose more space if the rectangle were not as long and skinny. A rectangle with a length of 30 feet and a width of 20 feet has a perimeter of 100 feet, but an area of 600 square feet.

The greatest amount of space is enclosed by a polygon with equal sides. A square does a better job than a rectangle. A square with sides of 25 feet has a perimeter of 100 feet but an area of 625 square feet: $A = S^2 = (25 \text{ ft})^2 = 625 \text{ ft}^2$.

Triangles show the same principle. A right triangle with unequal sides of 25.0 feet, 33.3 feet, and 41.7 feet has a perimeter of 100 feet and an area of 416 square feet. For a triangle to have the greatest area, it should have all three sides equal in length. Such a triangle is called an equilateral triangle. The word equilateral means equal sides. If each side had a length of $33\frac{1}{3}$ feet, then the perimeter is 100 feet, but the area is about 480 square feet.

Notice that the best triangle for enclosing a field can give only 480 square feet with 100 feet of fence, but a square field can enclose 625 square feet with the same 100 feet of fence. The square enclosed more space.

In fact, as the number of sides of the polygon increases, so does the area for the same perimeter. A pentagon (five sides) with all sides equal does a better job than a square, an octagon (eight sides) does better than a pentagon, and so on. As a polygon gains more and more sides, it takes on a more rounded shape. It looks more and more like a circle.

The Greeks discovered that a circle could have the smallest perimeter (or circumference) and enclose the greatest area. A circle with a circumference of 100 feet has an area of 796 square feet. Compare the area of the circle, 796 square feet, to the square, 625 square feet, and the equilateral triangle, 480 square feet. Of all plane figures having the same perimeter, the circle has the greatest area.

The Greeks believed the circle to be a perfect figure. They decided that because the heavens were perfect, planets must follow circular orbits. They used circles to describe the motion of the sun, moon, and planets. But the planets strayed from circular orbits. The Greeks did not abandon the circle. Instead, they used more and more circles to explain planetary motions. In their model of the planetary system, planets were carried by smaller circles that moved along larger circles. Eventually, the Greeks needed 70 circles to explain how the planets moved.

The circle is a member of a group of curves known as conic sections. They are called conic sections because the Greeks used a cone to describe them. Imagine an ice cream cone turned upside down on a table with the pointy end up. A cut through the cone parallel to the table gives a circle.

A cut across the cone at a slight angle to the table gives an ellipse (i-LIPS). An ellipse is like a circle that has been pulled on either side and stretched out. On the inside of an ellipse are two points. Each one is called a focus; together they are called foci.

An ellipse with foci far from one another is greatly flattened. An ellipse with the foci close together looks like a circle. If the foci are on top of one another, the ellipse becomes a circle. The two foci become the center of the circle.

Suppose that instead of being rectangular, a pool table is made with sides that follow the shape of an ellipse. A ball rolling across its flat surface that passes through one focus will hit the side and always bounce away so that it passes through the other focus. Some swimming pools are made in the shape of an ellipse. When a person dives into the water at one focus, the waves spread out in all directions, strike the walls, and then reflect back to the other focus and produce a splash there.

Some buildings have rooms with domes or archways shaped like part of an ellipse. Sounds made at one focus will radiate out in all directions. Those that strike the surface of the dome or archway will reflect to the other focus.

A person can stand at one focus and whisper to another person at the other focus.

The conic sections are described as slices through a cone.

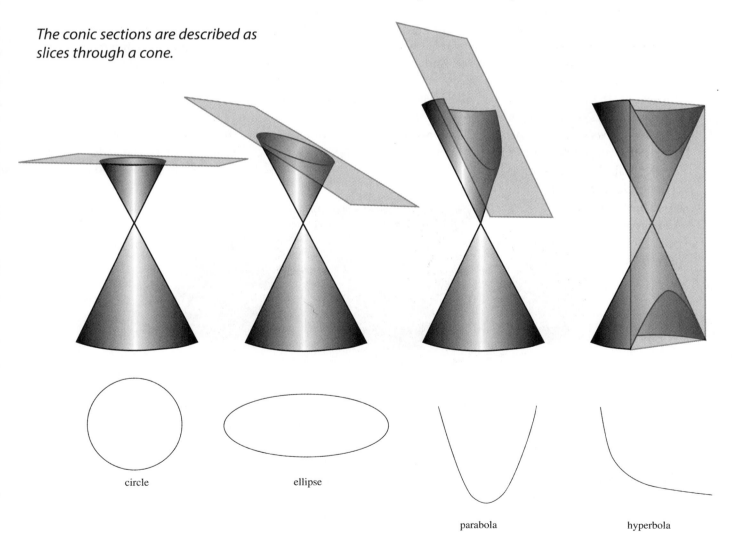

circle   ellipse   parabola   hyperbola

They can hear one another as if standing side by side. Buildings with the elliptical shape are called whispering galleries.

In 1610, Johannes Kepler, a German mathematician, investigated the orbits of planets. (Kepler was a student of Michael Maestlin who calculated the golden ratio as a decimal.) Kepler proved that the planets did not follow circular orbits. Instead, their paths were elliptical. The sun is at one of the foci. Kepler described planetary motions with a single ellipse for each planet. He did away with the 70 circles that the Greeks had been forced to use. Calculating astronomical events such as eclipses, predicting the time of full moon, and making calendars became easier.

Cutting a cone parallel to the slope of its side gives a parabola (puh-RAB-e-lah). A parabola looks like an ellipse that has been stretched out so far that one of the foci has been flung completely away. The second focus is at infinity.

The difference between parabolic and elliptical orbits for solar system objects is important. If an object follows an elliptical orbit, then it is on a closed path. No matter how far it goes out from the sun, the elliptical orbit will eventually bring it back.

A parabola, on the other hand, is open-ended. It does not close back on itself. An object on a parabolic path falls into the solar system, swings around the sun once, and then goes back into deep space, never to return.

Planets follow elliptical orbits that are nearly circular. However, some objects such as comets follow stretched out elliptical orbits. Others have parabolic paths. If a comet follows a very long and stretched

Halley's comet follows a greatly elongated elliptical orbit.

out ellipse, then it will take decades, maybe centuries, before it returns. But it will return. However, if it follows a parabolic orbit, then it will never return. Halley's comet, for instance, follows an elliptical orbit that takes about 76 years for a complete trip. However, some comets follow parabolic orbits. They visit the solar system once and disappear back into deep space.

A parabola has many important uses. A parabolic mirror brings rays of light from planets or the stars to a focus. Giant reflecting telescopes have mirrors whose surfaces have parabolic shapes. They bring the light of distant objects to a focus and form magnified images.

Parabolic mirrors can also be used to collect radio and television broadcast waves. Satellite television dishes have a parabolic shape.

Parabolic reflectors focus light and concentrate it. The United States government built a solar collector to generate electricity. It is in the Mojave (mo-HAH-vee) Desert in California where the sun shines nearly every day. Mirrors on the desert floor reflect sunlight onto a tank at the top of a tower 300 feet high. Although each mirror is flat, the array of individual mirrors is arranged to trace out a parabolic shape. They bring sunlight to a focus. The high temperature is used to boil water. The steam spins a turbine to produce enough electricity to power 3,000 homes.

A parabolic reflector can send out light rather than collect it. A searchlight has a parabolic mirror. A bright light is placed at the focus of the mirror. The mirror reflects the rays out as a tight, parallel beam. Automobile headlights have parabolic reflectors with light bulbs at the focus of each parabolic reflector. Light rays are directed to shine on the road far ahead of the car.

The hyperbola (hye-PUR-bu-luh) is the last conic section. Cutting two cones put pointed-end to pointed-end along the central axis gives a hyperbola. A hyperbola is made of two parts, each identical. Because both are identical, mathematicians often call each part a hyperbola and ignore the fact that it is made of two parts (and so will this book). The term hyper means over or beyond.

An object that enters the solar system along a hyperbolic path has not fallen into the solar system from a dead stop. Instead, it began with a high speed before the gravity of the sun began acting on it. Some subatomic particles such as cosmic rays enter the solar system as if they had been shot by something. They follow a hyperbolic path. One of the puzzles of science is what gives cosmic rays their hyperbolic speeds. A hyperbolic speed is a speed greater than can be accounted for due to the gravitational pull of the sun.

Air flowing around a hurricane follows a shape like a hyperbola. The wind can either be sucked into the swirling hurricane, or just miss it. This point is called the "stagnation point." Weather aircraft that fly into a hurricane look for the stagnation point because winds will be lightest there.

The four conic sections — circle, ellipse, parabola, and hyperbola — can also be described in words. A circle has all points the same distance from a fixed point called the center. An ellipse has two foci such that the straight-line distance from one focus to any point on the ellipse and back to the other focus is always the same distance. A parabola has all points the same distance from a fixed point and a fixed line. A hyperbola has all points for

A satellite dish has a parabolic shape.

which the difference in distance from two fixed points is a constant. However, the easiest way to visualize them is by cutting through the cone at different angles.

As the conic sections show, the mathematics of the Greeks was based mainly on geometry. The most important of the Greek books was Euclid's *Elements of Geometry*. Euclid was a mathematician and teacher who lived in the Greek city of Alexandria, Egypt. Euclid collected everything known about the subject. The 13 sections of his book cover plane geometry, ratios, and even solid geometry. Solid geometry is the study of figures with three dimensions such as pyramids and spheres.

Previous books had been merely collections of ways to solve problems. The Egyptian scribe Ahmes stated in his scroll that he was copying material from earlier scrolls. Euclid did more than merely collect information and copy it. He gave the book a structure that advanced from simple to complex.

Euclid started with a few key definitions and basic assumptions. He built upon discoveries previously proven with the basic assumptions.

Students studied geometry because it strengthened their ability to think and reason. But the subject did demand discipline and close attention. Ptolemy I, king of Egypt, studied geometry under Euclid. He asked for a simpler presentation. Euclid said, "There is no royal road to geometry."

On another occasion, a student asked, "What do I get by learning these things?"

Euclid said, "Give him a coin, since he must make a gain out of what he learns."

Euclid's *Elements* contained the basic mathematical knowledge of the ancient world. He wrote it on papyrus, the writing surface made of the grasslike reeds that grew along the Nile river. Papyrus scrolls were about 30 feet long. The material tended to crack and fray as students unrolled the scrolls. New copies had to be made often to replace well-used scrolls. As science advanced, some scrolls contained information that became out of date. They were discarded and never copied. They disappeared.

Euclid's *Elements* did survive because information in it remained useful. It was copied, recopied, and translated into other languages. Julius Caesar, Isaac Newton, George Washington, and Albert Einstein all learned geometry from various translations of *Elements*. More people have studied Euclid's *Elements of Geometry* than any other mathematics book.

Archimedes (ar-kuh-MEE-deez) is ranked as the greatest mathematician of the ancient world. He studied in Alexandria in Egypt. His instructor was one of the teachers that Euclid trained. After spending some time in Egypt, Archimedes returned to his home on Sicily, an island in the Mediterranean Sea. Hieron II ruled Syracuse, the city where Archimedes lived.

Archimedes became one of the best-known scientists of ancient times. He is generally considered equal to Isaac Newton in his mathematical ability. However, he was hampered by the lack of a convenient way to write numbers. The largest number in common use was 1,000. If objects numbered more than 1,000, then they were often said to be uncountable.

Archimedes realized that numbers continued well beyond 1,000. He invented the name myriad for 10,000. It was ten multiplied by itself four times: 10 x 10 x 10 x 10 = 10,000. He made a still larger number as a myriad myriad, or one

hundred million (100,000,000.) He called this number an octade because it was 10 multiplied by itself eight times. A still larger number would be an octade octade, or 10 multiplied by itself 16 times: 10,000,000,000,000,000.

Modern scientists use a similar way of showing larger numbers. The method is called powers of 10 notation. Powers of 10 is especially useful for very large numbers. Powers of 10 counts how many times 10 must be multiplied by itself to give the number.

The myriad of Archimedes can be expressed as 10^4. The expression 10^4 is read "ten to the fourth power." The number 10^4 and 10,000 are equal in value. For small numbers, powers of ten have no great advantage over writing out the numbers. Suppose however, the number is very large, say the octade octade that Archimedes used. An octade octade can be written as 10^{16}. That is certainly more compact and easier to read than 1 followed by 16 zeros.

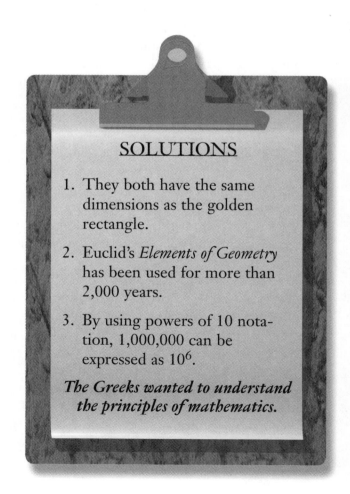

SOLUTIONS

1. They both have the same dimensions as the golden rectangle.

2. Euclid's *Elements of Geometry* has been used for more than 2,000 years.

3. By using powers of 10 notation, 1,000,000 can be expressed as 10^6.

The Greeks wanted to understand the principles of mathematics.

A B   1. The (A. Egyptians   B. Greeks) strove to understand the principles of mathematics.

            2. The sum of the _____ of the legs of a right triangle are equal to the _____ of the hypotenuse.

A B C   3. The figure that encloses the greatest area with the least perimeter or circumference is the (A. circle   B. square   C. triangle).

A B C D   4. A whispering gallery has a shape like (A. a circle   B. a hyperbola C. a parabola   D. an ellipse).

A B   5. If an object follows an elliptical orbit, then it is on (A. a closed B. an open) path.

Matching

6. _____ Archimedes
7. _____ Euclid
8. _____ Johannes Kepler
9. _____ Pythagoras
10. _____ Thales

a. discovered that the sum of the three angles of any triangle is 180 degrees
b. used ratios to find the heights of buildings
c. proved planets follow elliptical orbits
d. wrote *Elements of Geometry*
e. ancient Greek who worked out a way to show large numbers that he called myriads

Matching

11. _____ circle
12. _____ ellipse
13. _____ parabola
14. _____ hyperbola

a. a mirror of this shape will focus sunlight
b. all points are the same distance from the center
c. the first part of the name means over or beyond
d. the orbit of Halley's comet is of this shape

$$\tan\phi = \frac{X_C}{R}$$

$$E = \Delta mc^2$$

$$\sqrt{a^2 + b^2}$$

$$L = 2\pi fL$$

Names for Numbers

One of the first mathematical skills a child learns is to count. Ask a preschool child how old he or she is, and the child is most likely to hold up fingers. Three fingers means three years old. Or, the child may be able to say three (English), *tres* (Spanish), or *trois* (French.) Many children can count to ten by the time they enter kindergarten.

We count in groups of ten. From one to ten, a person can count on the fingers. Each of the numbers from one to ten has a separate name: one, two, three, four, five, six, seven, eight, nine, ten. After ten, the names begin repeating based on ten. The word eleven is from an old English word meaning one left after counting to ten. Eleven is ten with one more. Twelve means two left. Thirteen more clearly shows that it means three and

PROBLEMS

1. Why did "nothing" in math become so important?

2. How can five mean fifty?

3. Why should numbers be kept in their place?

Can You Propose Solutions?

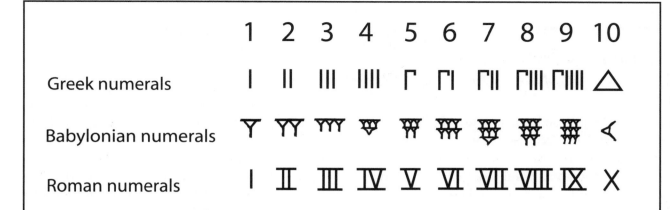

	1	2	3	4	5	6	7	8	9	10
Greek numerals	I	II	III	IIII	Γ	ΓI	ΓII	ΓIII	ΓIIII	△
Babylonian numerals	Υ	ΥΥ	ΥΥΥ	∇	∇∇	∇∇∇	∇∇∇	∇∇∇	∇∇∇	◁
Roman numerals	I	II	III	IV	V	VI	VII	VIII	IX	X

ten. Fourteen means four and ten, and so on to nineteen, meaning nine and ten. Twenty means two tens. The names are based on tens all the way to ninety-nine, meaning nine tens and nine.

One hundred, however, introduces a new word for the number. No one is quite sure of the origin of the word hundred. Ten hundreds make a thousand. The word thousand means great force. In the Middle Ages, an army was about 500 soldiers. An army that numbered 1,000 soldiers would be considered a great force.

Not every culture based their counting on tens. The Mayans of Mexico counted by 20s. The English language uses the word score for 20. The best-known example is in the Gettysburg Address. Several months after a terrible Civil War battle, President Lincoln spoke at the dedication of the national cemetery at Gettysburg, Pennsylvania. He began his speech with the words "Fourscore and seven years ago our fathers brought forth on this continent a new nation." The birthday of the United States was 1776, and fourscore and seven years are 87 years. Lincoln's speech was given in 1863: 1776 + 87 = 1863.

Any mark that is used to stand for a number is called a numeral. The symbol "1" is a numeral that stands for the number one. Some ancient people also used a mark much like our numeral 1 to stand for one. The Babylonians wrote with a wedge that made triangular marks in a wet clay tablet. They showed the number one by a single triangular mark. The Egyptian symbol for one was a single stroke of the pen, I, what we call a tally mark.

Sometimes people confuse numeral and number. For example, a first grade teacher wrote the numeral 5 on the board and asked a student to write a bigger number. The student made a gigantic 4. He made the numeral for 4 larger than the numeral for 5, but the number 4 represents a smaller quantity than the number 5. Most people, however, use the word number whether they are talking about the number or the numeral.

The value of a number does not depend on how it is represented. Four tally marks, I I I I, the word four, the numeral 4, and the Roman numeral IV, all represent the same quantity.

But some symbols are more difficult to use than others. The Greeks used letters of their alphabet to stand for their numbers. The first nine letters of the Greek alphabet stood for one through nine. The next nine letters stood for 10 through 90. Nine more letters stood for 100 through 900. This required 27 letters, but the Greek alphabet had only 24 letters. The Greeks borrowed three letters from the Phoenician alphabet to represent 700, 800, and 900. A person had to remember the value of all 27 letters.

The number 900 was the largest that the Greeks could represent with a single letter.

The Greeks made larger numbers by putting a small mark before the letter, so their

Roman Numerals Today

People use Roman numerals because they appear elegant or ornate. The Olympic games are numbered with Roman numerals, as are football superbowls. Kings and queens of England have Roman numerals after their name. Elizabeth II became queen of England in 1952 after the death of her father George VI. One of the best known kings of England was Henry VIII, read "Henry the 8th."

Clock faces on grandfather clocks have Roman numerals, and old books and movies use them to show the copyright date. Cornerstones of buildings use Roman numerals to show when construction began on the building. A cornerstone with MCMXVII gives a date of 1917.

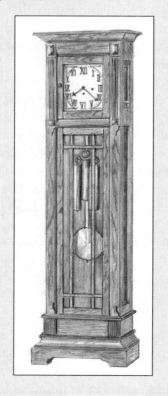

letter for A (called alpha) with a mark in front of it, 'A, meant 1,000.

The Romans used letters of their alphabet to stand for numbers, too. In the Roman system, the letter I stood for 1, V for 5, X for 10, L for 50, C for 100, D for 500, and M for 1,000.

The number 1,000 was the largest that the Romans could write with a single letter. The Romans made larger numbers by putting a bar over the letter. A bar over V showed 5,000 and a bar over X showed 10,000. However, they seldom needed to write a number greater than 1,000.

The Bible records in the Gospel of Luke that Joseph and Mary traveled to Bethlehem to be counted in a census. See Luke 2:1–5. The census and taxing were done with Roman numerals.

Roman numerals were added together to give the value of the number they represented. The expression VIIII meant nine: 5 + 1 + 1 +1 +1 = 9. (The use of IX for nine came later.) Fifty-five was written as LV: 50 + 5 = 55. The number 87 was shown as LXXXVII: 50 + 30 + 5 + 2 = 87.

Two numbers written with Roman numerals were added by first putting all of the letters together. Adding CLXXIII to XXXVIII gave CLXXXXXVIIIIIII. Then the expression was simplified. The five Xs could be replaced with L (50), and five of the six Is could be replaced with V. This gave CLLVVI, which could be simplified still farther. C replaced the two Ls, and an X replaced the two Vs. The final answer was CCXI.

Roman numerals required long and tedious calculations. Experts who did a lot of math used a simple calculator called an abacus. It had been invented in Babylon about 2,000 B.C. and spread throughout the world. The Roman abacus had markers called counters that could be moved in groves in a tablet. An improved model used beads strung on wooden rods. Adding and subtracting was a simple matter of quickly sliding the beads along the rods.

During Roman times, the order of Roman numerals did not matter. The Romans always added the values. So 23 could be written as XXIII or IIIXX. However, after the Roman Empire fell, scholars of the Middle Ages changed the writing of Roman numerals. The order of the letters now mattered. Should a single letter for a smaller number be in front of the letter for a larger number, then its value was subtracted from the value of the larger one. The change took less space. They changed four from IIII to IV. One was subtracted from five: IV = 5 - 1 = 4. Nine was written as IX. CM meant 1,000-100 = 900.

The year 1999 would be shown as MCMXCIX:

M + CM + XC + IX
1,000 + (1,000 - 100) + (100 - 10) + (10 - 1)
1,000 + 900 + 90 + 9
1999

With this new method, the number 23 was always written as XXIII but never IIIXX. The use of Roman numerals was clumsy to begin with, and the added complication of subtracting smaller numbers that came before larger ones added to the confusion.

The Romans conquered most of Europe, and parts of Africa and Asia. Their system of writing numbers became standard. Even after the Roman Empire collapsed, Europeans continued to use Roman numerals.

I	1
V	5
X	10
L	50
C	100
D	500
M	1000

The Romans used letters of their alphabet to stand for numbers

After the fall of the Roman Empire in A.D. 476, learning came to a standstill in Europe. Countries broke into small feuding kingdoms. Trade between cities nearly ceased. Schools closed. Few people learned to read, write, or solve simple arithmetic problems.

But the rest of the world continued to advance. People in India made the next great discovery in mathematics.

People in India did not rely on letters of the their alphabet to represent numbers. Instead, they invented separate symbols. The numerals, which they wrote by hand, did not look exactly like the ones printed in books today. However, their similarity clearly shows that they were the source of our modern digits: 1, 2, 3, . . . 9. The word digit means finger or toe, a reference to how counting began.

The Indian mathematicians used an abacus for calculations similar to the one the Romans used. Suppose a number on the abacus had three beads to the right on

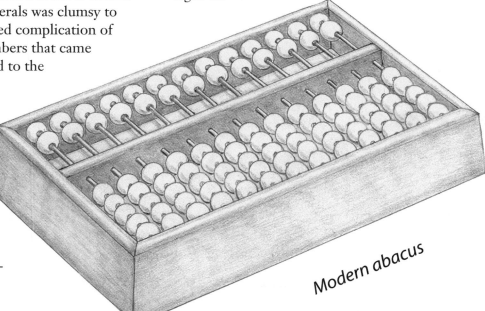

Modern abacus

the first rod and two beads on the second rod. The Indian mathematicians used digits to write this as 23, meaning two tens and three ones. Order of the digits mattered. Three beads on the second rod and two beads on the first rod would show 32, meaning three tens and two ones.

The number 23 was different from 32 because of place value. Place value gave a symbol a different value depending upon its location in a numeral. A symbol on the far right showed the number of ones. The next symbol gave the number of tens. The symbol in third place gave the number of hundreds, and so on.

The Roman system used three different symbols — V, L, and D — to stand for 5, 50 and 500. But in the new system, the digit 5 could stand for different values. The 5 in 15 meant 5 ones. The 5 in 57 meant 5 tens. The 5 in 538 meant 5 hundreds.

In most cases, place value took less room than the same number written with Roman numerals. Its value was easier to comprehend. The expression 538 and DXXXVIII both represented the same number, but the Roman version was longer and its value could not be easily grasped.

But the new system had one failing. The digits 1 through 9 could not show the absence of a bead on the abacus. Suppose the first row had three beads, the second row had no beads, and the third row had two beads. The beads showed a value of two hundreds, no tens, and three ones. Although you could read the number easily enough, how could you write it?

The digits 1 through 9 were in common use for 1,000 years before someone saw the need for a symbol for nothing. We don't know who made this important improvement. Sometime in the 700s (about 1,300 years ago) "0" was used to stand for nothing. The number with 2 hundreds, no tens, and 3 ones could be written as 203.

The origin of zero is unclear. At first, the number 203 may have been written with a blank for the missing tens: 2 3. But this could be confusing. Was it a poorly written 23, 203, or possibly 2003? So the person writing the number probably put a dot to show the missing digits: 2 • 3. Over time, the hastily written dot became a loop. Others think zero began as an empty circle, O, meaning a place with nothing in it.

Regardless of how it began, the numeral zero made a vast improvement in how people wrote numbers. With ten digits — 0, 1, 2, 3, 4, 5, 6, 7, 8, 9 — a person could easily write numbers from 0 to far beyond the myriad myriad of Archimedes.

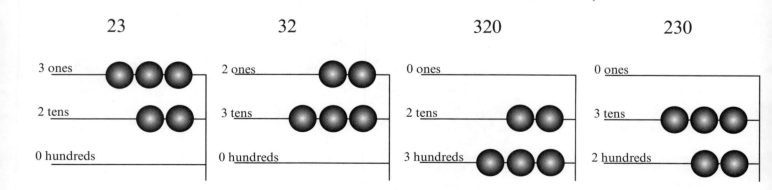

The abacus used beads to stand for the value of numbers.

A view of Pisa, the home of Leonardo Fibonacci, who convinced Europeans to use Arabic numerals

The great minds of Greece failed to see the need for a symbol for zero. Historians today are still puzzled by this fact. The zero in mathematics is as important as the wheel in transportation, but people invented the wheel at least 3,000 years before they invented zero.

The zero came into common use in India about A.D. 900. In less than 100 years, the new numbering system spread from India to the Arab world. The Arabs lived in the Middle East, which included southwest Asia, the Arabian Peninsula, and northeast Africa. Modern countries in this area include Saudi Arabia, Iran, and Iraq. The Arabs traded with India by sailing across the Indian Ocean, or by caravan along the Silk Road to China. The Arabs learned how to use the new numbering system as they traded for spices in India.

Spain was the first European country to use the new system. Moors ruled Spain until 1492. The Moors were people of North Africa who accepted the customs of the Arabs and married into their families. They learned the new math from the Arabs. The numerals became known as Arabic numerals, although the original inventors lived in India.

The rest of Europe remained mired in the Dark Ages. Few people could read and write. Even fewer could do mathematics, and they had been taught math using Roman numerals. They were unwilling to change. Most Europeans ignored Arabic numerals for more than 200 years.

Leonardo Fibonacci (fee-boh-NAHT-chee) of Pisa, Italy, convinced Europeans to use Arabic numerals. The Italian cities were

Leonardo Fibonacci

the first to come out of the Dark Ages. Pisa served as a center of commerce. Its merchants sent agents to buy products from the Arabs. When Fibonacci was 20 years old, he became an agent for Pisa merchants.

In Italy, merchants packaged goods in groups of 12, 60, 144, or 360. The numbers could be easily divided into smaller portions. For instance, a dozen items could be sold in smaller lots of 1, 2, 3, 4, or 6. Customers could pay $1/12$, $1/6$, $1/4$, $1/3$, or $1/2$ of the cost for a complete dozen. Merchants had to stick with these easily divisible numbers because Roman numerals did not lend themselves to complicated calculations. The lack of a good numbering system limited merchants in how they did business.

Everywhere he traveled, Fibonacci watched merchants make their calculations. He kept a record of shortcuts and improved methods. While in Algeria in Northern Africa, he saw that the Moors could easily divide large shipments into smaller ones, calculate weights and measures, change money from one currency to another, pay taxes, figure profit, and give each partner the right share. The Moors used Arabic numerals.

Fibonacci was astonished at the ease of doing math with Arabic numerals. It gave the Arabs and Moors an advantage over European merchants. He learned the new numbering system and how to calculate with it.

He returned to Pisa in the year 1200. He wrote several books about the new system. The best known one was *Book of Calculating*. (The actual title was *Liber Abbaci*, which means "book of the abacus.") The first seven chapters dealt with the way to write numbers. Fibonacci explained the benefit of separate symbols for digits, the advantage of place value, and the importance of zero. He gave step-by-step instructions on how to add, subtract, multiply, and divide. He solved practical problems of everyday business.

His *Book of Calculating* persuaded many Europeans to use this new system. Its ease attracted bankers, businessmen, engineers, and scientists. Of course, the change did not happen overnight. The Dark Ages lingered in

Galileo is rumored to have performed an experiment of dropping a cannonball and a wooden ball from the top of the Leaning Tower of Pisa.

Europe until about 1450. With the invention of the printing press, Europe again began making strides in science.

Mathematics is sometimes called the handmaiden of science. It is a tool that helps scientists do their jobs. In the late 1500s, Galileo in Italy measured the speed of falling bodies. In the early 1600s, Kepler in Germany described the motion of the planets around the sun. Later in that century, Newton in England developed the three laws of motion.

These and other advances in science became possible because of the new math introduced by Fibonacci. Today, he is credited with giving a fresh start to mathematics in Europe. He is honored with a statue near the Leaning Tower of Pisa.

Large numbers can be easily written with Arabic numerals. The need for larger numbers usually came when governments counted their people, and totaled the taxes collected from them.

In modern times, names for larger numbers have been invented. The word million (1,000,000) came into use in the 1300s, well after the time of the Greeks and Romans.

In 1790, the United States was made of 16 states with a total population of almost four million people — exactly 3,893,874 according to the national census — and a national debt of 40 million dollars. A national debt occurs when a government spends more money than it collects as taxes. It borrows money from its citizens or from foreign governments. The amount of money that a country owes is called the national debt.

The word billion did not come into use until the 1600s. It was made by combining the prefix bi with the word million. The prefix bi means two. In England, a billion meant two millions multiplied together: 1,000,000 x 1,000,000 = 1,000,000,000,000, or 10^{12}. But in the United States, a billion is a thousand millions, 1,000,000,000, or 10^9. In 1920, the United States had 48 states with a population in excess of 105 million people — 105,273,049 people according to the census — and a national debt of about 25 billion dollars.

Every time a number is multiplied by 1,000, three zeros are added, and a new name is given:

1,000	thousand
1,000,000	million
1,000,000,000	billion
1,000,000,000,000	trillion
1,000,000,000,000,000	quadrillion

An easier way to write these numbers is using the number 10 and an exponent. The exponent can be interpreted as showing how many zeroes are in the number:

10^3	3 zeroes	thousand
10^6	6 zeroes	million
10^9	9 zeroes	billion

A trillion also came into use in the 1600s. The word was made by combining the prefix tri with the word million. When the word was first coined, it equaled a million multiplied by itself three times: a million times a million times a million, or 10^{18}. However, in the United States, and everywhere else in the world except for England, a trillion means a thousand billion, or 10^{12}. In the year 2000, the United States had 50 states with a population of 281 million — exactly 281,421,906 according to the census — and a national debt between 5 and 6 trillion dollars.

Metric prefixes are also used for large numbers. Mega means one million, giga means one billion, and tera means one trillion. Today, these large numbers describe the speed and memory capacity of computers. Computers have disk drives that can store vast amounts of information. Large ones can store a terabyte of data. A byte is the space needed for a single character or letter of the alphabet. A disk drive with 1.0 terabytes of storage can hold 1,000,000,000,000 bytes (10^{12} bytes), which is enough space for four million books the size of this one.

Names for numbers larger than a trillion do exist. The names are based on the prefixes after tri. The prefix quad (4) makes quadrillion, 10^{15}, which is a thousand trillions. The prefix quin (5) makes quintillion, 10^{18}, which is a thousand quadrillions, and so on. The next prefixes are sext (6), sept (7), oct (8), non (9), and dec (10). A decillion is 10^{33}.

The largest named numbers are the googol and googolplex. The names appeared in 1940 in a book published by two mathematicians named Edward Kasner and James R. Newman. Edward Kasner asked his nine-year-old nephew, Milton Sirotta, to invent a name for a very large number. The boy called it a googol. Kasner defined a googol as 10 multiplied by itself 100 times (10^{100}). It is 1 followed by 100 zeros. Write it out if you wish. It will take about three lines on a piece of paper.

Be aware that expressing a number in Arabic numerals is not the same as the number of objects that it represents. As an example, one million can be written with seven digits (1,000,000), and it takes about an inch of paper. To make a million tally marks, I, takes about 12,000 feet of paper.

Edward Kasner invented a still larger number, the googolplex. He defined it as 10 multiplied by itself a googol number of times. A googol is 10^{100} and a googolplex is 10^{googol}. A googolplex is such a huge number that writing it as 1 followed by zeros simply cannot be done. A strip of paper that filled the entire known universe would not be long enough to hold all of its zeros. (Even the shortened exponential representation of this number would have an exponent of 1 followed by 100 zeros.)

Although googol and googolplex are fun numbers to talk about, most mathematicians and scientists prefer to use powers of ten and ignore the peculiar names.

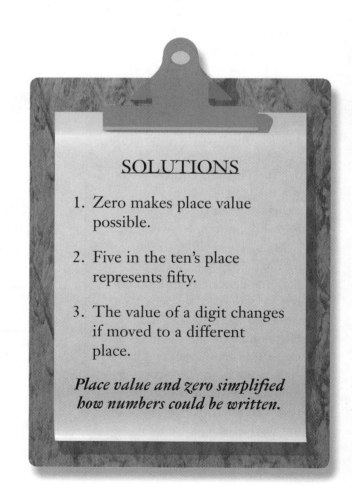

SOLUTIONS

1. Zero makes place value possible.

2. Five in the ten's place represents fifty.

3. The value of a digit changes if moved to a different place.

Place value and zero simplified how numbers could be written.

Questions

T F 1. Some cultures counted with 20 as the base.

T F 2. Any mark that is used to stand for a number is called a digit.

T F 3. The value of a number does not depend on how it is represented.

T F 4. Place value gives a symbol a different value depending upon its location.

T F 5. The digit zero was invented at the same time as the digits 1 through 9.

T F 6. The digit zero first came into use in India.

T F 7. Italian merchants packaged goods by the dozen because the number 12 could be divided into smaller portions.

T F 8. Mathematics is sometimes called the ruler of science.

T F 9. Isaac Newton introduced the use of place value and the numeral zero to Europe.

T F 10. Fibonacci wrote a book called *Elements of Counting*.

T F 11. The prefix bi means one half.

T F 12. The word billion has the same meaning in England as in the United States.

T F 13. Of the prefixes giga, mega, and tera, the one that has the greatest value is mega.

Number Patterns

In the English language, words such as radar and level are palindromes. They are spelled the same forward or backward. The proper names Eve and Anna are also palindromes. Entire sentences can be palindromes. "Madam, I'm Adam," has the letters in the same order when read forward or backward. "A man, a plan, a canal, Panama!" is still longer. One of the longest palindromes is this sentence that may sound like nonsense: "Straw? No, too stupid a fad, I put soot on warts." The sentence refers to the fact that at one time people thought they could get rid of warts by rubbing straw over them. Rewrite the letters in order from the end of the sentence toward the beginning and they will spell out the same sentence.

In Arabic numerals, the number 242 is a palindrome. It has the same value whether read forward or backward. The number 1881 is not only a

PROBLEMS

1. What do Eve, "Madam, I'm Adam," 121, and CXC have in common?

2. What is the largest prime number?

3. How did rabbits figure in a number problem?

Can You Propose Solutions?

palindrome, but also reads the same when held upside down! The Roman numeral expression for 242 is CCXLII, and that is not a palindrome. The number 1881 in Roman numerals is MDCCCLXXXI. It is not a palindrome, and it does not read the same right side up as upside down. On the other hand, CXC is a palindrome in Roman numerals. But 190 is not a palindrome in Arabic numerals.

Whether a number is a palindrome or not depends on the notation. The notation for the number and not the number itself has the property of being a palindrome. That property can change if the notation changes.

Number patterns can also be based on the way the numbers are written and not the numbers themselves. For instance, most mathematicians would be puzzled by why numbers are listed in this sequence: 8, 5, 4, 9, 1, 7, 6, 3, 2, 0. However, the pattern is easy to see when the values of the numbers are written as words: eight, five, four, nine, one, seven, six, three, two, and zero. Expressed as words, digits in the series 8, 5, 4, 9, 1, 7, 6, 3, 2, and 0 are in alphabetical order.

But many properties of numbers remain true regardless of how they are written. They are properties of the numbers themselves. The study of the properties of whole numbers is called number theory. Mathematicians are interested in facts about numbers that are true regardless of the notation. These facts include whether a number is even, odd, or prime.

The numbers, 2, 4, 6, 8, and so on are even numbers in any notation system. An even number can be divided evenly by two. The division by two does not leave a remainder. Mathematicians state the same idea in terms of multiplication. They say that an even number can be written as two times some other whole number. For instance, 10 is even because it can be written as two times five: $2 \times 5 = 10$, and 14 is even because it can be written as two times seven: $2 \times 7 = 14$.

An even number can be written in symbols as $2 \times n$, where n is a whole number. We know that 22 is even because it can be written as

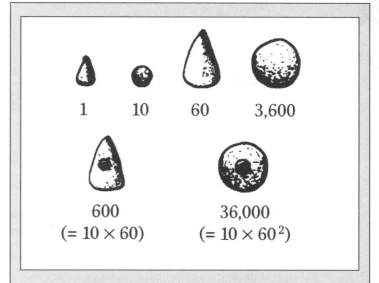

From about 3300 B.C., the Sumerians represented numerical units with ordinary objects. These symbolized 1, 10, 60, and 60^2.

$2 \times n$ by setting n equal to 11. The expression $2 \times n$ can also be written as 2n. It is understood to mean multiply 2 and n.

When written using Arabic numerals, even numbers always end in 0, 2, 4, 6, or 8. We know that 3,586 is even because it ends in 6. It can be written in the mathematical form of $2 \times n$ with n = 1,793 because $2 \times 1,793 = 3,586$.

The numbers 1, 3, 5, 7, 9, and so on are odd numbers. An odd number gives a remainder of one when divided by two. Mathematicians use multiplication to say that an odd number can be written as an even number plus one. For instance, 11 is odd because it can be written as the even number 10 plus one: $10 + 1 = 11$, and 15 is odd because it can be written as $14 + 1 = 15$.

An odd number can be written in symbols as $2n + 1$, where n is a whole number. We know that 23 is odd because it can be written as $2 \times 11 + 1$.

Two is a factor of all even numbers. A factor will divide into a number without giving a remainder. Two is a factor of 10 because two will divide into 10 and not leave a remainder. Five is also a factor of 10 because it will divide into 10 without a remainder.

Figure 8-1

Prime Numbers

Is 221 prime? Here is a table of the divisions:

$$221 \div 2 = 110 \text{ remainder } 1 \qquad 221 \div 7 = 31 \text{ remainder } 4$$

$$221 \div 3 = 73 \text{ remainder } 2 \qquad 221 \div 11 = 20 \text{ remainder } 1$$

$$221 \div 5 = 44 \text{ remainder } 1 \qquad 221 \div 13 = 17 \text{ remainder } 0$$

Mathematicians define factors in terms of multiplication. Two is a factor of 10 because 10 can be written as the product of two and another whole number: 2 x 5 = 10. Five is also a factor of 10 because 5 x 2 = 10. The other factors of 10 are 1 and 10 because 1 x 10 = 10. The number 10 has four factors: 1, 2, 5, and 10.

The number 12 has six factors: 1, 2, 3, 4, 6, and 12: 1 x 12 = 12, 2 x 6 = 12, and 3 x 4 = 12. Five is not a factor of 12 because no whole number can be found that will make 12 when multiplied by five. (It is true that 5 x 2.4 = 12, but 2.4 is not a whole number.)

Some numbers such as 12 have many factors, but other numbers have only two factors. The number seven can only be written as 1 x 7.

A prime number is one that has only itself and one as factors. Mathematicians do not consider the number one prime. The first prime number is two. It is the only even prime. Three is prime, and so is five, seven, 11, and 13.

After the number two, all prime numbers are odd. It is easy to see why this is true. An even number has two as a factor, so it is not prime because it has factors other than itself and one. All other prime numbers after two must be odd numbers.

However, being odd alone is not enough to make a number prime. The number nine is odd, but it can be written as 3 x 3 = 9, so it has factors other than one and itself. It is not prime.

A number that is not prime is called composite. The word composite means to put together from smaller parts. Nine is composite because multiplying 3 x 3 will make it.

The prime numbers less than 100 are 2, 3, 5, 7, 11, 13, 17, 19, 23, 29, 31, 37, 41, 43, 47, 53, 59, 61, 67, 71, 73, 79, 83, 89, 97. All the rest are composite, except for 1, which is considered a special case. It is neither prime nor composite.

As you count higher and higher to larger numbers it is often difficult to decide if the number is prime or not. You can eliminate some numbers right away. Those that end in 0, 2, 4, 6, and 8 are even so they will have two as a factor. Except for five itself, numbers that end in 0 or 5 will have five as a factor. For example, 125 cannot be prime because 125 is divisible by five without a remainder: 125 / 5 = 25. Or, stating the same idea as a multiplication, 5 x 25 = 125.

But merely looking at a number that ends in 1, 3, 7, or 9 will not tell you whether it is prime or not. The numbers 51, 87, and 91 may appear to be prime, but they are not prime: 3 x 17 = 51, 3 x 29 = 87, and 7 x 13 = 91.

Finding prime numbers is not easy. To test whether a particular number is prime, you must divide it by the prime numbers below it. For instance, to test whether 221 is prime, divide by 2, 3, 5, 7, 11, 13, and 17. See figure 8-1.

The number 221 is composite and has prime factors of 13 and 17: 13 x 17 = 221. A similar test of the number 223 reveals that it has no factors. It is a prime number.

Mathematicians have found that testing for primes can end when a prime number times itself is greater than the number being tested. In the test of 223, only the primes up to 13 must be tested. The product of 13 x 13 = 169, which is less than 223. But 17 does not have to be tested because 17 x 17 = 289, which is greater than 223.

A moment's thought reveals why this is so. As the size of a divisor increases, the answer decreases. For instance, two divided into 100 is 50. Five divided into 100 is 20, and 11 divided into 100 gives nine and a remainder. Any divisor of 100 that is larger than 10 will give an answer that is less than 10.

This means that at a certain point there is no need to divide by larger and larger primes. If the number being tested is composite, then a smaller prime will reveal the larger prime factor. For instance, when 13 was divided into 221, it gave 17. If you divide 221 by 17 you get 13, which you have already tried.

A Greek mathematician named Eratosthenes (er-uh-TAHS-theh-neez) invented a way to test for primes that did not require multiplication or division. His method was called the sieve of Eratosthenes. A sieve is a device that separates objects. Flour is passed through a sieve during milling to remove straw, husks, pebbles, and other foreign material.

The sieve of Eratosthenes removed composites from a list of numbers. To use his method, begin by writing the whole numbers to 100. Skip two and then strike out every second number. Skip three and strike out every third number. Move to the next number that has not been struck out.

Four was struck out by two, so the next number is five. Skip five and strike out every fifth number. The next number is seven because six was struck out by both two and three. Strike out every seventh number after seven.

Figure 8-2

Sieve of Eratosthenes finds prime numbers to 100.
The prime factors 2, 3, 5, and 7 will reveal all of the prime numbers.

#		#		#		#		#	
1	special	21	3, 7	41	prime	61	prime	81	3
2	prime	22	2	42	2, 3, 7	62	2	82	2
3	prime	23	prime	43	prime	63	3, 7	83	prime
4	2	24	2, 3	44	2	64	2	84	2, 3, 7
5	prime	25	5	45	3, 5	65	5	85	5
6	2, 3	26	2	46	2	66	2, 3	86	2
7	prime	27	3,	47	prime	67	prime	87	3
8	2	28	2, 7	48	2, 3	68	2	88	2
9	3	29	prime	49	7	69	3	89	prime
10	2, 5	30	2, 3, 5	50	2, 5	70	2, 5, 7	90	2, 3, 5
11	prime	31	prime	51	3	71	prime	91	7
12	2, 3	32	2	52	2	72	2, 3	92	2
13	prime	33	3	53	prime	73	prime	93	3
14	2, 7	34	2	54	2, 3	74	2	94	2
15	3, 5	35	5, 7	55	5	75	3, 5	95	5
16	2	36	2, 3	56	2, 7	76	2	96	2, 3
17	prime	37	prime	57	3	77	7	97	prime
18	2, 3	38	2	58	2	78	2, 3	98	2, 7
19	prime	39	3	59	prime	79	prime	99	3
20	2, 5	40	2, 5	60	2, 3, 5	80	2, 5	100	2, 5

Striking out the multiples of seven finishes the test for primes through 100. Any number that has not been struck out will be prime. We can stop at 11, the next prime number, because 11 x 11 = 121, which is greater than 100.

In quick order, the sieve of Eratosthenes revealed all prime numbers below 100. See figure 8-2. The same procedure can find the prime numbers less than 1,000 by striking out multiples of 2, 3, 5, 7, 11, 13, 17, 19, 23, 29, and 31. After every 31st number is struck out, the test is finished because the next prime, 37, times itself is greater than 1,000: 37 x 37 = 1,369.

The top number in the sieve can be far greater than 1,000. Eratosthenes's method was the first efficient way to test for primes. It is still used today to find prime numbers, although high-speed computers do the striking out electronically.

Mathematicians used computers to test large numbers to see if they were prime. In 2001, a prime number was found that had more than four million digits. At 72 digits per line and 50 lines per page, you would need more than 1,000 sheets of paper to write it out.

As you count higher and higher, prime numbers become rarer and rarer. Between 1 and 100, a total of 25 prime numbers are found. Between 1,001 and 1,100, only 16 numbers are prime. Prime numbers occur less often, and they are more difficult to detect. The early mathematicians asked, "Do the prime numbers end? Do you finally come to the last prime number?"

For More Study:
Euclid's Proof that There Is No Largest Prime Number

Euclid's proof that prime numbers go on without end is both simple and unusual. Rather than trying to prove that there is no largest prime number, he assumed the opposite.

His proof goes like this. Assume that the prime numbers do end. Let the letter p stand for the largest prime number. Now make a number that is the product of every prime number from two up to p and add one to it. Let N stand for this number: N = 2 x 3 x 5 . . . x p + 1

What can be said about N? None of the prime numbers will divide N evenly, because each will have a remainder of one. According to the original assumption, p is the last prime, so N cannot be prime because it is greater than p. Yet, none of the known primes will divide it, so it must either be prime, or some prime number not in the list 2 x 3 x 5 . . . x p must divide it.

Either way, another prime exists that wasn't counted originally.

The fact that there is no largest prime number is sometimes stated as "The number of prime numbers is infinite." Or, "prime numbers go to infinity." In ordinary usage, a person may say that something is infinite but mean that it is very large. But in mathematics, infinite means without limit. An infinite series of numbers is one that never ends. The prime numbers are an example of an infinite series.

Euclid

In section nine of Euclid's book *Elements of Geometry*, he proved that prime numbers go on without end. Euclid assumed the opposite of what he wanted to prove, but arrived at a conclusion that contradicted his original assumption. This showed that his original assumption was false. Mathematicians often use Euclid's roundabout method of proof. They assume the opposite of what they think is true and then see if it leads to a contradiction.

Mathematicians need to use every trick they can find because some math problems are easy to state but extremely difficult to prove. Since the time of Euclid, mathematicians believed that every composite number could be written as the product of prime numbers in only one way. The number 10 can be written as 2 x 5 and both 2 and 5 are prime numbers. No other pair of primes multiplied together will give 10. The number 30 can be written as 2 x 3 x 5. No other prime numbers will give 30.

Changing the order of the prime factors is not a different way of making the product. The number 12 can be written as 2 x 2 x 3 or as 3 x 2 x 2 or as 2 x 3 x 2. But the prime factors are 2, 2, and 3, and they are the only prime factors that will make the number 12.

Centuries passed before anyone proved that a composite number could be written as the product of prime numbers in only one way. The German mathematician Carl Fredrick Gauss made the proof in 1801.

Another simple statement is that every even number greater than two is the sum of two primes: 4 = 2 + 2; 6 = 3 + 3; 8 = 3 + 5; 10 = 5 + 5; 12 = 5 + 7; and so on. Every even number that mathematicians have looked at can be written as two primes added together. However, no one has been able to prove that this is always true. It is one of the great unsolved problems of number theory.

Notice that some prime numbers come in pairs: 3 and 5, 11 and 13, 17 and 19, 41 and 43, 59 and 61, and 71 and 73. Members of each prime pair have a single even number between them. The next prime pair is 101 and 103. As you go higher and higher, the number of primes and the number of prime pairs become less common. Euclid proved that you never run out of primes. There is always a larger one. But no one has proven whether you run out of prime pairs. That, too, is an unsolved problem.

For generations, prime numbers appeared to have no particular practical use. Then, when computers sent data such as banking records over the Internet, people realized the data needed to be encrypted. Encrypted data is in a code that can only be read by the sender and receiver. To prevent a dishonest person from breaking the code, the secret transmission is based on very large prime numbers. Prime numbers have an important use after all.

Odd, even, and prime are not the only properties of numbers that are studied by mathematicians. The series 1, 1, 2, 3, 5, 8, 13, 21, 34, and so on is known as Fibonacci numbers. The first two numbers in the series are the two ones, then every number after that is equal to the sum of the previous two: 1 + 1 = 2, 1 + 2 = 3, 2 + 3 = 5, 3 + 5 = 8, and so on.

Leonardo Fibonacci, the mathematician who introduced Arabic numerals to Europe, developed this sequence of numbers. In his books, he made up problems to solve with Arabic numerals.

In Fibonacci's *Book of Calculating*, published in 1202, he posed a riddle to help readers practice their arithmetic. The problem was about multiplying rabbits. Suppose that after becoming two months old, a female rabbit gives birth to exactly one female rabbit every month. Her offspring begin giving birth in the same way after two months. Fibonacci asked, "Provided no rabbits escape and none die, how many rabbits will there be at the end of a year?"

In the first month, there is but one rabbit. The second month begins with only one rabbit. At the end of the second month, she gives birth. The third month begins with two rabbits. At the start of the fourth month, she gives birth again so there are three rabbits. In the fifth month both she and her first daughter give birth, so there are a total now of five rabbits. In the sixth month, she continues to give birth, her daughter continues to give birth, and now her granddaughter gives birth. The rabbits number eight.

The number of rabbits for each month is: 1, 1, 2, 3, 5, 8, and so on. The numbers form a predictable pattern. Starting with two, any number in the series is equal to the sum of the previous two numbers: $1 + 1 = 2$, $1 + 2 = 3$, $2 + 3 = 5$. Mathematicians describe the Fibonacci series by the equation $F_{n-2} + F_{n-1} = F_n$. The sum of the previous two Fibonacci numbers gives the next Fibonacci number.

What comes after eight? Add five and eight to give the next number: $5 + 8 = 13$. The series continues through a year with 21, 34, 55, 89, and 144 rabbits. At the end of 12 months, there will be 144 rabbits.

The Fibonacci series of numbers does not end at 144, nor does it ever end. Merely add the previous two values to give the next one. The Fibonacci number following 144 is 233: $89 + 144 = 233$.

The number of petals on some flowers is often a Fibonacci number. For instance, lilies have 3 petals, buttercups have 5 petals, corn marigolds have 13 petals, black-eyed Susans have 21 petals, and some types of daises have 34. All of these are Fibonacci numbers.

These petal counts are generally the same within a species, but not always. Some daises may have 35 petals rather than 34, but 34 petals is the most common. As another example, clover usually has three leaves, and three is a Fibonacci number. But sometimes you will find a four-leaf clover. Four is not a Fibonacci number. However,

three-leaf clovers are far more common than four-leaf clovers.

When people cut an apple, they usually slice it in half along the core from top to bottom. However, if you cut the apple horizontally across the middle, you will see that the apple has five seeds arranged in a star pattern. The number five is a Fibonacci number.

As the seed head of a large sunflower grows, its seeds come out in a spiral shape. The number of spirals is always a Fibonacci number. Some pinecones also show the spirals. The spiral shape helps pack more seeds into less space.

Numbers should never be thought of as "magic." In the special creation of God, some quantities show the best way to pack together growing things such as leaves, petals, and seeds. Fibonacci numbers reflect a pattern to nature put there by God.

The chambered Nautilus, a marine creature, builds a larger chamber as it grows. It moves into the new chamber and closes off the old one to trap air and help it float. The chambers in the shell follow a design of Fibonacci numbers.

Figure 8-3

Squares with sides that are Fibonacci numbers pack together without wasted space.

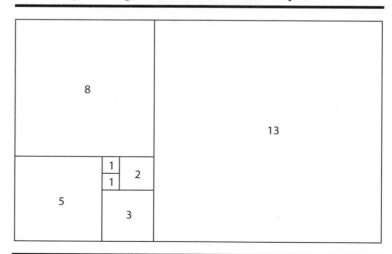

You can see the packing advantage of Fibonacci numbers by making squares that have sides with lengths equal to Fibonacci numbers. Make two squares with 1 unit on a side and then squares with sides of 2, 3, 5, 8, and 13 units. The length of the unit does not matter. It could be millimeters, centimeters, or inches provided all squares use the same unit of measure.

Now pack the squares together. The result shows that the squares fit together perfectly with no wasted space. See figure 8-3.

Suppose you start making fractions of pairs of Fibonacci numbers $\frac{1}{1}$, $\frac{2}{1}$, $\frac{3}{2}$, $\frac{5}{3}$, $\frac{8}{5}$, $\frac{13}{8}$, $\frac{21}{13}$ and so on. Written as decimal numbers, the fractions are 1.000, 2.000, 1.500, 1.667, 1.600, 1.625, 1.615. The pattern gets closer and closer to 1.618, which is the approximate decimal value for the Golden Ratio. The fraction formed by Fibonacci numbers 89 and 144, $\frac{144}{89}$, have a decimal value of 1.618, which is the same as the Golden Ratio to three decimal places.

Look at the outer perimeter of the rectangle made from the squares. It has pleasing proportions of the golden rectangle.

Figure 8-4

Arcs of circles in the Fibonacci squares form a Fibonacci spiral.

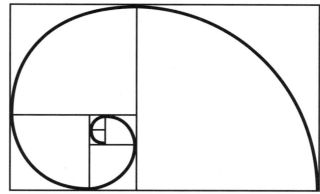

Suppose arcs of circles are drawn diagonally from one corner of the one unit square to the other corner and then into the next square. The result is a beautiful spiral called a Fibonacci spiral. See figure 8-4.

The spiral is also found in nature. The shell of the chambered nautilus, the curl of the horns of some animals, the spiral of an orb weaver spider web, and the arrangement of the inner ear of humans all have the spiral shape. It is found as the whirl on the surface of

Figure 8-5

A series of square numbers

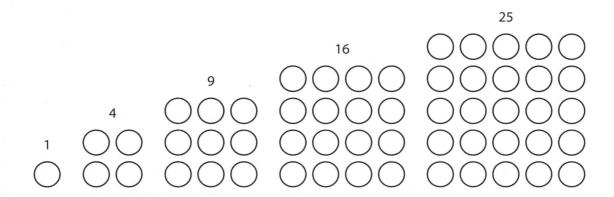

Figure 8-6

A series of triangular numbers

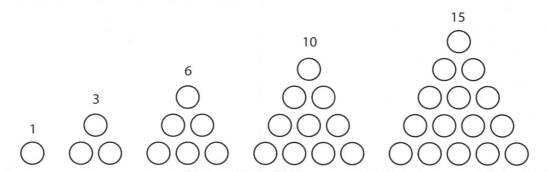

pineapples and in the arrangement of stars in distant galaxies.

Some number series in this chapter are easy to identify. The numbers 2, 4, 6, 8, 10, and so on are easily seen as a sequence of even numbers. The numbers 1, 3, 5, 7, 9, and so on are the odd numbers. Now that you have read about them, you will recognize the series of Fibonacci numbers: 1, 1, 2, 3, 5, 8. . . .

Some series can be figured out with a moment's thought. What do the numbers 1, 4, 9, 16, and 25 have in common? They are a series of square numbers. Ancient mathematicians thought of the square numbers as patterns that formed squares. See figure 8-5.

However, they can also be represented as the multiplication of a number times itself: $1 \times 1 = 1$, $2 \times 2 = 4$, $3 \times 3 = 9$, $4 \times 4 = 16$, and $5 \times 5 = 25$. Exponents can also show the square numbers: $1^2 = 1$, $2^2 = 4$, $3^2 = 9$, $4^2 = 16$, and $5^2 = 25$. The formula for this series is n^2, with n representing any number. The 7th member of the series is given by squaring n. You can quickly jump to the 10th square number by putting 10 in the formula: $n^2 = 10^2 = 100$.

The ancient mathematicians showed the series 1, 3, 6, 10, 15, and so on as triangular numbers. See figure 8-6.

The triangular numbers go on endlessly, but what is the next one? The next one will have a row of six circles at the bottom, so it will be six more than the previous one. The next triangular number is $15 + 6 = 21$. By using

a formula, you can leap ahead to the 10th triangular number without calculating those before it. The formula for triangular numbers is $n(n + 1)/2$. You can immediately find the 10th triangular number by replacing n with 10: $n(n+1)/2 = 10(10+1)/2 = (10 \times 11)/2 = 110/2 = 55$.

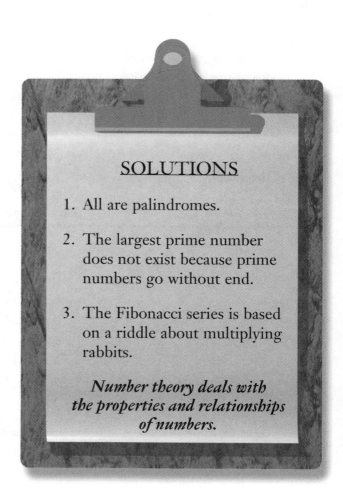

SOLUTIONS

1. All are palindromes.

2. The largest prime number does not exist because prime numbers go without end.

3. The Fibonacci series is based on a riddle about multiplying rabbits.

Number theory deals with the properties and relationships of numbers.

A B C D   1.   The sentence, "Madam, I'm Adam" is an example of a (A. composite statement   B. palindrome   C. permutation   D. Roman oration).

A B C D   2.   The study of the properties of whole numbers is called (A. algebra   B. geometry   C. number theory   D. real analysis).

A B   3.   The general form of an even number is (A. 2n   B. 2n + 1) with n a whole number.

A B   4.   Two is a factor of all (A. even   B. odd) numbers.

A B   5.   The number with the greater number of factors is (A. 12   B. 13).

A B C   6.   Nine is an example of (A. a prime   B. an even   C. an odd) number.

A B   7.   An example of a composite number is (A. 11   B. 12).

A B C D   8.   Prime numbers can be found with the sieve of (A. Eratosthenes   B. Euclid   C. Gauss.   D. Pythagoras).

A B   9.   As you count higher and higher, prime numbers become (A. more and more common   B. rarer and rarer).

T F   10.   The statement "A composite number can be written as the product of prime numbers in only one way" has not yet been proven to be true.

T F   11.   The statement "Every even number greater than two is the sum of two primes" has not yet been proven to be true.

A B   12.   Encrypted data (A. is especially easy for any computer to read and display   B. can only be read by the sender and receiver).

A B C D   13.   Fibonacci numbers could also be called (A. calculating with an abacus   B. the problem of adding Adder snakes   C. the problem of multiplying rabbits   D. the problem of the Leaning Tower of Pisa).

   14.   The next Fibonacci number after 89 and 144 is _____.

T F   15.   The Fibonacci series of numbers is seldom found in nature.

Matching

16.   _____ 1881, 121, 1001   a. Fibonacci numbers

17.   _____ 2, 3, 5, 7, 11, 13, . . .   b. palindromes

18.   _____ 1, 1, 2, 3, 5, 8, 13, . . .   c. prime numbers

19.   _____ 1, 4, 9, 16, 25, . . .   d. square numbers

20.   _____ 1, 3, 6, 10, 15, . . .   e. triangular numbers

$$\tan\phi = \frac{X_c}{R}$$

$$E = \Delta mc^2$$

$$\sqrt{a^2 + b^2}$$

$$L = 2\pi f L$$

Endless Numbers

Counting numbers are 1, 2, 3, 4, and so on. When zero is included, 0, 1, 2, 3 . . . then the numbers are called whole numbers. Another name for whole numbers is integers (IN-tuh-jurz). The word integer means whole or complete. An integer does not have a fractional part.

Addition is a mathematical operation that produces the sum of two numbers. The sum of two whole numbers will always be a whole number and never a fraction.

Whole numbers can be even (2, 4, 6, 8 . . .) or odd (1, 3, 5, 7 . . .) Will the sum of two even numbers be odd or even? What about the sum of two odd numbers? Will it be odd or even? Suppose an odd number and an even number are added. Will the sum be odd or even?

PROBLEMS

1. Is division of whole numbers "closed"?

2. Does calling a number "irrational" refer to its mental condition?

3. What do π, 2, and the golden ratio have in common?

Can You Propose Solutions?

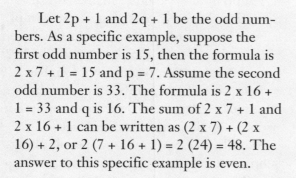

For Further Study:
Prove that the sum of two odd numbers is an even number

Let 2p + 1 and 2q + 1 be the odd numbers. As a specific example, suppose the first odd number is 15, then the formula is 2 x 7 + 1 = 15 and p = 7. Assume the second odd number is 33. The formula is 2 x 16 + 1 = 33 and q is 16. The sum of 2 x 7 + 1 and 2 x 16 + 1 can be written as (2 x 7) + (2 x 16) + 2, or 2 (7 + 16 + 1) = 2 (24) = 48. The answer to this specific example is even.

Prove that the sum of two odd numbers will always be even by using the formulas. Let 2p +1 be one odd number and 2q + 1 be the other odd number. The sum is (2p +1) + (2q + 1) = 2p + 2q + 2. The expression 2p + 2q + 2 can be written as 2(p + q + 1). Let n = p + q + 1, and the expression 2(p + q + 1) becomes 2n, the form of an even number.

Testing the addition of a few pairs of even and odd numbers gives a table that shows the results:

E + E = E
O + E = O
E + O = O
O + O = E

The letter E stands for even and O stands for odd. If both numbers are the same — either both even or both odd — the sum is even. But if one number is even and the other is odd, then the sum is odd.

We could try a few sample problems to illustrate that the sum of two even numbers gives an even number: 12 + 18 = 30 and 1,792 + 3,014 = 4,806. However, no matter how many pairs we tested, other pairs of even numbers would still need tested. Mathematicians rely on proofs, not examples, to show whether a statement is true or false.

How can you prove that the sum of even numbers will always be even? First, notice that all even numbers can be written as two times some whole number. For example, 14 is two times 7. An even number has the form 2n. The letter n stands for a whole number. The letter that stands for the whole number is not

important. It could be n, p, q, or some other letter. Suppose 2p is an even number and 2q is another even number. If the first even number is 14, then the formula is 2 x 7 = 14 and p = 7. Assume the second number is 32. The formula is 2 x 16 = 32 and q = 16. The sum of (2 x 7) + (2 x 16) can be written as 2 (7 + 16) = 2 x 23, or 46, which is even.

The example with actual numbers can be changed into a proof by using letters that stand for any number. Let 2p + 2q be the sum of the two even numbers. But 2p + 2q can be written as 2(p + q), which is the form of an even number, 2n, with p + q taking the place of n. The sum of two even numbers is even.

The sum of an even number and an odd number gives an odd number. The form for an odd number is 2n + 1 with n a whole number. Suppose 2p is the even number and 2q + 1 is the odd number. Their sum is 2p + (2q + 1) or 2p + 2q + 1, which can also be written as 2(p + q) + 1, or 2n + 1 with n = p + q. The expression 2n + 1 is the definition of an odd number, so the sum of an even and odd number is odd.

A similar proof will show that the sum of two odd numbers is an even number.

Another mathematical operation is multiplication. The word multiplication comes from a Latin word meaning many folds.

The product is the answer to a multiplication problem.

Multiplication is a shorthand way of showing repeated additions. The answer to the multiplication 5 x 7 can be found by adding seven five times. For small numbers, multiplication is simple. However, as the numbers become larger, the process is not very simple. Addition of whole numbers gives a whole number, so the product of two whole numbers is always a whole number, too.

The product of two even numbers appears to always give an even number. A few test cases such as 4 x 8 = 32 and 6 x 12 = 72 seems to show that even times even gives even. But to prove that this is true, one must use the formula for even numbers: 2p x 2q = 2(p x q), and that is the same form as 2n, so the statement is true.

What if an odd number is multiplied by an even number? Will the result be odd or even? Once again, a few examples makes you think the result will always be even. Multiply 4 x 7 and 6 x 11, and both results, 28 and 66, are even. The formulas for even and odd numbers settle the matter for certain. An even number can be written as 2p, and odd number as 2q + 1. The product is 2p(2q + 1). This is the same as an even number 2n, with n = p(2q+1). The final result is even.

Only in the case of the two odd numbers will their product be odd.

Facts about the multiplication of even and odd numbers can be summarized as:

E x E = E
E x O = E
O x E = E
O x O = O

Subtraction is another mathematical operation. In early times, people thought of subtraction as finding the difference between two numbers. If one bag of wool weighed 128 pounds and another bag of wool weighed 120 pounds, then the bags differed in weight by 8 pounds. Today, the answer to a subtraction problem is still called the difference.

Until about 500 years ago, people always subtracted the smaller number from the larger one. The difference between 128 and 120 was always thought of as 128 - 120 and never 120 - 128. Today we would say that 120 - 128 = -8. The number -8 is read as "negative eight." At first, people did not accept the idea that a number could be less than zero. Negative numbers did not come into common use until the 1500s.

The negative whole numbers -1, -2, -3, and so on are also called negative integers. The numbers greater than zero are called positive integers. Sometimes they are shown plain, 1, 2, 3, and so on. Sometimes the plus sign is used to make it clear that they are positive numbers, +1, +2, +3, and so on.

No one is quite sure of how the plus, +, and minus, -, signs came to mean positive or negative. But they were in use in the 1400s to show that a shipment of goods was underweight, -,

For More Study:
Product of two odd numbers

Proof that the product of two odd numbers, 2p +1 and 2q + 1, is odd requires algebra to multiply the two expressions. It is given here:

$(2p + 1) \times (2q + 1)$
$4pq + 2p + 2q + 1$
$2(2pq + p + q) + 1$
$2n + 1$ with $n = 2pq + p + q$

or overweight, +. Work-men chalked a minus on a crate or barrel to show that it weighed too little. Workmen added goods to bring it up to the right weight. Then they drew a vertical bar through the minus sign to show the shortage had been corrected. The vertical bar changed the minus sign, -, into a plus sign, +.

Plus, +, and minus, -, signs do double duty. They show the operations of addition and subtraction, and they stand for positive and negative integers. The plus sign can be used for the mathematical operation of addition as in 2 +

Whalers were paid in shares to make the math calculations easier.

3 = 5. The plus sign can also be used to show that an integer is positive, for example, +2. The usage may seem similar, but one is an operation and the other is a property of a number.

Sometimes positive and negative signs are raised to keep them from being confused with addition and subtraction: $^+5 + ^-3 = ^+2$ and $^-8 - ^+2 = ^-10$. Two entirely different signs for positive and negative would have been better. However, the use of + and - for both purposes have been in use for years and change is not likely.

The use of negative integers ensures that there is always an answer to a subtraction problem. The difference of two whole numbers is always a whole number, although in some cases it can be negative. Mathematicians say that the whole numbers are closed with respect to subtraction. This means that the final result will be a whole number, too. The whole numbers are also closed with respect to addition, subtraction, and multiplication.

Division is the fourth mathematical operation after addition, subtraction, and multiplication. The answer to a division problem is the quotient. The word quotient means how many as in, "How many times will 5 go into 32?"

Whole numbers that are added, subtracted, or multiplied will give answers that are also whole numbers. But division can produce fractions. Dividing five into 32 gives a quotient of six with a remainder of two. Or, as a fraction the answer is 6⅖ and as a decimal 6.4.

Before the use of calculators, division of large numbers was a difficult task and one prone to errors. Businessmen reduced the necessity of doing division by using shares. For example, owners of whaling ships paid the crew in shares. The number of shares depended on the size of the ship. The profit from an average size vessel would be divided into 4,000 shares. The owners of the ship and those who put up the money for the voyage received 1,000 shares.

They gave the remaining shares to the crew: 400 shares to the captain, 300 shares to the first mate, 200 shares to the second mate, and 100 shares to the third mate, and

Long John Silver and Captain Flint

100 shares to each of three harpooners. Experienced seamen, 20 in all, received 75 shares each. Finally, the remaining 200 shares were given to the cabin boy and seamen in training, 40 shares each for five people in this category.

A whaling voyage might last as long as two years. During that time, the crew would harpoon whales and render them for whale oil, the main fuel for lamps. A ship could return with a cargo worth $13,200.00. Dividing $13,200.00 by 4,000 showed that one share was worth $3.30. After that single division, the rest of the figuring could be done with multiplication. The captain would get 400 shares x 3.30 per share = $1,320.00, and a seaman would get 75 shares x $3.30 per share = $247.50.

The seaman's share of $247.50 for two years' work may not sound like much. However, money was worth more back then. In the early 1800s, a working person earned only about $100.00 a year.

Prices were cheaper in the 1800s, so many people paid for their purchases with coins rather than paper money. A silver coin, called a *real*, was a popular coin in the American colonies. The value of a real was too much for ordinary trade, so the coin was cut into eight parts. Each part was called a bit. There were eight bits to a real. Sometimes they were called pieces of eight.

In the book *Treasure Island* by Robert Louis Stevenson, Long John Silver's green parrot, Captain Flint, cries out "Pieces of eight!" He squawked about the eight pieces, or bits, of a Spanish coin.

Even after the Declaration of Independence, Americans continued to think in terms of pieces of eight. The eighth part of a dollar was 12½ cents. Merchants often measured out their products to be sold in lots worth 12½ cents. In the early 1800s, people could pay for items priced to the half penny because the United States minted ½-cent coins.

Two bits was 25 cents. As recently as the 1940s, a barber would give a shave and a hair cut for 25 cents or two bits. Even today, a code knock on a door keeps time with the sentence, "Shave and a haircut — two bits!" And the phrase "two bits" describes something that is cheap or cheaply made.

The use of fractional parts of a dollar rather than decimal parts of the dollar, continued until the end of the 1900s. Stock prices on the New York Stock Exchange were given as bits or eighths of a dollar. A stock is a paper document that shows ownership of shares in a business. In 1792, when the New York Stock Exchange began operating, the price was given

The place value of numbers

The value of a digit is determined by its place within the number:

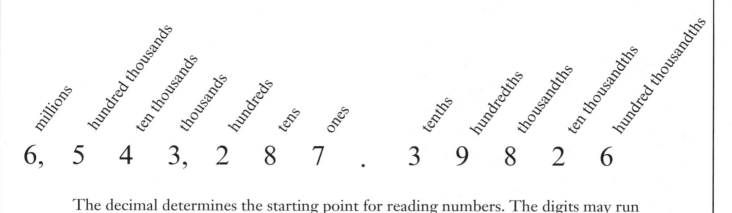

millions	hundred thousands	ten thousands	thousands	hundreds	tens	ones		tenths	hundredths	thousandths	ten thousandths	hundred thousandths
6,	5	4	3,	2	8	7	.	3	9	8	2	6

The decimal determines the starting point for reading numbers. The digits may run infinitely in either direction.

in dollars and eighths of dollars. A stock price might be $\$7\frac{1}{8}$ or $\$30\frac{3}{8}$.

Care must be taken in comparing one fraction to another. Given that the same number is in the numerators, or top part of the fraction, a larger number in the denominator, or bottom part of the fraction makes the fraction smaller: $\frac{1}{8}$ is smaller than $\frac{1}{4}$. A larger number in the numerator, with the same denominator as another fraction makes the fraction larger: $\frac{3}{8}$ is larger than $\frac{2}{8}$.

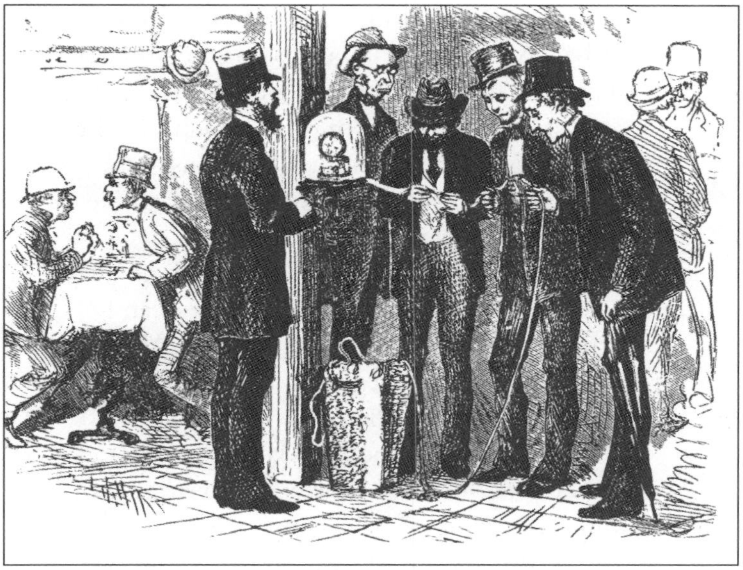

Until the end of the 1900s, stock prices were given in eighths of a dollar rather than dollars and cents.

Confusion arises when the denominators are different. It is difficult to compare fractions directly that have different denominators. Which is larger: $\frac{3}{4}$ or $\frac{2}{3}$? How about $\frac{5}{6}$ or $\frac{7}{9}$? They have to be given common denominators. The lowest common denominator is the smallest number that has both denominators as factors.

The lowest common denominator for 4 and 3 is 12. It is the smallest number that has 4 and 3 as factors. The fraction $\frac{3}{4}$ equals $\frac{9}{12}$ (4 goes into 12 three times, and $3 \times 3 = 9$) and $\frac{2}{3}$ equals $\frac{8}{12}$ (3 goes into 12 four times, and $4 \times 2 = 8$). The fractions $\frac{9}{12}$ and $\frac{8}{12}$ are easily compared, and $\frac{3}{4}$ is the larger fraction.

To compare $\frac{5}{6}$ and $\frac{7}{9}$, first write them as $\frac{15}{18}$ and $\frac{14}{18}$ because 18 is the lowest common denominator of six and nine. The fraction $\frac{5}{6}$ is larger than $\frac{7}{9}$ because $\frac{15}{18}$ is larger than $\frac{14}{18}$. The two fractions have the same denominator but the numerator 15 is larger than the numerator 14.

Decimals make the comparison easier. The decimal fractions 0.75 and 0.67 are easy to compare. The digit to the right of the decimal is the tenths place, the next one to the right is the

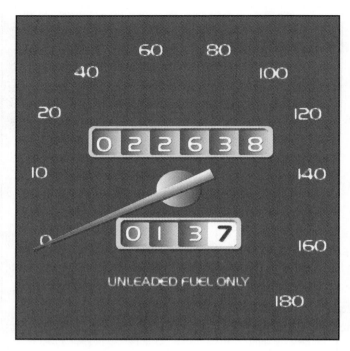

Car odometers are marked in miles and decimal miles; this ones reads 13.7 miles.

hundredths place, and so on. The decimal fraction 0.75 is larger than 0.67 because the tenths place digit, 7 in 0.75, is larger than the tenths place digit, 6, in 0.67.

To compare the size of decimal numbers, one merely needs to scan left to right across the numbers and the first one with a larger digit is the larger number. Compare 0.385294 and 0.385278. They are the same until you reach the 5th place, which is the hundred-thousandths place. The decimal fraction 0.385294 is the larger number because 9 is larger than 7.

Today, using decimals rather than common fractions makes a lot of sense. They are easier to type in a document, they are easier for a calculator to display, and decimal prices are easier to understand than prices written as common fractions.

Because of these advantages, in August of the year 2000, the New York Stock Exchange switched over to decimal values for stock. They list prices for stock in decimal dollars rather than fractions: $7⅛ became $7.12 and $30⅜ became $30.37. They gave the value to the nearest penny or hundredth of a dollar.

Although common fractions appear to be on their way out, it is still necessary to know the decimal values of some common fractions in everyday life. A customer at a deli may order ¼ pound of potato salad. Most modern scales in delis and grocery stores measure weight in decimal pounds. The deli clerk must know that the scale should read 0.25 pound for ¼ of a pound.

The odometer of a car in the United States measures distance in tenths of a mile. A driver who is told to drive 13¾ miles and then turn left must know that 13¾ miles is 13.75 miles. The odometer measures to the nearest tenth of a mile. The driver must know to turn after the odometer shows 13.7 miles but before it changes to 13.8 miles.

A common fraction can be changed into a decimal fraction by dividing the numerator by the denominator. As examples, ¼ = 1 ÷ 4 = 0.25 and ⅔ = 2 ÷ 3 = 0.6666 with the 6 repeating without end. The fraction ¼ gives a terminating decimal. But ⅔ is a repeating decimal because the 6 repeats over and over.

Any common fraction expressed as a decimal will either terminate or repeat. The part that repeats can be a single digit or a group of digits. The fraction ⅔ repeats a 6, but ⅐ = 0.142857142857142857 . . . which repeats the group 142857 without end.

A common fraction is known as a rational number. A rational number has whole numbers in both the numerator and denominator. The word rational comes from ratio, which was the early way of writing common fractions. The common fractions ¼, ⁵⁄₁₂, and ²²⁄₇ are examples of rational numbers.

The whole numbers, 1, 2, 3, and so on are also rational numbers because they can be written as ¹⁄₁, ²⁄₁, ³⁄₁, and so on with 1 as the denominator. The integers, then, are special types of rational numbers.

Mixed fractions such as 5⅜ are rational numbers, too, because they can be written as common fractions. For instance, 5⅜ is equal to ⁴³⁄₈. To change a mixed fraction to a common fraction you multiply the whole number by the denominator and add the numerator: $5\frac{3}{8} = (5 \times 8) + 3 = 40 + 3 = 43$. Keep the original denominator as the denominator in the new fraction.

A rational number cannot have zero as the denominator. The expression $\frac{5}{0}$ is equivalent to five divided by zero. Division by zero is meaningless. If $\frac{5}{0} = n$ then $5 = n \times 0$, but any number times zero is zero, so the equation becomes $5 = 0$, and that can never be a true statement.

Are rational numbers the only types of numbers possible? The question can be asked several different ways. Do some numbers exist that cannot be written as a rational numbers? Do some numbers exist that cannot be expressed as common fractions? When expressed as decimals, do some numbers go on forever without terminating and without repeating?

The answer is that numbers do exist that are not rational. They cannot be written as n/d

For More Study:
Square Root of Two

The proof that the square root of two is irrational follows the pattern of first assuming the opposite and see if that assumption leads to a contradiction.

First, notice that for a perfect square to be even, its square root must be even. For instance, 4 is a perfect square and its square root is the even number 2; 16 is a perfect square and its square root is the even number 4. In general, if n^2 is even, then n must be even. We showed earlier that the product of two even numbers is even and the product of two odd numbers is odd. If n x n gives an even number, then n must be even.

Assume that $\sqrt{2}$ is rational and the whole number p/q exists so that $p/q = \sqrt{2}$. Reduce the fraction p/q to lowest terms by dividing out any common multiples. For instance, if p = 12 and q = 9, then cancel the common factor of 3 and make p = 4 and q = 3.

Multiply $p/q = \sqrt{2}$ by q and then square both sides.

$p/q \times q = \sqrt{2} \times q$
$p = \sqrt{2}\, q$
$p^2 = (\sqrt{2} \times q)^2$
$p^2 = (\sqrt{2})^2 \times q^2$
$p^2 = \sqrt{2} \times \sqrt{2} \times q^2$
$p^2 = 2q^2$ because $\sqrt{2} \times \sqrt{2} = 2$

The equation $p^2 = 2q^2$ shows that p^2 is even. But the only way for the square of p to be even is for p itself to be even. If p x p gives an even number, then p must be even. Replace p with the even number 2n.

$(2n)^2 = 2q^2$
$4n^2 = 2q^2$ divide both sides by two
$2n^2 = q^2$ but this shows that q^2 and q are even

Now we have reached a contradiction because both p and q are even, giving them a common factor of two, but in the first step we began by canceling all common factors. The contradiction shows that our original assumption that $\sqrt{2}$ could be written as p/q is in error. We must conclude that $\sqrt{2}$ is an irrational number.

where n and d are whole numbers. If expressed as a decimal they neither terminate nor repeat. Instead, they go on forever without repeating. Such a number is called irrational. The word irrational means "cannot be written as a ratio."

Early mathematicians discovered irrational numbers when they worked with the square roots of numbers. Mathematicians write the square root of the number n as $\sqrt{n}$. The square root of a number is a second number that times itself gives the first number: $\sqrt{n} \times \sqrt{n} = n$. One could write $\sqrt{4} \times \sqrt{4} = 2 \times 2 = 4$, but the middle part is not needed. The definition alone tells us that the square root of four times the square root of four is equal to four: $\sqrt{4} \times \sqrt{4} = 4$.

The square root of four is a rational number because $\sqrt{4} = 2$ and 2 can be written as the rational number $\frac{2}{1}$. Other numbers also have rational square roots: $\sqrt{9} = 3$ because $3 \times 3 = 9$, and $\sqrt{16} = 4$ because $4 \times 4 = 16$. The numbers 1, 4, 9, 16, 25, 36, 49, and so on are called perfect squares. The square root of a perfect square is a rational number.

If a number is not a perfect square, then its square root will be irrational. The square root of two, $\sqrt{2}$, was the first irrational number discovered.

The fact that $\sqrt{2}$ is irrational arose from a study of the length of the diagonal of a square. A diagonal is a straight line that connects one

corner of the square to the opposite corner and goes through the center of the square.

The length of the diagonal can be calculated using the Pythagorean theorem which states that the legs of a right triangle are related to the hypotenuse by the equation: $a^2 + b^2 = c^2$ with a and b the legs and c the hypotenuse.

In a square, the diagonal separates the square into two identical right triangles. The legs of the triangle are sides of the square and the hypotenuse of the triangle is the diagonal of the square. The Pythagorean triangle gives the length of the diagonal by the equation $a^2 + b^2 = c^2$. For the right triangle made in a square, the equation is $side^2 + side^2 = diagonal^2$.

Suppose the sides of the square have a length of one. When one is squared the answer is one: $1^2 = 1 \times 1 = 1$. The length of the diagonal, represented by c, is given by $1^2 + 1^2 = c^2$, or $1 + 1 = c^2$, or $2 = c^2$.

The expression $2 = c^2$ can also be written as $c = \sqrt{2}$. Now $\sqrt{2}$ has the property that $\sqrt{2} \times \sqrt{2} = 2$. That number, whatever it is, is called the square root of two.

The number $\frac{10}{7}$ is close to being the square root of two because $(\frac{10}{7})^2 = \frac{100}{49}$ or about 2.04. That is close to two but not exact. In fact, no fraction when multiplied by itself will give two exactly. No decimal can equal it exactly.

The first few digits of the square root of two, $\sqrt{2}$, are 1.4142135623731. . . . The digits go on forever without terminating and without repeating and no pattern emerges. One cannot predict what the next digit will be without working it out.

Multiplying the approximate value of $\sqrt{2}$ by itself shows that one can get very close to two, but never exactly two:

1.4 x 1.4 = 1.96
1.41 x 1.41 = 1.9881
1.414 x 1.414 = 1.999396
1.4142 x 1.4142 = 1.99996164

The last number, 1.4142, when squared gives a value so close to two that for all

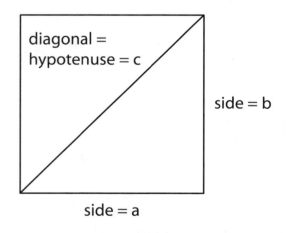

diagonal =
hypotenuse = c

side = b

side = a

$a^2 + b^2 = c^2$ or
$side^2 + side^2 = diagonal^2$

Length of the diagonal

practical purposes it can be used as the square root of two. Although it is a very close approximation, it is nevertheless merely an approximation.

The number 3 is not a perfect square, and its square root, $\sqrt{3}$, is irrational. The first few digits of $\sqrt{3}$ are 1.7320508, but to say that it is the square root of 3 is an approximation: 1.7320508 x 1.7920508 = 2.9999999737806, rather than 3 exactly.

In chapter 6, we explored the properties of the golden ratio and said that it was approximately equal to 1.618. However, the exact expression for the golden ratio is $(1 + \sqrt{5})/2$. Because $\sqrt{5}$ is an irrational number, the golden ratio is also an irrational number. Written as a decimal, the golden ratio is 1.6180339887498948482. . . . The digits never terminate, never repeat, and never form any pattern that gives a clue as to what the next number will be.

Calculating square roots can be difficult mathematical problems. But one simple way to calculate square roots is by a process called iteration. The word iteration is from a Latin word meaning "do it again." A series of identical mathematical steps are repeated until the desired result is obtained.

Suppose you wanted to find the square root of 125. The number 125 is not a perfect square, so you know that you will not be able to give its square root exactly. Instead, you must be satisfied with an approximation. You know that $\sqrt{125}$ is near 11 because 11 x 11 = 121. Divide 125 by 11. The result is 11.363636. Now average 11 (the divisor) and 11.363636 (the quotient): (11 + 11.363636)/2 = 22.363636/2 = 11.181818. Divide 125 by this average: 125/11.181818 = 11.178862. Average

Pythagoras

11.181818 (the new divisor) and 11.178862 (the new quotient): (11.181818 + 11.178862)/2 = 11.18034.

The value 11.18034 is a very accurate approximation to the square root of 125. Multiplying 11.18034 by 11.18034 gives 125.0000025156, which differs from 125 in the millionths place. The approximate value for the square root of 125 was found after only three iterations. Mathematicians say that the iterative process converges quickly to an acceptable value.

Use a calculator to find the square root of 39 by iteration. Use six as the first approximation; divide 39 by 6; average 6 and the answer and use the average to divide again. After three steps, you will have a very good value for the square root of 39. Some calculators have a square root key. When you enter a number and press the square root key, the calculator uses the iterative method to find the square root of the number.

Pi, π, is the number given by dividing the circumference of a circle by its diameter. The ancient Greek mathematician Archimedes was the first person to find an accurate approximation to pi.

Archimedes worked with figures that had straight sides. He put a 96-sided polygon inside a circle. He calculated the polygon's circumference divided by diameter to be $^{223}/_{71}$, or about 3.14085. He then put a slightly bigger 96-sided polygon outside the circle. He calculated its circumference divided by its diameter to be $^{22}/_{7}$, or about 3.142857. He had trapped pi between $^{223}/_{71}$ and $^{22}/_{7}$. The modern value for pi to five decimal places is 3.14159, which is between the two values Archimedes calculated.

A calculator with a square root function uses the iterative method to extract square roots.

Another way to find pi is by the expansion $\pi = \frac{4}{1} - \frac{4}{3} + \frac{4}{5} - \frac{4}{7} + \frac{4}{9}$. . . . Notice that it is a series of fractions with four in the numerator and odd numbers in the denominator. The fractions are alternatively added and subtracted. The series is called an infinite series because more and more terms can be added to it. The next one is $-\frac{4}{11}$. Unfortunately, this equation does not converge quickly. You must work out a lot of terms to find an acceptable value for pi. However, other but more complicated expansions do converge more quickly.

In 1873, an Englishman named William Shanks announced that he had calculated the value of pi to 707 places. He spent 15 years at the task. It was not until 1949 that a computer named ENIAC calculated pi to more places. The computer worked for 70 hours and gave pi to 2,035 places. In comparing the answer with Shanks's value, they found that he had made an error in the 528th place. So all of the rest of his digits from there were wrong.

By the year 2003, computers had calculated pi to 200 billion decimal places. It may seem senseless to carry out pi to so many places, but mathematicians continue to be fascinated by pi. They are interested in seeing if certain facts are true. For instance, most mathematicians believe that each of the digits 0, 1, 2, . . . 9, will occur with the same frequency in pi. No one digit will be used more than the others. However, that idea has yet to be proven true.

For years, school textbooks gave $\frac{22}{7}$ as the value of pi. It is off by about 12 parts in 10,000. Today, the value of pi is often given as the decimal 3.14. That value is off by about 16 parts in 10,000. Either value is a good approximation for ordinary use.

For greater accuracy, pi = 3.14159 can be used. However, pi is an irrational number. Like $\sqrt{2}$, when pi is written as a decimal, the decimal never terminates, never repeats, and never forms a pattern that will predict the next digit. The only way to find out what the next digit will be is to calculate it.

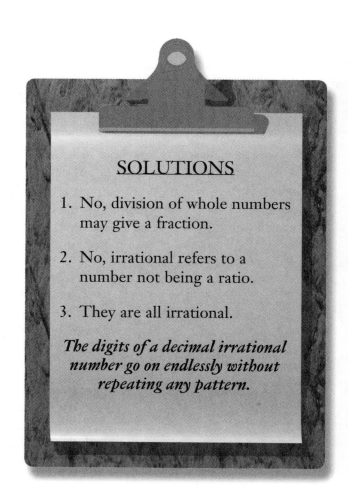

SOLUTIONS

1. No, division of whole numbers may give a fraction.

2. No, irrational refers to a number not being a ratio.

3. They are all irrational.

The digits of a decimal irrational number go on endlessly without repeating any pattern.

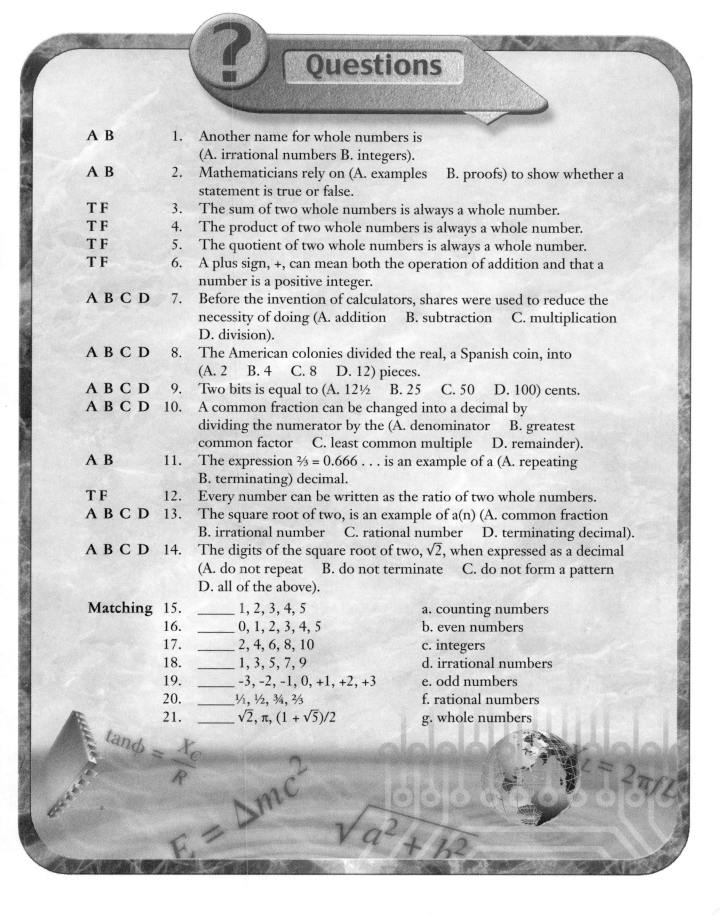

A B   1.   Another name for whole numbers is
       (A. irrational numbers B. integers).

A B   2.   Mathematicians rely on (A. examples   B. proofs) to show whether a
       statement is true or false.

T F   3.   The sum of two whole numbers is always a whole number.

T F   4.   The product of two whole numbers is always a whole number.

T F   5.   The quotient of two whole numbers is always a whole number.

T F   6.   A plus sign, +, can mean both the operation of addition and that a
       number is a positive integer.

A B C D   7.   Before the invention of calculators, shares were used to reduce the
       necessity of doing (A. addition   B. subtraction   C. multiplication
       D. division).

A B C D   8.   The American colonies divided the real, a Spanish coin, into
       (A. 2   B. 4   C. 8   D. 12) pieces.

A B C D   9.   Two bits is equal to (A. 12½   B. 25   C. 50   D. 100) cents.

A B C D   10.   A common fraction can be changed into a decimal by
       dividing the numerator by the (A. denominator   B. greatest
       common factor   C. least common multiple   D. remainder).

A B   11.   The expression ⅔ = 0.666 . . . is an example of a (A. repeating
       B. terminating) decimal.

T F   12.   Every number can be written as the ratio of two whole numbers.

A B C D   13.   The square root of two, is an example of a(n) (A. common fraction
       B. irrational number   C. rational number   D. terminating decimal).

A B C D   14.   The digits of the square root of two, $\sqrt{2}$, when expressed as a decimal
       (A. do not repeat   B. do not terminate   C. do not form a pattern
       D. all of the above).

Matching   15.   _____ 1, 2, 3, 4, 5   a. counting numbers

         16.   _____ 0, 1, 2, 3, 4, 5   b. even numbers

         17.   _____ 2, 4, 6, 8, 10   c. integers

         18.   _____ 1, 3, 5, 7, 9   d. irrational numbers

         19.   _____ -3, -2, -1, 0, +1, +2, +3   e. odd numbers

         20.   _____ ⅟₁, ½, ¾, ⅔   f. rational numbers

         21.   _____ $\sqrt{2}$, π, $(1 + \sqrt{5})/2$ g. whole numbers

Math for Scientists

Mathematics is called the handmaiden of science. The assistance of mathematics is essential to understanding the natural world. Without mathematics to summarize discoveries, scientists would be overwhelmed with the data generated by their experiments. Equations state complex laws briefly and concisely. Equations often reveal discoveries that would otherwise be concealed.

Arithmetic is the study of numbers and the mathematical operations of addition, subtraction, multiplication, division, raising numbers to powers, and taking their roots.

Arithmetic textbooks might pose a question such as, "What number plus three is equal to eight?" In symbols, the question would be written: $? + 3 = 8$. The question mark, ?, represents the missing number. A box could be used instead of a question mark to stand for the number:

PROBLEMS

1. Why is math called a handmaiden?

2. How can scientific data be shown?

3. What ancient problem did analytical geometry solve?

Can You Propose Solutions?

❏ + 3 = 8. The question mark and the box are placeholders. They hold the place for the unknown number.

Algebra is similar to arithmetic, but symbols are used to stand for numbers. In algebra, the letter x is often used as a placeholder: $x + 3 = 8$. The letter x is also called a variable. Normally, a variable can have more than one value. That is what variable means. However, in $x + 3 = 8$, x can have but one value and that value is 5.

Some equations have two variables. The equation $3x - 2 = y$ is an example of an equation with two variables, x and y. The x and y can take on different values. If x is 3, then y is 7 because $3 \times 3 - 2 = 9 - 2 = 7$. Other values for x and y are possible. If x is 10 then y is 28, and if x is 8 then y is 22. An endless number of solutions are possible.

Discovering the value of x when y is equal to zero is called solving the equation. Mathematical operations move numbers to one side of the equal sign and leave x on the other side by itself. The word equal means level. An algebraic equation is like a teeter-totter balanced on the equal sign. To keep the equation in balance, whatever is done on one side must also be done on the other side. Here are the steps for solving the equation $3x - 2 = y$:

$3x - 2 = 0$	set y equal to zero
$3x - 2 + 2 = 0 + 2$	add 2 to each side
$3x = 2$	
$3x * \frac{1}{3} = 2 * \frac{1}{3}$	divide each side by 3 (or multiply by $\frac{1}{3}$)
$x = \frac{2}{3}$	

The solution to the equation is $x = \frac{2}{3}$. That value of x makes y equal to zero.

The equation $3x - 2 = 0$ can also be written as $3x + (-2) = 0$. The number 3 is called a coefficient. The word coefficient means "acting together." The number 3 acts with the x to produce a single term, 3x. The term -2 is called the constant.

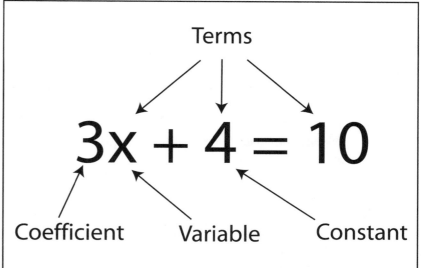

$$3x + 4 = 10$$

Terms → (pointing to 3x, 4, and 10)
Coefficient (pointing to 3)
Variable (pointing to x)
Constant (pointing to 10)

Parts of an Equation

Other equations may have different coefficients and constants. The equation $5x + 2 = 0$ has 5 as a coefficient and +2 as the constant. The equation $-2x + 12 = 0$ has -2 as the coefficient and +12 as the constant. And $1x - 5 = 0$ has 1 as the coefficient and -5 as the constant. The term 1x can also be written as x with the 1 understood but not shown.

The general form of the equation is $ax + b = 0$ with a the coefficient and b the constant. The letters a and b have special meaning. Rather than being variables such as x or y, they have a specific value that cannot change in any one equation. Letters at the end of the alphabet — x, y, z — are used as names for variables, and letters at the first of the alphabet — a, b, c — are used as names for constants. Compare $ax + b = 0$ to $4x + 2 = 0$. The a is equal to the coefficient 4 and the b is equal to the constant 2.

The advantage of using the general form for the equation is that it can be solved once to give all solutions of equations of the same type.

$ax + b = 0$	
$ax = -b$	subtract b from each side (or add -b)
$x = -b/a$	divide both sides by a (or multiply by $\frac{1}{a}$)

Substitution of the coefficient and constant term for $-b/a$ solves all equations of the form $ax + b = 0$. Solve $5x + 2$ by putting 5 in for a and 2 in for b: $x = -b/a = -2/5$. Algebra is powerful because a single formula solves an endless number of equations.

The equation $ax + b = 0$ is called an equation of the first degree. The x is raised to a power of +1, and can be written as x^1. The first power is seldom shown, and x^1 is usually written as x (without the exponent).

An equation such as $ax^2 + bx + c = 0$ is called an equation of the second degree. The highest power is the exponent 2 in ax^2 of the first term. The equation $ax^2 + bx + c = 0$ is also known as a quadratic equation. The word quadratic means "to make square," because x^2 is read as "x squared."

Examples of quadratic equations include:

$$x^2 + x + 2 = 0$$
$$x^2 + 4x - 4 = 0$$
$$2x^2 - 3x - 1 = 0$$
$$-3x^2 + 7x - 15 = 0$$

Hooke's law is the principle behind spring scales.

The x^2 term must be present for the equation to be a quadratic equation. However, either or both of the other terms can be missing. The following are quadratic equations, too:

$$x^2 = 0$$
$$5x^2 + 4x = 0$$
$$-3x^2 - 1 = 0$$

Algebra is often thought of as a difficult topic, yet algebra was invented to make hard problems easier. The word algebra dates from about the 800s. It comes from the Arab word *al-jabr* meaning restoration. At first, symbols for the unknowns and operations such as addition and subtraction were not used. But in 1637, the French mathematician René Descartes (day-KAHRT) published a book on geometry that included a long section on algebra. He used symbols for numbers and for mathematical operations. His book looked much like a modern algebra text.

Descartes, Galileo, Johannes Kepler, Robert Boyle, Robert Hooke, and Isaac Newton founded modern science. Most of these great people of science believed that God the Creator had designed nature with a basic harmony that they could trace out. They were convinced that experiments should not lead to a bewildering array of contradictory facts. Instead, those facts should fit into simple, easily understood laws.

The founders of science discovered that most physical laws followed one of four basic equations:

Equation 1: $y = kx$ y equals the product of a constant and x

Equation 2: $y = kx^2$ y equals the product of a constant and x squared

Equation 3: $y = k\sqrt{x}$ y equals the product of a constant and the square root of x

Equation 4: $y = k/x$ y equals the product of a constant and the reciprocal of x

An example of equation 1 is Hooke's law. Robert Hooke (1635–1703) measured how far weights would cause a spring to stretch. He discovered that the spring would stretch by a predictable amount. If he doubled the weight, then the spring stretched twice as far. When he tripled the weight, then the spring stretched three times as far.

Hooke's discovery is the principle behind how spring scales work. Many grocery stores have a spring scale in the produce aisle. Customers weigh apples, carrots, and other fruits and vegetables on the scales. Hooke's law explains how the spring scale gives accurate readings.

Robert Hooke wrote his discovery as an equation: $D = kF$, with D the distance the spring stretched and F the force (or weight) that pulled down on the spring. In words, Hooke's law can be stated as "the length a spring stretches is directly proportional to the force pulling on the spring." The word proportional means "forming a relationship."

What is k in the equation $y = kx$? The letter k stands for a coefficient that relates force to distance. The k is similar to the conversion factor that changes one measurement to another. The conversion factor of 12 inches to the foot changes feet to inches. You multiply feet by 12 to get inches. In the same way, the coefficient k relates the length that a spring stretches to the weight hanging on it.

Suppose you repeat Robert Hooke's experiment and suspend a paper cup from a rubber band. You add quarters to the cup and measure how far the weight of the coins stretches the rubber band.

Robert Hooke

The weight of the coins does not equal the distance: $D = F$. But you can set them equal by finding the value of k. The data shows that the rubber band stretches 0.4 millimeters for each coin. The coefficient k is equal to 0.4 millimeter per coin, which can be written as 0.4 mm/coin. The slash mark is read "divided by." The equation becomes $D = (0.4 \text{ mm/coin}) \times F$. The letter D represents the distance in millimeters, F the force measured by the weight of a coin, and 0.4 mm/coin the coefficient that relates distance to force.

The equation shows that 30 coins give a distance of 12.0 millimeters.

$D = kF$
$D = (0.4 \text{ mm/coin}) \times (30 \text{ coins})$
$D = 12.0 \text{ mm}$

An equation can predict values not in the table. You can predict that 50 coins will cause the rubber band to stretch 20.0 millimeters:

$D = 0.4 \text{ mm/coin} \times F$
$D = 0.4 \text{ mm/coin} \times 50 \text{ coins}$
$D = 20 \text{ mm}$

The value of k will change if a different rubber band is used — one that is wider, longer, or made of a different type of rubber. It

Hooke's Law Using Coins and a Rubber Band

F = Force (weight) Number of Coins	D = Distance (Millimeters, mm)
0	0
5	2
10	4
15	6
20	8
25	10
30	12
35	14

Figure 10-1

Hooke's Law with a Rubber Band

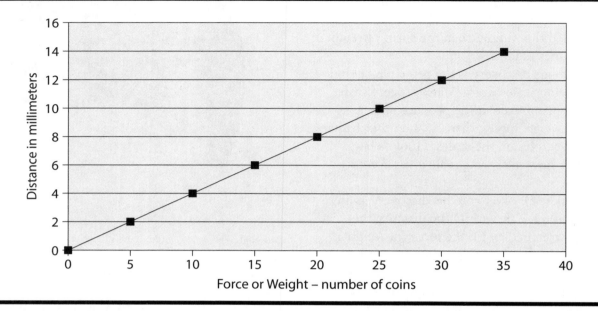

would also be different if a metal spring were used instead of an elastic band.

The information from the table or from values given by the equation can also be presented in the form of a graph. The number of coins is marked off on the vertical axis and the distance on the horizontal axis. The line goes up because distance and force are directly related. As the weight increases, so does the distance the rubber band stretches.

The graph (figure 10-1) shows that a straight line connects the values of force and distance. For that reason, an equation of the type y = kx is called a linear equation. A straight line connects different values of x and y.

The relationship between two quantities may not be a straight line. The Italian scientist Galileo (1564–1642) was one of the leaders of the scientific revolution. He studied the motion of falling objects.

Galileo used mathematics to summarize the data he collected about falling objects. Until his experiments, scholars believed an object fell at a constant speed. Galileo experimented with balls rolling down ramps. From those experiments, he proved that an object would gain speed as it fell. Each second saw it falling through a

greater distance. He compared distance to time and gave the results in a table.

Galileo's Experiments with a Falling Object

Time	Distance
Seconds	Feet
0	0
1	16
2	64
3	144
4	256
5	400

Notice that an object fell 16 feet in one second, but fell 64 feet in two seconds. The time doubled but the distance more than doubled. This showed that the relationship was not linear. In doubling the time from one second to two seconds, the distance became four times as great: 16 feet x 4 = 64 feet. In tripling the time from one second to three seconds, the distance became nine times as great: 16 feet x 9 = 144 feet.

Galileo discovered that the distance was proportional to the square of the time. Let D represent distance and T represent time.

The equation is $D = kT^2$. In words, Galileo's discovery can be stated as "the distance an object falls under the influence of gravity is directly proportional to the square of the time it has fallen."

Examine the table and you can see that the coefficient k must have a value of 16. The units are ft/sec^2. Those units are needed so that the conversion of seconds to distance gives an answer in feet. The equation relating distance to time for a falling object is $D = 16$ ft/sec^2 x T^2. For example, if the time is 5 seconds, then the distance is 400 feet.

$D = 16 \text{ ft/sec}^2 \text{ x } T^2$
$D = 16 \text{ ft/sec}^2 \text{ x } (5 \text{ sec})^2$
$D = 16 \text{ ft/sec}^2 \text{ x } 25 \text{ sec}^2$
$D = 400 \text{ ft}$

Once the equation is figured out, then the table of data is no longer needed. All of the data in the table can be produced by putting the number of seconds — 0 sec, 1 sec, 2 sec, 3 sec, and so on — in the equation for time and calculating distance.

An equation can give values not in the table. Suppose you drop a pebble into a deep well and it takes 2.5 seconds for it to splash into the water at the bottom. You can calculate the distance by putting 2.5 seconds in for T.

$D = 16 \text{ ft/sec}^2 \text{ x } (2.5 \text{ sec})^2$
$D = 16 \text{ ft/sec}^2 \text{ x } 6.25 \text{ sec}^2$
$D = 100 \text{ ft}$

A scientific law is true regardless of the units of measure used. The only change is that k must have the right value and units for the two quantities that are being measured. For instance, the metric unit for distance is meter. Stated in the metric system, Galileo's equation for falling objects is still $D = kT$, but with k equal to 4.9 m/sec^2.

Plotting data from Galileo's experiment gives a rising curve (figure 10-2). The curve is the right hand side of a parabola. The parabola has its axis (a line down its center) along the vertical number line. The vertical number line is called the y-axis.

Figure 10-2

Distance an Object Falls

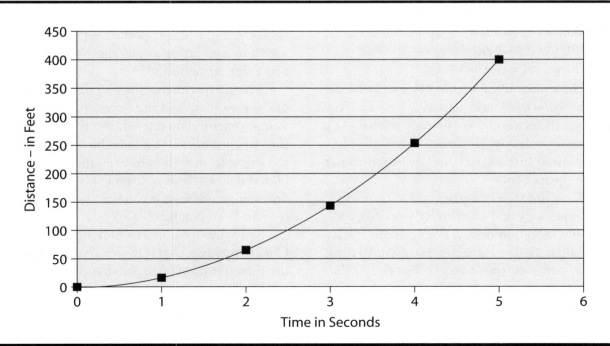

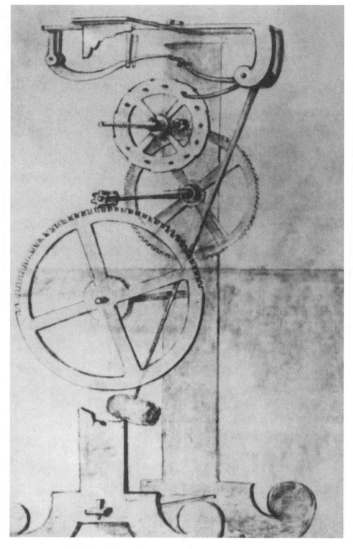

1659 drawing by Vincenzio Viviani, a pupil of Galileo, depicting a pendulum and escapement for making a pendulum clock

The equation for a falling object, $D = kT^2$, has the same form as Equation 2: $y = kx^2$. The two quantities x and y are directly related. As x increases, so does y. However, the relationship is not linear. Instead, y is directly proportional to the square of x.

The third type of equation is $y = k\sqrt{x}$. In this equation, y and x are directly related, too. As x gets larger, so does y. For example, if x is 4, then y is 2k. If x increases from four to nine, then y increases from 2k to 3k. But the y value does not increase as rapidly as the x value. If pairs of x and y values are plotted on a graph,

the figure is not a straight line. Instead, it is a parabola, but one that is lying on its side.

As an example of this type of relationship, the period of a pendulum is directly proportional to the square root of the length of the pendulum. A pendulum is a length of string tied at the top but free to swing at the bottom where a weight is attached. The period is the time for the pendulum to make a complete swing from one side to the other side and back again to its starting position.

Galileo was the first scientist to experiment with a pendulum. When he pulled the weight to one side and released it, the pendulum swung back and forth. For a pendulum 40 inches long, a complete swing took about two seconds. The 40-inch pendulum had a period of two seconds.

Galileo could think of several properties of the pendulum that might change the period of its swing. Did it matter if the weight at the bottom, called the bob, was made of metal, glass, wax, or wood? No, the period was still two seconds. He could pull the bob only slightly to one side or far to one side before releasing it. This made no difference in the period either.

The only way to change the speed of the swing was to change the length of the string. A pendulum with a longer string swung more slowly. It had a longer period. A pendulum with a shorter string swung more rapidly. It had a shorter period.

These experiments showed that the length of the pendulum and the time for a complete swing were directly related. But the relationship was not linear. When Galileo shortened the string from 40 inches to 20 inches, the period did not shorten from two seconds to one second. Instead, it changed from two seconds to 1.4 seconds.

Several years later, the Dutch scientist Christian Huygens (HOY-genz) investigated the principle of the pendulum more thoroughly. He made the first accurate clocks. In his clocks, the regular back and forth motion of a pendulum measured off the seconds.

Huygens found the equation that related the period, T, to the length, L, of the pendulum: $T = k\sqrt{L}$. In words, the law of the pendulum can be stated as "the period of a pendulum is directly proportional to the square root of the length of the pendulum."

Here are some sample values for the length of a pendulum and its period.

The Period of a Pendulum

Length of Pendulum in Inches	Period in Seconds
0.0	0.00
2.5	0.51
5.0	0.72
10.0	1.01
15.0	1.24
20.0	1.43
25.0	1.60
30.0	1.76
35.0	1.90
40.0	2.03

If L is in inches and T is in seconds, the value of k is 0.321. The units for k are sec/√in, or seconds per square root of inches. The peculiar looking unit of sec/√in is required so that the final unit for T will be seconds. A pendulum with a length of 15 inches gives a period of 1.24 seconds:

$T = k\sqrt{L}$
$T = (0.321 \text{ sec}/\sqrt{in}) \times \sqrt{(15 \text{ in})}$
The square root of 15 is about 3.87.
$T = 0.321 \text{ sec}/\sqrt{in} \times 3.87 \sqrt{in}$
$T = 1.24 \text{ sec}$

The equation can predict periods of pendulums that are not in the table. For instance, a person would need almost 16 seconds to swing back and forth on a rope 200 feet (2,400 inches) long.

$T = k\sqrt{L}$
$T = (0.321 \text{ sec}/\sqrt{in}) \times \sqrt{(2.400 \text{ in})}$
The square root of 2,400 is about 49.0.
$T = (0.321 \text{ sec}/\sqrt{in} \times 49.0 \sqrt{in}$
$T = 15.7 \text{ sec}$

Figure 10-3

Period of a Pendulum

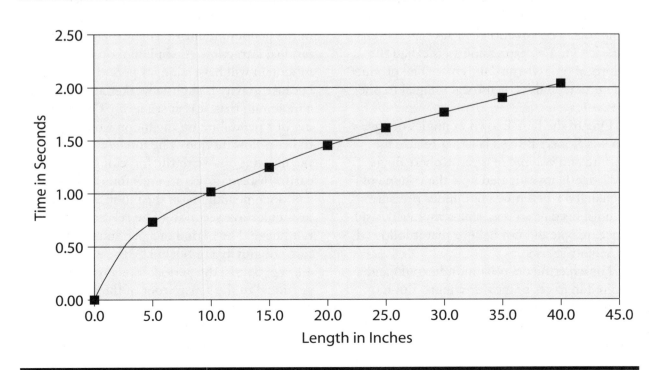

Galileo studied the motion and speed of falling objects.

If the values for T and L are plotted, then the graph is the top half of a parabola that is parallel to the horizontal number line (figure 10-3). The horizontal number line is called the x-axis.

Equation 4 is $y = k/x$. It is the fourth type of equation that scientists are likely to encounter when they study the laws of nature. The statement $y = k/x$ means that as x gets larger, y gets smaller. As one goes up, the other goes down. Scientists say that y is inversely proportional to x. The equation can also be written as $y = k * \frac{1}{x}$. The expression $\frac{1}{x}$ is called the reciprocal (ri-SIP-ruh-kuhl) of x. The product of a number and its reciprocal is equal to one: $x * \frac{1}{x} = 1$.

One of the best-known examples of equation 4 is Robert Boyle's law that relates the pressure and volume of a gas. Robert Boyle (1627–1691) investigated how the volume of air changed when it was put under pressure. Up until his day, air was such a mysterious substance, people did not believe that it followed any scientific laws.

His experiments took months to do and resulted in pages of measurements. But he summarized his discovery by the equation $V = k/P$, with V the volume of the gas and P the pressure on the gas. Doubling the pressure squeezed the gas into a volume one-half as great. Tripling the pressure squeezed the gas into a volume one-third as great. In words, Boyle's law can be stated as "the volume of a gas is inversely proportional to the pressure acting on the gas."

Plotting the values for volume and pressure gives a graph that is a hyperbola (figure 10-4). Although the hyperbola may look similar to a parabola, the two figures have different properties. For instance, the hyperbola runs along each axis and gets closer and closer, but never touches them.

A scientist who does an experiment tries to keep everything constant except for the two quantities under study. In his experiment with the pressure and volume of air, Robert Boyle kept the temperature constant.

Galileo realized that as an object fell faster and faster, air resistance would slow it. He said the distance and speed would be as predicted provided the object fell in a vacuum without air resistance.

Often, new information changes scientific laws. Scientists have found that the principle of the pendulum must take into account gravitational attraction. A pendulum on top of a mountain will have a longer period of swing because gravity is slightly weaker at the top of a mountain than it is at sea level. The swinging of a pendulum on the moon would appear to be in slow motion. The force of gravity on the moon is one-sixth the force of gravity on earth. Instead of two seconds for a full swing, a 40-inch pendulum on the moon would take just under five seconds. (The relationship is not linear. The period of a pendulum and the force of gravity are related by the expression $T = k/\sqrt{g}$; that is, the period, T, is inversely proportional to the square root of the acceleration due to gravity.)

In addition, a scientist must be careful to keep the results of his study within the limits of his or her data. For example, Robert Hooke knew a spring that is stretched too far becomes sprung. Anything that bends or stretches has an elastic limit. Too much weight will cause it to break or snap. A rubber band will stretch only so far. If pulled beyond its elastic limit, then it will snap. Hooke's Law stops working as the object being stretched nears its elastic limit.

A graph is often a simple way to show how two quantities are related to one another. At other times, an algebraic equation is the best way to show data. However, geometric proofs can often mystify a person skilled in algebra, while algebra can bewilder a person knowledgeable in geometry.

In the 1600s, the French mathematician René Descartes discovered a way to combine algebra with geometry and use the best features of both. He invented a new type of

mathematics called analytical geometry. The key idea was to use a coordinate system to locate a point exactly.

Navigators used latitude and longitude to locate points on the earth's surface. Latitude measured distance north or south of the equator and longitude measured distance east or west of a central meridian. English sailors used the prime meridian that passed through Greenwich, England.

Descartes's system used two number lines at right angles to one another. One ran left to right, the x-axis, and the other one ran up and down, the y-axis. They crossed at the origin. It was the zero point on both axes. Numbers to the right of the origin on the x-axis were given positive values: +1, +2, +3, and so on. Numbers to the left of the origin on the x-axis were given negative values: -1, -2, -3, and so on.

Figure 10-4

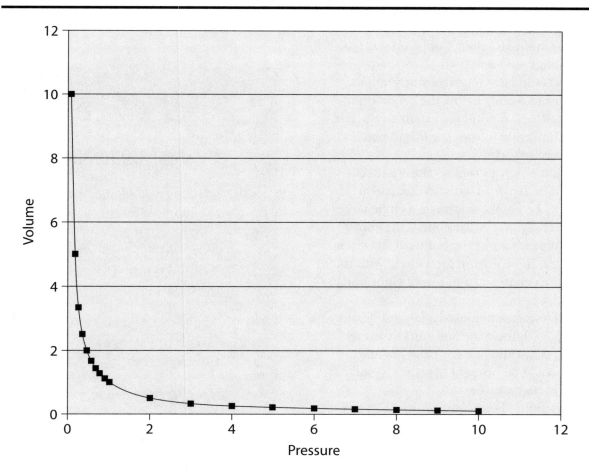

Pressure and Volume

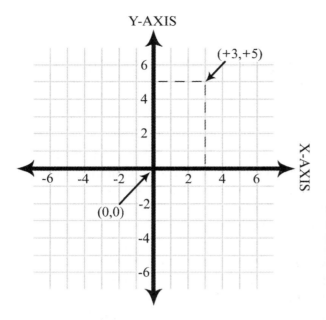

Numbers going up from the origin on the y-axis were positive while those going down were negative.

Any point on the sheet of paper could be labeled based on its distance from the x- and y-axis. The x value was always first and the y value second. The origin was (0, 0), meaning that x = 0 and y = 0. A point five units over to the right on the x-axis was labeled (+5, 0), meaning that x = +5 and y = 0. A point three units to the right and then 4 units up was (+3, +4), meaning x = +3 and y = +4.

Points could have negative x or y values, too. A point two units below the origin on the y-axis was (0, -2). A point four units to the left and three units down from the origin had the coordinate of (-4, -3).

Geometric figures such as the conic sections could be replaced with mathematical equations. The points that made a circle were written as $x^2 + y^2 = r^2$ with x and y the coordinates of the point and r the radius of the circle. For instance, the equation for a circle with its center at the origin and a radius of eight units was $x^2 + y^2 = 8^2$.

René Descartes first used analytical geometry in 1637. Mathematicians quickly saw its advantage. All of the power of algebra and geometry could be brought together to solve problems in mathematics.

For example, the ancient Greeks had proposed three problems that resisted all efforts to solve them. They wanted to square a circle (construct a square with the same area as a given circle), trisect an angle (cut an angle into three equal angles), and double a cube (make a cube with a volume twice as great as a given cube.) In trying to work these problems, the Greeks limited themselves to a straight edge for drawing straight lines and a compass for drawing circles.

The Greeks failed to solve the three problems. Over the next 2,000 years, the best mathematicians also tried and failed to solve any one of the three classic Greek geometry problems. They had begun to suspect that none of the three could be done using the rules that the Greeks laid down.

In 1882, Carl Louis Lindemann (LIN-duh-mahn), a German mathematician, proved that squaring a circle was impossible with straight edge and compass alone. He did it by changing the problem from a geometric one to an algebraic one. Algebra also showed the other two Greek problems were impossible, too.

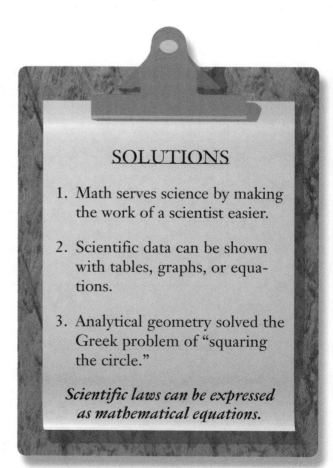

SOLUTIONS

1. Math serves science by making the work of a scientist easier.

2. Scientific data can be shown with tables, graphs, or equations.

3. Analytical geometry solved the Greek problem of "squaring the circle."

Scientific laws can be expressed as mathematical equations.

T F   1. Normally, a variable can have more than one value.

A B C D   2. Discovering the value of x when y is equal to zero is called
(A. modernizing   B. normalizing   C. solving   D. zeroing) the equation.

A B C D   3. The 5 in the equation $5x + 2 = 0$ is called (A. a coefficient
B. a constant   C. an equalizer   D. a variable).

A B   4. An equation such as $ax^2 + bx + c = 0$ is called an equation of the
(A. first   B. second) degree.

T F   5. An equation of the type $y = kx$ is called a linear equation.

T F   6. A scientific law must be stated in the metric system of units to be true.

A B C D   7. The expression $\frac{1}{x}$ is called the (A. base   B. identify   C. reciprocal
D. square root) of x.

A B C D   8. In the 1600s, the French mathematician René Descartes discovered
a way to combine algebra with (A. computer programming
B. geometry   C. number theory   D. physics).

A B C   9. The three problems that had resisted solutions since ancient Greek
times were trisecting the angle, doubling a cube, and (A. bisecting
an angle   B. making a right angle   C. squaring the circle).

Match the equation with the figure on right.

10. _____ $y = kx$

11. _____ $y = kx^2$

12. _____ $y = k\sqrt{x}$

13. _____ $y = k/x$

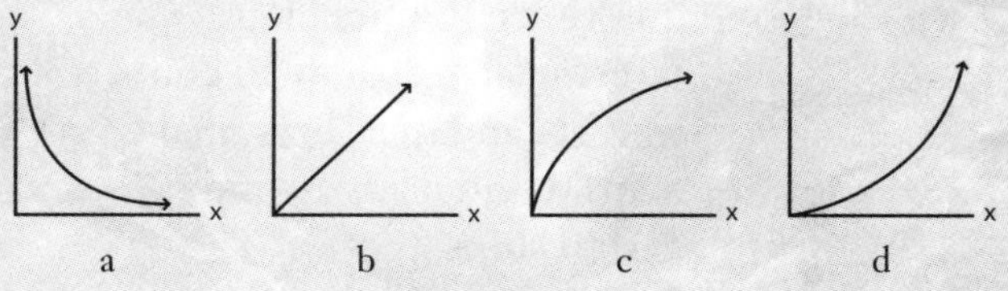

a   b   c   d

Match the statement with the figure above.

14. _____ The length a spring stretches (y-axis) is directly proportional to the
force pulling on the spring (x-axis).

15. _____ The distance an object falls (y-axis) under the influence of gravity is
directly proportional to the square of the time it has fallen (x-axis).

16. _____ The volume of a gas (y-axis) is inversely proportional to the pressure
acting on the gas (x-axis).

17. _____ The period of a pendulum (y-axis) is directly proportional to the square
root of the length of the pendulum (x-axis).

Pure and Applied Math

Mathematics that can be put into practice for a particular use is called applied mathematics. Calculating the orbits of planets, making accurate calendars, and using computer programs to predict the path of storms are examples of applied math. Applied mathematics answers questions of immediate interest such as how to convert weights and measures, make maps, build bridges, and design ships.

Pure mathematics investigates numbers without any particular real-life use. Discovering the properties of prime numbers was pure mathematics for thousands of years. However, early in the 1900s, bank records and other vital information began to be sent through telephone lines. Later, in the 1990s, the Internet began to be used for transmitting personal information. The records must be protected so only the sender and person receiving the records

PROBLEMS

1. How did a walking tour of a city start a new branch of mathematics?

2. How did ringing church bells start a new branch of mathematics?

3. Does probability play a role in scientific laws?

Can You Propose Solutions?

Figure 11-1

Königsberg and Its Seven Bridges

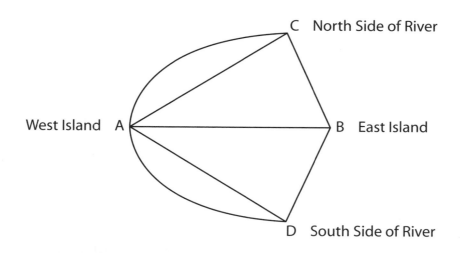

C   North Side of River

West Island   A

B   East Island

D   South Side of River

Taking a Sunday stroll across the bridge

can read them. Mathematicians discovered how to encode the data using very large prime numbers. Discovering large prime numbers changed from an exercise in pure mathematics to one of applied mathematics.

Almost all branches of mathematics that started out as pure mathematics eventually found a practical use. For instance, people living in Königsberg, Prussia (present-day Kaliningrad, Russia), had an interesting puzzle. In the 1700s, the city spread across both sides of the Pregel River and occupied two islands in the middle of the river. Seven bridges connected various parts of the town. People who took a Sunday stroll wondered if they could walk through the city and cross all seven bridges only once. No one succeeded. The puzzle became known as the Königsberg Bridge puzzle.

A mathematician named Leonhard Euler (Oi-ler) tackled the problem. He redrew the map of the city, islands, and bridges as a simple network diagram. He showed the west island (A), east island (B), north side of the river (C), and south side of the river (D) as points. He connected the points with lines to represent the bridges.

Figure 11-2

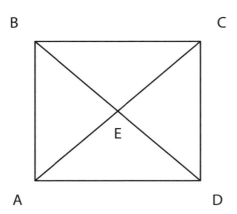

*The Envelope
Puzzle*

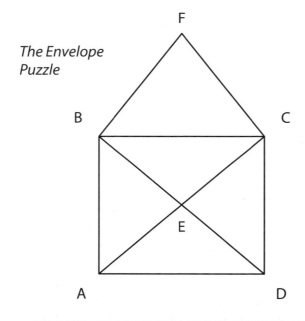

to either begin there or end there but could
not do both.

The north shore also had three bridges. A
person had to either begin there or end there
but could not do both. The south shore also
had three bridges. The person had to begin
there or end there, too.

The city had three points (C, B, D, see
figure 11-1) where walkers had to either begin
or end but could not do both. Walkers could
not begin or end in three different places. This
made it impossible to walk across all seven
bridges without crossing one a second time.

As Leonard Euler solved the Königsberg
bridge problem, he developed a whole new
field of mathematics known as network design.
Nodes are points in a network where lines
meet. An even node has an even number of
lines connected to it. An odd node has an odd
number of lines connected to it. Euler showed
that a network with any number of even nodes
could be traced in one continuous route provided it had either no odd nodes or exactly two
odd nodes.

Suppose a figure is given and you are asked
to draw the diagram with one continuous
motion of a pencil without lifting it from the
paper and without retracing a line. Count the
nodes that are odd or even. If all are even, or
even with exactly two odd nodes, then it can be
done.

For example, a rectangle with diagonals
cannot be traced without going over a line or
lifting the pencil. (See figure 11-2, top.) Of
the five points, only point E is even. The other
four nodes — A, B, C, and D — are odd.

The envelope puzzle can be done
because there are two odd nodes, A and D,
and four even nodes. One possible route is
ABFCBECDAED. (See figure 11-2, bottom.)

At first, Euler's network studies had no
apparent real-world application. But network
design became applied mathematics with the
invention of the telephone, computers, and the
Internet. Large volumes of data are broken into
individual packets at the source and routed
through a network in the most efficient way.

His diagram showed that the east island
had three bridges connected to it. With three
bridges, a person who started walking from the
island would leave it by one bridge, return by
a second bridge, and then leave again by the
third bridge. The person could not end on the
island. A person who started elsewhere had
to come to the island by one bridge, leave by
another bridge, and return by the third bridge.
He would end up on the island. A person had

Four Corners is the only point in the United States where four states touch a single point.

The packets do not all have to travel the same route. If one route is too busy, some of the packets are sent a different way. A particular node can malfunction and drop out of the network, but the packets will get through by an alternate route. Software at the destination reassembles the packets to give the complete document. Problems in data throughput can be worked on with network design that Euler pioneered.

A problem involving areas and how they touch each other is the four-color map problem. Mapmakers colored maps so borders between regions could be easily seen. They found that any map, no matter how complicated, never needed more than four colors. However, no one could prove this statement true. Mathematicians became aware of the question in 1852 and it became known as the four-color map problem.

How many colors are needed to color an ordinary map so that no two regions that share the same border have the same color? The regions can touch at a single point and have the same color. For example, the four states of New Mexico, Colorado, Utah, and Arizona share a single point. It is called Four Corners. A person can get on hands and knees at the common point and a different part of his or her body is in four different states. Two colors are enough to color the map so the four states have different colors along their borders. At the single intersecting point of the Four Corners at least two of the states share the same color. However, that is all right.

But other maps had regions where two or three colors were definitely too few, and four colors were needed. Mathematicians quickly proved that five colors would always be enough no matter how complicated the map. But showing that four colors would always be enough was not proven for more than 100 years.

In the 1970s, a group of mathematicians at the University of Illinois tackled the problem. They worked on it for four years. A computer program generated 1,936 shapes for possible maps. In 1976, they had the answer. Four colors are enough to color any map no matter how complicated. The solution ran to several hundred pages.

Mathematicians often face problems in which numbers grow large very quickly. Answers to problems about combinations and permutations (per-myoo-TA-shuns) often give large numbers. A combination is any selection of objects without regard to their order.

For instance, you can pay for a 75-cent purchase at a vending machine with two quarters, a nickel, and two dimes. The order does not matter. You can put in the quarters first, then the other coins. Or, you can put in the nickel, then a dime, the two quarters, and then the last dime. Vending machines will take change in any order. A situation in which order is not important is called a combination.

On the other hand, if you go to a ballpark and your seat number is 971, then you look for the digits in that order. Seats numbered 917, 719, 791, 197, or 179 will not do. The order of the digits does matter. Each different arrangement is called a permutation.

A permutation is an arrangement of things in a definite order. The word permutation is based on the Latin word mutation meaning change. Each change in the order is a different permutation.

The question of how many permutations are possible began with church bell ringing in the 1400s. Before the invention of clocks, most churches rang a bell to call the faithful to worship. The first church bells were installed in the 900s. As time passed, more bells were added to the bells in the bell tower. The bells were of different sizes and produced different tones. One person was assigned to each bell. He pulled on a rope fastened to a wheel that rotated the bell and caused it to strike the clapper.

The first permutations came about because of bells in church bell towers.

Bell ringers challenged themselves to ring the bells in all possible orders. During any one permutation, each bell had to be rung, but no bell could be rung more than once. With 3 bells labeled A, B, and C, the first order might be ABC, the next one would be ACB, then BAC, BCA, CAB, and finally CBA. The sequence AAB was not allowed because no bell can be used twice in a single sequence. Ringing only 2 bells, AB, would not be allowed because bell C would be left out.

Rewriting the six possible permutations shows how the order of ringing the bells is shifted around:

ABC, ACB	A goes first, then B and C switch positions
BAC, BCA	B goes first, then A and C switch positions
CAB, CAB	C goes first, then A and B switch positions

At the start, the bell ringers had a choice of any 1 of the 3 bells. They could begin with A, B, or C. After they chose a bell, they had but two choices remaining. After choosing the second bell, they had but one bell left, and they had to ring it last. The bell ringers had three choices, then two choices, and finally one choice.

The permutations of 3 bells is given by the product of 3, 2, and 1: 3 x 2 x 1 = 6. The expression 3 x 2 x 1 is called three factorial. Mathematicians use a symbol that looks like an exclamation mark but is called a factorial. The expression 3! is read as "three factorial" and means 3 x 2 x 1.

Four factorial is equal to the product of 4 and all whole numbers smaller than 4: 4! = 4 x 3 x 2 x 1 = 24. Four factorial gives the number of different ways that 4 things can be arranged such as how 4 bells can be rung.

Ringing bells in all possible ways is called a peal. Assume that ringing an individual bell took about ⅓ of a second. For 3 bells, each sequence took about one second and the entire group of 6 permutations took about 6 seconds.

The total number of possible permutations went up quickly as more bells were added. With 4 bells, the permutations numbered 24:

ABCD ACBD BACD BCAD CABD CBAD
ABDC ACDB BADC BCDA CADB CBDA
ADCB ADCB BDAC BDCA CDAB CDBA
DACB DACB DBAC DBCA DCAB DCBA

The bell ringers had 4 choices for the first bell that they rang, 3 choices for the next one, then 2 choices, and finally 1 choice. The number of permutations is given by four factorial: 4! = 4 x 3 x 2 x 1 = 24. Each sequence had 4 bells, and there were a total of 24 sequences. Ringing a complete peal took 32 seconds.

But most churches had from 5 to 12 bells. How many permutations are possible with 5 bells? Rather than listing them, we can calculate the value of five factorial, 5! If we already know the value of 4!, then we can calculate 5! easily because 5! = 5 x 4!. The value of four factorial is 24, so five factorial is 5 x 24 = 120.

How long does it take to make a peal of 5 bells? Each sequence has 5 bells and there are 120 sequences. The total number of bells rung is 600 (5 x 120 = 600.) Each bell takes about ⅓ of a second, so ringing them all would take 3 minutes 18 seconds: (600 bells x ⅓ bell per second) / (60 second per min) = 3.3 minutes or 3 minutes 20 seconds.

What about a church with 12 bells? The number of sequences is twelve factorial: 12! = 12 x 11 x 10 x 9 x 8 x 7 x 6 x 5 x 4 x 3 x 2 x 1 = 479,001,600. Each sequence rings 12 bells. Ringing all 12 bells a total of 479,001,600 times would take about 60 years!

Bell ringing is still practiced as a hobby today. Should the bell ringers make a mistake and ring a bell before its time or out of its order, they have to start over. The bell ringers cannot stop to take a rest. Normally, peals for more than 7 bells are not attempted. A successful 7-bell peal (5,040 sequences) takes about three hours and 16 minutes. The actual time may differ because of the skill of the bell ringers and the size and weight of the bells. Most bell ringers are happy to get to 5,040 different combinations without a mistake, and they call that a full peal, even if the church has more than 7 bells.

If bells can be repeated during a peal, then the number of permutations is even greater. Suppose bell ringers decide to ring groups of 3 rings and let bells repeat. Rather than 6 sequences, they could make 27 sequences.

To calculate the number of ways that items can be arranged, multiply the number of choices for each position. For first place, the bell ringers who ignore the rule not to repeat a bell have a choice of 3 bells, for second place the same 3 bells, and for third place the same 3 bells. The total number of sequences is 3 x 3 x 3 = 27.

Imagine a small island nation that decides to make license plates for vehicles on the island. Only the digits 0 and 1 will be used for license plate numbers. The island government decides to have plates with room for only 4 digits. How many plates with different numbers can be made?

A choice of 2 different digits can be put in each of the 4 places on each license plate. The total number of different license plates is 2 x 2 x 2 x 2 = 16. Here are all possible four-digit numbers using 0 and 1:

0000	1000
0001	1001
0010	1010
0011	1011
0100	1100
0101	1101
0110	1110
0111	1111

The island decides that 16 plates would not be enough for all the vehicles on the island. If they use all of the digits, 0 through 9, how many plates can they make? If you number the plates as 0000, 0001, 0002, 0003, and so on, the numbering will end at 9999. There are 10,000 different plates (9,999 plates plus the one plate numbered 0000.)

Another way to solve the same problem is to remember that each of the 4 positions can be filled with any one of 10 digits: 10 x 10 x 10 x 10 = 10,000.

Later, the number of vehicles on the island increased to be more than 10,000. Unless something was done, new vehicles would have the same number on their license plate as older vehicles. The island decided to use letters instead of numbers. How many license plates were possible? Answer: Each of 4 positions can be filled with any one of 26 letters of the alphabet. The total is 26 x 26 x 26 x 26 = 456,976. You can get more license plates using four letters than four digits because there are more letters in the alphabet (26) than digits from zero through nine.

Place four coins in a row on a table. How many different ways can you line them up by heads or tails? A person might say, "All heads, one head and three tails, two heads and two tails, one head and three tails, or all tails. That is five different ways." That is five different combinations, but it is not the number of permutations.

Each of four coins can be turned to show two different sides. The overall total is 2 x 2 x 2 x 2 = 16. Here is a list of how they could be arranged:

HHHH	THHH
HHHT	THHT
HHTH	THTH
HHTT	THTT
HTHH	TTHH
HTHT	TTHT
HTTH	TTTH
HTTT	TTTT

The 16 permutations are the same as the number of four-digit license plates using the digits 0 and 1. In both cases, there are four positions and each position has two choices. The choices are H or T in this case and 0 or 1 in the island license plates example.

Order is important in the arrangement of heads and tails. A head in first place followed by three tails is different than three tails followed by a head. A summary shows

1 way to have all heads and zero tails
4 ways to have three heads and one tail
6 ways to have two heads and two tails
4 ways to have one head and three tails
1 way to have all heads and zero tails

Figure 11-3

Pascal's Triangle

Row 1	1	row sum = $1 = 2^0$
Row 2	1 1	row sum = $2 = 2^1$
Row 3	**1** 2 1	row sum = $4 = 2^2$
Row 4	1 **3** 3 1	row sum = $8 = 2^3$
Row 5	1 4 **6** 4 1	row sum = $16 = 2^4$
Row 6	1 5 10 **10** 5 1	row sum = $32 = 2^5$
Row 7	1 6 15 20 **15** 6 1	row sum = $64 = 2^6$

The numbers 1, 4, 6, 4, 1 make up one row of a mathematical series of numbers known as Pascal's triangle. Blaise Pascal (pas-KAL) developed this special triangle. He was a French mathematician and philosopher who lived in the 1600s. He called it an arithmetic triangle, but it was soon named after him (see figure 11-3).

In Pascal's triangle, each number is the sum of the two numbers immediately above it. The next row in the triangle can be found by adding the two numbers above each entry. Row 8 starts with 1, then it has the sum of 6 and 1, the sum of 6 and 15, the sum of 15 and 20, and so on. Row 8 is 1, 7, 21, 35, 35, 21, 7, 1.

The triangle has many interesting mathematical patterns. Recall the triangular numbers from chapter 8: 1, 3, 6, 10, 15. They can be found in the diagonal line that starts in row three. They are shown in bold in the triangle. The square numbers are in the table, too, because if you add two of those triangular numbers that are next to one another, you will get a square number:

$$1 + 3 = 4 = 2^2$$
$$3 + 6 = 9 = 3^2$$
$$6 + 10 = 16 = 4^2$$
and so on.

The sum of each row is a power of two. Row 1 is $2^0 = 1$. Mathematicians define any number to the zero power as equal to one. The second row is $1 + 1 = 2$, which equals 2^1. The sum of the numbers in the third row is $1 + 2 + 1 = 4$, which is 2^2, and so on.

Ignore the 1's and look at the other numbers. If the first number is prime, then all the other numbers in the row will be divisible by it. Row 6 has 5, 10, 10, 5, and all of them are divisible by the prime number five. Row 8, as previously calculated, has 7, 21, 35, 35, 21, 7. All of those numbers are divisible by the prime number 7.

The numbers also give what is called the binomial expansion, discovered by Isaac Newton. Isaac Newton (1642–1727) is considered the greatest mathematician who ever lived. He made important discoveries in physics, astronomy, optics, and mathematics.

Raising a binomial to a power was one of the problems in mathematics that captured Newton's attention. The word binomial was from bi meaning two and nomial meaning names. A binomial was an expression in algebra made of two numbers. It could be written as a + b, with the letter "a" standing for one number and "b" standing for the other number.

Binomials can be added, subtracted, multiplied, divided, and raised to powers. However, raising a binomial to a power was difficult because it expanded into a series of complicated terms. The simplest binomial raised to a power was $(a + b)^2 = (a + b) \times (a + b)$. Isaac carried out the multiplication and gave the answer as $1a^2 + 2ab + 1b^2$. You calculate a cross product in a way that is similar to how you multiply numbers with two digits. Recall that a x b can be written as ab.

$$
\begin{array}{r}
a + b \\
a + b \\
\hline
a \times b + b \times b \\
a \times a + a \times b \\
\hline
1a^2 + 2ab + 1b^2
\end{array}
$$

What about $(a + b)^3$? The answer is $(a + b) \times (a + b) \times (a + b) = 1a^3 + 3a^2b + 3ab^2 + 1b^3$. As the powers increased, the expression became more tangled. When Isaac multiplied out a binomial raised to the fourth power, it had five terms: $(a + b)^4 = 1a^4 + 4a^3b + 6a^2b^2 + 4a^2b^3 + 1b^4$.

Isaac Newton

As he pored over the calculations, Isaac saw a pattern emerge. He discovered he could calculate the terms in his head. For instance, the number in front of the second term was always the power to which the binomial was raised.

The numbers are also given by the rows of Pascal's triangle. For example, the coefficients for $(a + b)^4$ are 1, 4, 6, 4, 1 that are found in Row 5 of Pascal's triangle. Recall that this sequence of numbers is also the number of ways that the heads and tails for four coins can be arranged: one with all heads, four ways with three heads and one tail, six with two heads and two tails, four with one head and three tails, and one with all four tails. People are fascinated by the surprising connections between what appears to be different areas of math.

Pascal developed his triangle when studying combinations and permutations. For this project he worked with Pierre de Fermat (fehr-MAH), a lawyer and amateur mathematician.

Pascal and Fermat did not live in the same city, and they never met. But they were both interested in working out the mathematics of combinations and permutations. This was in the 1600s. For the first time, mail delivery became reliable enough for two people to work together on the same problem by exchanging letters. In 1654, they sent a flurry of letters back and forth to one another as they developed the rules governing combinations and permutations. Pascal and Fermat are often called the founders of modern number theory.

For years, one of the most interesting unsolved problems of mathematics was known as Fermat's last theorem. He would read a book and take notes, often by jotting them in the margins of the book.

In one book, he wrote that if x, y, z, and n were all integers (whole numbers) then $x^n + y^n = z^n$ had no solutions for n greater than two. He said that he'd found a truly wonderful proof of this fact, although the margin of the book was too small to contain it.

Fermat claimed that in some instances you could add the squares of two whole numbers and get the square of a third whole number. In fact, when n = 2, the equation becomes the Pythagorean theorem: $x^2 + y^2 = z^2$, and numbers such as 3, 4, and 5 are one answer: $3^2 + 4^2 = 5^2$. Another solution is 5, 12, and 13: $5^2 + 12^2 = 13^2$.

But the equation could be solved only when n = 2. According to Fermat, you could not add the cubes to two whole numbers and get the cube of a third whole number. The equation $x^3 + y^3 = z^3$ had no solution using whole numbers. The sum of the fourth power of two numbers never gave the fourth power of a number. The equation $x^4 + y^4 = z^4$ had no solution. Except for the well-known case of n = 2, no equation with a higher power for n had a solution.

A statement in mathematics that something is true based on explicit assumptions is called a theorem. Fermat also made many other claims. Mathematicians began to trust what he said. If he said he had proven an idea to be true, then later they would find that it was true. One by one, all of his statements were shown true.

Because $x^n + y^n = z^n$ was the last of Fermat's theorems that had not been proven one way or another, the problem became known as Fermat's last theorem. Fermat was a brilliant mathematician. Most people believed that his statement was true that only the power of 2 would work. Fermat's simple theorem turned out to be surprisingly difficult to prove. Practically every great mathematician and countless amateurs tackled the problem. Prizes were offered for a solution to Fermat's last theorem. Many regretted that Fermat's book had such narrow margins. It they had been wider, maybe he would have given the proof.

For more than 350 years, many mathematicians tried and failed to prove that $x^n + y^n = z^n$ had no solution except for n = 2. Andrew Wiles, an English mathematician living in the United States, devoted seven years to the problem. With the help of Richard Taylor, a former student, he supplied the proof in 1995. Fermat

Blaise Pascal

was right: $x^n + y^n = z^n$ has no solution with whole numbers except for $n = 2$.

Andrew Wiles used methods that were totally unknown to Fermat. If Fermat did have a proof, then it probably would have been a simpler and shorter one. Mathematicians are still looking for a way to prove the theorem using the mathematics that was known in Fermat's day.

The study by Fermat and Pascal of combinations and permutations turned out to have applications in many branches of science. Genetics is the study of how traits are passed from one generation to the next in living organisms including humans. Inheritance of traits depends on how the genes that carry those traits combine with one another.

The DNA (deoxyribonucleic acid) molecule in each living cell carries heredity information. The molecule is shaped like a twisted ladder called a double helix. The steps of the ladder are made of only four different chemical molecules called bases. Biologists identify the bases by the letters A, G, C, and T. The bases are found in pairs going between the two rails of the ladder. Each gene for a particular trait has a sequence of different combinations of base pairs. Calculating the possible combinations makes use of the mathematics that Fermat and Pascal developed.

Fermat and Pascal began their study of combinations and permutations because of a question about probability. They expressed probability as a fraction between 0 and 1. An unlikely event had a probability near 0. A likely event had a probability near 1.

The number of permutations helps calculate the probability. Suppose you were on the island that had license plates of 0s and 1s. What is the probability that the next vehicle you see has all ones on the license plate, 1111?

Earlier we calculated that there could be 16 license plates. But only one of them is all ones. So the probability of all ones is 1 in 16, $\frac{1}{16}$ or 0.0625.

Probability is used in a number of different scientific fields, today. People who sample public opinion about a particular issue use probability. From a small sample, they can predict what a larger group is thinking about the issue. The polltakers do not claim that their results are 100 percent accurate. Instead, they use a percentage, based on calculations involving probability, to express how much error the poll may have. A well-designed poll that interviews 1,600 people can often predict the opinion of millions of people with an error of only three or four percent.

Probability became a useful subject because scientists often deal with objects that individually may not seem to follow a pattern, but as a group do follow a pattern. The molecules that make up a gas in a container seem in random motion with the molecules darting in every direction. But as a group their action can be predicted.

Each day our life is touched by discoveries that Fermat and Pascal made. A weather forecaster may predict a "20 percent chance of rain." The forecaster uses software that calculates the percentage using the rules of probability.

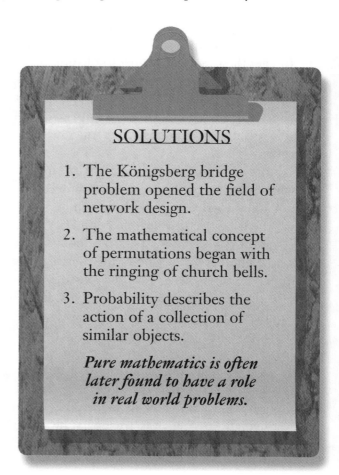

SOLUTIONS

1. The Königsberg bridge problem opened the field of network design.

2. The mathematical concept of permutations began with the ringing of church bells.

3. Probability describes the action of a collection of similar objects.

Pure mathematics is often later found to have a role in real world problems.

A B   1. Mathematics for practical use is called (A. applied   B. pure) mathematics.

A B   2. Discovering large prime numbers to encode data is an example of (A. applied   B. pure) math.

A B C D   3. The problem that a computer helped solve was the (A. bell peal problem   B. binomial theorem   C. four-color map problem D. Königsberg bridge problem).

A B   4. Each arrangement of the letters ABC, ACB, BAC, BCA, CAB, and CBA is called a (A. combination   B. permutation).

A B C D   5. The expression 3! is read as "three (A. combinations"   B. factorial" C. permutations"   D. probabilities").

A B C D   6. The value of 5! is (A. 24   B. 25   C. 120   D. 125).

A B   7. To calculate the number of ways that items can be arranged, (A. add   B. multiply) the number of choices for each position.

T F   8. The study of combinations and permutations has no application in everyday life.

Matching

9. _____ Andrew Wiles
10. _____ Blaise Pascal
11. _____ Isaac Newton
12. _____ Leonhard Euler
13. _____ Pierre de Fermat

a. discovered how to calculate the coefficients of a binomial raised to a power.

b. he called his triangle an arithmetic triangle.

c. his last theorem was solved in 1995.

d. solved the Königsberg bridge problem.

e. proved that $x^n + y^n = z^n$ has no solution with whole numbers except for $n = 2$.

Try Your Math

14. The state of Missouri has license plates with three letters followed by three digits. How many license plates are possible?

$\tan\phi = \dfrac{X_c}{R}$

$E_c = \Delta mc^2$

$\sqrt{a^2 + b^2}$

$L = 2\pi fL$

Computing Machines

S cientists who lived a few hundred years ago faced a daunting task when they did difficult calculations. They had no calculators, computers, or other aids for the difficult computations. Johannes Kepler, who lived at about the same time as Galileo, spent six years calculating the orbit of Mars. He worked long and lonely hours by candlelight late into the night.

Kepler wrote to instrument makers and encouraged them to build a calculating machine. A few people tried, but none of the machines proved satisfactory. Kepler himself built a small mechanical calculator that could do simple addition.

In the 1600s, instrument makers had not gained the skill to make small gears and dials with the precision that calculators required. Clocks were the most intricate devices

PROBLEMS

1. When is a log table not made of wood?

2. What were the step reckoner, difference engine, and analytical engine?

3. Lady Ada, Countess of Lovelace, is credited with what mathematical accomplishment?

Can You Propose Solutions?

being built at that time. Some of them used wooden cogs, and the smallest clocks took up an entire cabinet.

Every 30 years or so, a person would read about the previous attempt and then decide that instrument making had improved enough to try again. In 1639, Blaise Pascal started building a calculator. His father, who was a tax collector, had the tedious chore of adding long columns of numbers. Pascal spent three years building his machine, which was intended mainly to add numbers.

Pascal's machine used a series of gearlike wheels that connected with one another. Each gear had ten teeth. Ten full turns of the first wheel rotated the next wheel by one turn. Ten turns of the second wheel advanced the third wheel by one turn. The wheels counted by 1, 10, 100, and so on. An answer appeared in little windows at the top of the machine. Pascal is credited with building the first adding machine. But the one he built had limited use.

Other inventors improved on his basic idea. German mathematician Gottfried Leibnitz (LIPE-nits) said, "It is unworthy of excellent men to lose hours like slaves in the labor of calculation." In 1671, he constructed an updated version of Pascal's machine. Leibnitz called his calculator the "Step Reckoner." He chose that name because it did multiplication by a series, or steps, of repeated additions.

His machine and others like it added by turning gears. Multiplication was done by repeated additions. To multiply 263 by 81, he input 263 and added it 81 times. Division was done by repeated subtractions. To divide 263 by 81, the machine counted how many times 81 could be subtracted from 263.

During the 1700s, instrument makers succeeded in making practical mechanical calculators. The machines were improved over the years and stayed in use until the late 1960s. They were often built for a specific purpose, and were large, heavy, expensive, and noisy.

Blaise Pascal invented a calculator in 1642.

At first, a person turned a hand crank or pressed down on a lever to crank the gears. Electric motors powered later models, but multiplication remained a matter of repeated additions. Once a problem was typed in on keys, the electric-powered mechanical calculator worked with loud clatter. The machine made a grinding noise as the gears meshed against one another. It printed out intermediate steps by banging keys against a strip of paper. A single problem could take two or three minutes. Because of the loud noise, people said the machine was "crunching numbers."

The first electronic hand-held calculators did not come into use until 1967. Except for the keys, they had no large moving parts. Electrons coursed through circuits and did the work of gears. Rather than printing numbers on paper, light-emitting diodes displayed the answers.

Electronic calculators could add, subtract, multiply, divide, raise numbers to powers, and extract square roots. Expensive ones could also

A slide rule added logarithms to multiply numbers.

calculate other functions such as factorials, n!, up to about the number n = 69, and calculate the values of trigonometric functions.

Until the 1970s, most engineers and scientists did their calculations with a slide rule. A slide rule was a handy device that used a mathematical shortcut based on writing numbers using exponents.

Scientists must often deal with very large or very small numbers. One simple way to write large numbers is with exponents. The expression 10^6 is read "10 to the sixth power" or "10 raised to the sixth power." It means to multiply 10 times itself six times: $10^6 = 10 \times 10 \times 10 \times 10 \times 10 \times 10 = 1,000,000$. The expression 10^6 is a shorthand way of writing one million.

The reciprocal of 10 is $\frac{1}{10}$. Scientists define a negative exponent as the reciprocal of the number: $n^{-1} = \frac{1}{n}$, and $10^{-1} = \frac{1}{10}$. The number 10^{-6} is equal to $\frac{1}{10}$ times itself six times: $10^{-6} = \frac{1}{10} \times \frac{1}{10} \times \frac{1}{10} \times \frac{1}{10} \times \frac{1}{10} \times \frac{1}{10} = \frac{1}{1,000,000}$ or 0.000001. The expression 10^{-6} is a shorthand way of writing the fraction one millionth.

Mathematicians define 10^0 to be one: $10^0 = 1$. Any number raised to the zero power is one: $n^0 = 1$.

One advantage of exponents is that numbers are multiplied by adding their exponents: $10^2 \times 10^3 = 10^{(2+3)} = 10^5$. The exponents can only be added if the base (10 in this case) is the same for all of the numbers. It is true that $2^2 \times 2^3 = 2^{(2+3)} = 2^5$ because the base, 2, is the same throughout. But the solution to $2^3 \times 10^5$ cannot be found by adding exponents because the bases, 2 and 10, are not equal.

Exponents can also be fractions. The square root of a number is equal to the number raised to the one-half, or 0.5, power: $\sqrt{2} = 2^{0.5} = 1.414$ (approximate) and $\sqrt{25} = 25^{0.5} = 5$ (exact).

John Napier (NAY-pee-ur, 1550–1617) realized that every number is equal to 10 raised to some power. It would be easier to add exponents rather than multiply numbers. Napier was a Protestant religious leader in Scotland who had an inventive mind. He invented the decimal point to show where the decimal part of a decimal fraction began. Before then, the decimal part was circled. This worked all right for handwritten manuscripts, but could not be set to type and printed. A decimal point was a simpler solution for printed documents because it could be shown as a period.

Napier's greatest achievement was the invention of logarithms. A logarithm (LOG-uh-RITH-um) is the power to which a base such as 10 is raised to give a number. Napier coined the word logarithm, which means roughly logical arithmetic.

The number 3 is 10 raised to the 0.477 power, $3 = 10^{0.477}$, so 0.477 is the logarithm of 3 in base 10. Mathematicians abbreviate logarithm as log. The expression $\log_{10} 3 = 0.477$ is read as "The logarithm of the number 3 in base 10 is 0.477." The two expressions below show how logs are related to exponents.

$\log_{10} 3 = 0.477 \longleftrightarrow 10^{0.477} = 3$

Napier began working on logarithms in 1594. For them to be useful, a table of logarithms had to be made. Except for numbers that were powers of 10 (1, 10, 100, 1,000), logarithms were irrational numbers. Calculating them took a lot of effort. Napier spent 20 years at the task and published his table of logarithms in 1614.

Log tables became a popular short cut to long calculations. French astronomer Pierre Simon Laplace (1749–1827) said that Napier's development had halved the labors of astronomers. He also remarked that reducing the stress of complicated calculations had probably doubled the astronomers' lifetimes.

Tables of logarithms simplified multiplication, division, raising numbers to powers, and taking square roots. But the procedure did require mental effort. Suppose a person wanted to multiply 1,280 by 283. First, the numbers

For More Study:
Significant Digits

In 1999, the record time for running the 100-meter dash was 9.79 seconds. American sprinter Maurice Green set the record. His average speed is given by 100 m / 9.79 sec = 10.030090270812 m/sec. But such an answer implies far more accuracy than can be achieved in measuring distance and time. A better answer would be to say that his average speed was 10.0 m/sec, about 22.4 miles per hour.

Mount Everest

The final answer can be no more accurate than the starting data. Scientists state the accuracy by counting the significant digits. A significant digit is one that shows the accuracy of a measurement.

Non-zero digits are always significant. Numbers such as 98.6, 3.14, and .333 have three non-zero digits, so they have three places of accuracy.

When is zero a significant digit? The statement that the height of Mount Everest is 29,035 feet has a zero between the other digits. Anytime a zero is sandwiched between non-zero digits, then it is significant. The number 29,035 has five significant digits. The accuracy is to the nearest foot. It means that Mount Everest is 29,035 feet high give or take one-half foot.

Zeros that are not between non-zero digits are the ones that give the most trouble. One has to use judgment or some other information to decide. The number 100 to describe a 100-meter track used by world-class runners has at least three significant digits. The zeros in measuring 100 meters are significant. It has an accuracy of at least three places. The statement that the speed of light is 186,000 miles per second probably has only three significant digits. The actual speed has been rounded off to the nearest 1,000.

Scientists put numbers in standard form to show the significant digits. In the 1800s, when Mount Everest was measured for the first time, the answer came out to be 29,000 feet. The number 29,000 looks like it has been rounded off to the nearest 1,000 feet and that the accuracy is only two digits. But that turned out not to be the case. The scientist who made the calculations believed his answer to be accurate to four significant places, or to the nearest 10 feet. To show this, the number 29,000 was written as 2.900×10^4 feet.

If a zero is not needed to show the value of a number, but it is given anyway, then the zero is used to help show accuracy of the number.

John Napier

were written in what was called standard form: $1,280 = 1.28 \times 10^3$ and $283 = 2.83 \times 10^2$.

Standard form was always a single digit, then a decimal point followed by the rest of the number. The number part was multiplied by a power of ten to make it equal to the original number. For example, $1.28 \times 10^3 = 1.28 \times 1,000 = 1,280$.

Writing numbers in standard form broke the problem into two parts, the number parts, 1.28×2.83, and the powers of ten part, $10^3 \times 10^2$. The second part was easy to figure mentally: $10^2 \times 10^3 = 10^5 = 100,000$.

Next, the numbers in the first part were looked up in a table of logarithms and then the logarithms were added:

$$\log 1.28 = 0.107$$
$$\log 2.83 = 0.452$$
$$\text{sum} = 0.559$$

The sum of the logarithms, 0.559, was not the answer. The number 0.559 was the logarithm of the answer. Again, the person doing the math turned to a table listing antilogarithms and did a reverse look-up to find the number. According to the log table, the answer to the

number part was 3.62. It was multiplied by the powers of ten part to give the final answer:

$$3.62 \times 10^5 = 3.62 \times 100,000 = 362,000.$$

If you calculate $1,280 \times 283$ by hand, or use a calculator, the answer is 362,240, not 362,000. This difference did not bother scientists. Scientific measurements could be no better than the instruments used to make the measurements. Instruments such as scales for weighing, rulers for measuring distance, and thermometers for measuring temperature were accurate to only three or four places. Writing a number so that it gave the appearance of five or six places of accuracy would be misleading. It would imply an accuracy that did not exist.

People who did many calculations learned to quickly rewrite numbers in standard form. The speed of light, for instance, is 186,000 miles per second. Its value in standard form is 1.86×10^5 mi/sec. The distance from the earth to the sun is 93,000,000 miles, and this can be written as 9.30×10^7 mi.

Some people even memorized the logarithms of common numbers, such as π, because they used them so often. Gifted individuals memorized entire tables of logarithms. The German mathematician and astronomer Karl Fredrick Gauss lived in the days before computers and pocket calculators. He did all calculations in his head or with pen and paper. To make his calculations go faster, Gauss memorized a table of logarithms. The table had 10,000 numbers, each four digits long.

The slide rule was another device that used logarithms. It was made of two rulers, one that was fixed in place, and a second one that could slide along the fixed ruler.

Take two ordinary rulers and put them flat on a table. Leave one of them in place and slide the second one so that its beginning point aligns with the number two on the fixed ruler. Now look along the second ruler to the number three. Below it will be the number five on the first ruler. In other words, you can use rulers to add numbers: $2 + 3 = 5$.

A slide rule added numbers, too. However, it added the logarithms of numbers. The two rulers were marked off from 0.00 to 1.00, but the numbers were scaled so their spacing was by logarithms. A sliding window with a fine crosshair helped align numbers. To multiply 1.28 by 2.83, a person set the end of the sliding ruler at 1.28, then moved the crosshair to 2.83 on the sliding part, and then looked down on the fixed ruler to see the answer, 3.62.

The slide rule did away with the need of looking up logarithms in a table. Of course, all of the work of keeping up with the powers of

John Napier Had an Inventive Mind

John Napier was a Protestant religious leader of Scotland. He wrote a commentary on the Book of Revelation in the Bible. He also had meetings on religious matters with King James VI of Scotland. James VI later became James I of England and authorized the King James Translation of the Bible.

In addition to his logarithms, Napier invented another aid to calculations known as Napier's bones. He inscribed on rods, or bones, multiples of the digits from 0 to 9. Each rod had the multiples of a different digit. The rod for the number 5 was marked with the multiples of 5: 0, 5, 10, 15, and so on to 45. To multiply the number 125 by 3, a person placed rods for 1, 2, 5 side by side. The third row gave the third multiple of each number: the third multiple of 1 (3), the third multiple of 2 (6), and the third multiple of 5 (15). Combining the three multiples and taking into account their place value gave the answer: 300 + 60 + 15 = 375.

John Napier had a creative approach to problems in areas outside of science. Once,

A later version of Napier's bones used rods that could be quickly rotated to multiply numbers.

he discovered that one of his servants had been stealing from him, but he did not know which one. He put a coal-black rooster in a cage in a dark room. He instructed the servants to go in, place their hands on the back of the rooster, and then come out. He solemnly told them that the rooster would reveal the culprit. The seven servants did as he directed. At the end of the test, Napier announced the name of the culprit and the man confessed.

Napier, and not the rooster, had done the successful crime solving. He had chosen a rooster with black feathers for a special reason. Black concealed the fact that he had sprinkled black soot all over the bird. The innocent servants with clear consciences touched the rooster and came out with soot on their hands. The guilty servant feared the rooster would reveal his crime. He decided not to touch the bird. He revealed himself because he was the only one to leave the darkened room with soot-free hands.

10 had to be done in the head, or jotted down on paper.

The calculations could be done rapidly, but the answers were only approximate. Working with a slide rule, a person had to be careful to achieve accuracy to three places. The slide rule was entirely satisfactory for doing rough and ready calculations. Engineering students prided themselves with their skill at using slide rules. They would carry their slide rules in leather holders on their belts. However, they quickly gave them up in the 1960s for electronic calculators.

Before the invention of scientific calculators, mathematicians calculated common quantities such as logarithms, squares, cubes, factors, primes, and trigonometric functions and saved the values in books as look-up tables. An average-size handbook of mathematical tables ran to 300 pages of closely spaced numbers.

Each of the numbers had to be calculated by hand. Unfortunately, now and then a number in one of the tables would be found to be in error.

In the 1820s, the English inventor Charles Babbage built a machine to calculate mathematical tables automatically. He called his machine a difference engine. It changed a series of long and difficult multiplications into a series of simple additions.

Babbage's first difference engine gave answers to eight places. He considered it merely a preliminary machine to prove that his idea worked. In 1823, Babbage asked the British government for money to build a full-

Charles Babbage
(Courtesy of the Smithsonian)

sized model. It would be accurate to 20 places. Over the next ten years, he spent 6,000 pounds of his own money and 17,000 pounds from the government. At that time a working person made about 100 pounds a year. The total of 23,000 pounds that Babbage spent on the machine was an immense amount of money.

He interrupted construction to make improvements. Typewriters and printers had not yet been invented. The answers would have to be copied down by hand and then set to type to print the tables. Babbage decided his machine should set type automatically to avoid the possibility of human error in printing the book.

Despite pressure from the government to complete the machine, Babbage would think of an improvement, take the machine apart, and rebuild it with his improvement. To the government inspectors, the difference engine always seemed to be in a state of disrepair.

After 11 years, the government gave him a deadline to complete the machine. Finally, they cut off the money. By then, he had thought of an even grander machine. He called it an analytical engine. Rather than a calculator to do a specific task, the analytical engine would be a general-purpose mechanical computer. He would spend the rest of his life working on it.

Except for being mechanical rather than electrical, his design contained the five essential components of a modern computer: input, control program, memory, central processing unit, and output.

Babbage's Difference Engine

Babbage called his machine a difference engine by the way he programmed it to generate numbers. To calculate the squares of numbers, Babbage worked the first few problems himself. Then he took differences between each answer, and then differences of those differences until a constant difference showed up.

Next, Babbage entered the first value for n^2 (0), the first difference (1), and the second difference (2). The machine printed out the sequence of square numbers:

0	1	2
1	3	2
4	5	2
9	7	2
16	9	2

Once the machine was programmed, it could continue to generate larger and larger square numbers. What numbers are after 16, 9, and 2? The first number in the next row is found by adding 16 and 9. The answer is 25, which is the square of 5. The second number in the next row is 11 found by adding 9 and 2. The third number in each row is always the constant number 2.

25	11	2

The table of squares by differences from 6^2 to 25^2.

36	13	2
49	15	2
64	17	2
81	19	2
100	21	2
121	23	2
144	25	2
169	27	2
196	29	2
225	31	2
256	33	2
289	35	2
324	37	2
361	39	2
400	41	2
441	43	2
484	45	2
529	47	2
576	49	2
625	51	2

Table of Differences for Squares

value of n	value of $y = n^2$	
0	0	
	difference 1 - 0 = 1	
1	1	difference 3 - 1 = 2
	difference 4 - 1 = 3	
2	4	difference 5 - 3 = 2
	difference 9 - 4 = 5	
3	9	difference 7 - 5 = 2
	difference 16 - 9 = 7	
4	16	

The input into a computer is made of two parts. One is the data. In a modern computer, data can be entered by the keyboard, by clicking with a mouse, by reading the data from a hard drive or CD, downloading (transferring) it from the Internet, scanning in text or pictures, or by a variety of other methods such as a joystick used for games. Some computers accept voice commands and can read handwriting.

In Babbage's machine, data was entered primarily by punched cards. Punched cards remained the main way to get information into a computer for more than 100 years. Herman Hollerith of the United States perfected the cards in the 1880s. He made the cards a little larger than a dollar bill out of a thin, slick cardboard. Holes punched in the cards represented letters, numbers, and special symbols. Hollerith built a machine that could read punched cards and summarize the information they contained. It was called a tabulating machine. The punched cards were used during the 1890 census. The work was done in just six weeks, far faster than the 1880 census.

Hollerith's company merged with other companies and became known as International Business Machines Corporation, or IBM. The first computers that IBM made used punched cards for input of data. Computers continued to receive data by punched cards well into the 1970s.

In addition to data, the second type of input into a computer is the control program. Data alone is not enough. A computer must know what to do with the data. A computer

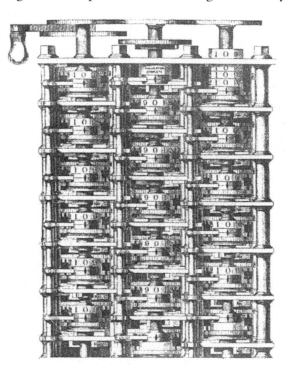

A small part of Babbage's analytical engine, a mechanical computer

program is an ordered sequence of instructions that tell the computer what to do with the data. The computer program is often described as software to distinguish it from the computer itself that is called hardware.

Augusta Ada Byron wrote the first computer program. Her father was Lord Byron, the notorious English poet. He left for Europe when she was six months old, and she never saw him again. Her mother steered Ada toward science rather than poetry.

Ada was educated by tutors that included Augustus De Morgan, who taught her how to use the logical operators of OR and AND that would later become important in query languages and computer programming.

During her studies, Ada learned about Babbage's analytical engine. Ada became as enthused about the machine as Babbage. She wrote to him and they soon began exchanging ideas about the machine. In one letter she wrote, "The analytical engine weaves algebraic patterns, just as the Jacquard loom weaves flowers and leaves."

Babbage believed the machine's chief use would be to calculate mathematical results. Ada, however, believed the machine could do other tasks, even compose music. She was ahead of Babbage himself because she understood what a programmable computer might do.

In 1835, Ada married William King, and when he was made an earl, she became Countess of Lovelace. As she raised their three children, she continued to correspond with Babbage. She encouraged him to use the 0's and 1's of binary notation for calculations.

BASIC Computer Programming Language

The letters in BASIC stand for Beginners All-purpose Symbolic Instruction Code. John Kemeny and Thomas Kurtz at Dartmouth College invented BASIC in the mid-1960s. In 1975, William H. (Bill) Gates and Paul H. Allen converted the language so it would run on personal computers (known as microcomputers at that time). They sold BASIC to computer uses through Microsoft, the company they founded. The name Microsoft came from the words *micro*computer and *soft*ware.

one? But the statement does not say they are equal. It is an assignment. It assigns the value of KOUNT + 1 to the variable KOUNT.

Lines 70 through 130 make a loop that is repeated until KOUNT reaches 100. The GOTO in line 130 is considered poor programming today. Modern programming would do the loop using a DO WHILE statement. Line 70 would be written as DO WHILE KOUNT < 101 (< means "less than") and Line 130 would be WEND (meaning "end the whole loop").

```
10    REM CALCULATE FIBONACCI NUMBERS
20    LET X = 1
30    LET Y = 1
40    PRINT X
50    PRINT Y
60    LET KOUNT = 2
70    CONTINUE
80    LET Z = X + Y
90    PRINT Z
100   LET X = Y
110   LET Y = Z
120   LET KOUNT = KOUNT + 1
130   IF KOUNT < 100 THEN GOTO 70
140   PRINT "FINISHED"
150   END
```

The first line begins with REM, which stands for remark. It is a comment added by the programmer and the computer ignores it as it works through the program. Lines 20–50 assign the first two Fibonacci numbers to the variables X and Y and prints them out. Line 60 gives the value of 2 to the variable KOUNT. It will be used to keep track that the first 100 Fibonacci numbers have been printed.

The statement in 120 that KOUNT = KOUNT + 1 may seem to be a contradiction. How can a number equal itself plus

BASIC and most other computer languages have a few essential features. One is the assignment statement that gives a value to a variable. Operations such as addition, subtraction, and so on, act on the variables. The program has provisions to change the flow of control from one statement to another. Tests can be made that two numbers are equal, or that one is larger than the other, or that a statement is true or false. Finally, the program must display the results.

She realized that the analytical engine could be programmed by punched cards. She wrote instructions to calculate Bernoulli (ber-NOOL-ee) numbers. The numbers, named after the Swiss mathematician Jakob Bernoulli, were used by the insurance industry. Lady Ada's sequence of steps is regarded as the first computer program.

During the last ten years of her life, she struggled to raise her three daughters while being treated for a medical condition. Her medication included opium that left her dazed and weak. Like her father, Lady Ada lived only half of a normal life span. She died at the age of 36.

The heart of any computer is the central processing unit, or CPU. It is made of three parts: memory, an arithmetic unit for doing calculations, and a control unit that keeps the parts of the computer working together. It acts on the input data based on the instructions received from software. Babbage called his CPU the mill.

A CPU saves intermediate results in memory. A modern computer uses memory chips known as random access memory, RAM for short. Babbage used rods, gears, and punched cards to save data. He called it the store.

Output from Babbage's machine was also by punched cards. Modern computers use a variety of output methods. They can display information on a screen, save it to magnetic media, or send it to a printer. Early computers had speakers that made an attention-getting beep to warn the computer operator that something was wrong. Today, computers can generate music, and sound is an example of output, too.

Babbage's machine had bells and whistles to announce intermediate steps and announce the final answer. Today, people say a computer software has "bells and whistles" to mean that it informs the computer user of what is happening as it runs a program.

Babbage devoted 50 years to the design and construction of the analytical engine. It proved too difficult to build with the technol-ogy of his day. Neither Babbage nor Ada lived to see the machine finished.

Sixty years after the death of Babbage, Howard H. Aiken, a student at Harvard University, discovered a description of the analytical engine. Technology had improved enough to make a mechanical computer possible. Aiken, working with IBM, constructed Mark I, the first general-purpose calculating machine. It used both mechanical and electrical parts.

By the end of the 1960s, electronic devices replaced mechanical adding machines and calculators. By the start of the year 2000, a CPU with millions of individual electronic components could be made on a silicon chip the size of a postage stamp. Today, the simplest laptop computer has far more power than Babbage dreamed possible. Yet, all the main features of Babbage's analytical engine are still found in a modern computer.

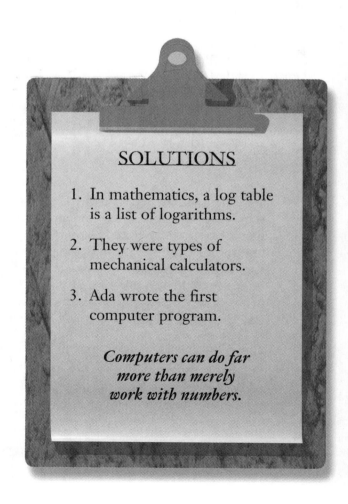

SOLUTIONS

1. In mathematics, a log table is a list of logarithms.

2. They were types of mechanical calculators.

3. Ada wrote the first computer program.

Computers can do far more than merely work with numbers.

A B C D   1.   Any number raised to the zero power, is (A. 0   B. 1   C. 2   D. undefined).

T F   2.   Babbage completed the analytical engine shortly before his death.

T F   3.   Powers of ten can be multiplied by adding their exponents.

T F   4.   Fractional exponents are not allowed.

T F   5.   A logarithm is an exponent.

6.   The expression $\log_{10}3 = 0.477$ is read as "The logarithm of the number _____ in base _____ is _____."

A B C D   7.   The number 5,280 changed to standard notation is (A. $.5280 \times 10^1$ B. $5,280 \times 10^3$ C. 5.28×10^2 D. 5.28×10^3).

A B C   8.   Scientific measurements are (A. less accurate   B. no more accurate   C. significantly more accurate) than the instruments used to make the measurements.

T F   9.   A slide rule multiplies two numbers by adding their logarithms.

A B C D   10.   In the early days of computers, input was mainly by (A. colored ribbons   B. punched cards   C. spoken commands   D. switches and relays).

11.   In this list, which one is considered the "heart" of a computer: input, control program, memory, central processing unit, output.

A B C D   12.   The letters RAM stand for (A. random access memory   B. reasonably accurate member   C. recent abacus modification   D. Robert A. Morley).

Matching

13. _____ Augusta Ada Byron, Lady Lovelace

14. _____ Howard H. Aiken

15. _____ Charles Babbage

16. _____ Herman Hollerith

17. _____ Johannes Kepler

18. _____ Gottfried Leibnitz

19. _____ John Napier

20. _____ Blaise Pascal

a. built a calculator called the Step Reckoner

b. built a calculator to help his father, a tax collector

c. built first general purpose calculating machine

d. built the difference engine

e. invented logarithms

f. invented tabulating machines used in the 1890 census

g. spent six years calculating the orbit of Mars

h. wrote the first computer program

Bits and Bytes

Ten is the base of our usual number system. All numbers are written with the ten digits 0 through 9. The number 573 uses the digits 5, 7, and 3 to multiply different powers of ten:

$5 \times 10^2 + 7 \times 10^1 + 3 \times 10^0$
$5 \times 100 + 7 \times 10 + 3 \times 1$
$500 + 70 + 3$
$573.$

The number 5,280 in base ten means:

$5 \times 10^3 + 2 \times 10^2 + 8 \times 10^1 + 0 \times 10^0$
$5 \times 1000 + 2 \times 100 + 8 \times 10 + 0 \times 1$
$5,000 + 200 + 80 + 0$
$5,280.$

Binary numbers are limited to only two digits, 0 and 1. Chapter 11 described an island with vehicle license plates numbered only with the digits 0 and 1. The 16 different license plates also showed the binary numbers from 0 to 15: 0000 equals zero, 0001 equals one, 0010 equals two, 0011 equals three, 0100 equals four, and so on.

PROBLEMS

1. In computer lingo, what is the origin of the term "bug"?

2. How can time be saved when downloading large files?

3. What toy was used as a unique demonstration of using the binary system to answer questions?

Can You Propose Solutions?

Each position in a binary number shows if a power of two is used or not. The binary number 10011 means

$$1 \times 2^4 + 0 \times 2^3 + 0 \times 2^2 + 1 \times 2^1 + 1 \times 2^0$$
$$1 \times 16 + 0 \times 8 + 0 \times 4 + 1 \times 2 + 1 \times 1$$
$$16 + 2 + 1$$
$$19 \text{ (in base 10).}$$

A number such as 1111 in base two means

$$1111$$
$$1 \times 2^3 + 1 \times 2^2 + 1 \times 2^1 + 1 \times 2^0$$
$$1 \times 8 + 1 \times 4 + 1 \times 2 + 1 \times 1$$
$$8 + 4 + 2 + 1$$
$$15 \text{ (in base 10).}$$

Any number, regardless of its size, can be expressed in binary notation as some combination of 1s and 0s. Gottfried Wilhelm Leibnitz, the German mathematician who built the calculator known as the "Step Reckoner," worked out the binary system in 1695. Although the idea of writing numbers with zero and one had been around for years, Leibnitz put the matter on firm mathematical footing. Leibnitz was a religious person who saw religious significance in the digits one and zero. God (number one) made all things from nothing (zero.)

The multiplication table for binary numbers is especially simple:

$$0 \times 0 = 0$$
$$0 \times 1 = 0$$
$$1 \times 0 = 0$$
$$1 \times 1 = 1$$

Gottfried Wilhelm Leibnitz

The addition table is nearly as simple:

$$0 + 0 = 0$$
$$0 + 1 = 1$$
$$1 + 0 = 1$$
$$1 + 1 = 10$$

The last entry, 10, is not 10 but 2. Mathematicians use subscripts to avoid confusion when they are talking about numbers in different bases: 10011_2 means a number in base 2 while 19_{10} means a number in base 10. Usually, however, subscripts are not needed. In the expression $1 + 1 = 10$, the 10 is understood to be base two, 10_2, not base ten, 10_{10}.

Leibnitz's binary numbers were interesting but of no practical value for well over 150 years. Binary numbers gained importance with the invention of electronic digital computers in the 1940s. Computers used binary code to represent data.

In computer usage, a single position for a binary digit is called a bit. The word bit is a blending of the phrase "binary digit." A bit can be either 0 or 1. Binary numbers have the advantage of being readily applied to electrical devices. Electrical devices have switches to turn them on or off. Either the current flows (1) or it does not flow (0). Today, many electrical switches are not labeled with the words off or on. Instead, they are marked with 0 for off and 1 for on.

A single bit can have but two values, 0 or 1. Bits are combined into larger groups to represent more values. Two bits can show four values: 00, 01, 10, and 11.

A byte of data is made of eight bits, at least for personal computers. Some larger computers use more bits to the byte. The word byte came from the alternate definition of bit — a small morsel of food. If a bit is a small amount of food, then a bite is a larger amount. The "i" in bite was changed to "y," but byte is pronounced the same as bite.

An eight-bit byte can form 256 different values because $2^8 = 256$. The different bytes are formed using only zero and one: The first number is 00000000 and the last number is 11111111.

Most computer software writes the letters of a text file in binary code. One such code is called ASCII (American Standard Code for Information Interchange.) The code assigns binary numbers to letters of the alphabet, numerals, and punctuation marks. ASCII codes also mark the end of a line, end of a paragraph, end of page, and stand for other special symbols.

The letter "A" is coded as binary number 65_{10} or 01000001_2, "B" is 66_{10} or 01000010_2, and so on. The lowercase character "a" is coded as binary number 97_{10} or 01100001_2, "b" is 98_{10} or 0110010_2, and so on.

A byte can display 256 different ASCII codes. Only the first 128 are needed to show plain text. The other 128 characters can be used for special purposes. For example, some text documents need to show accented characters, such as é in "René Descartes." ASCII code 130, 10000010, is used to represent é, and code 228, 11100100, is used to represent pi, π.

A full page of text in a book like this one is about 350 words or 1,750 characters. A character can be a letter, punctuation mark, numeral, or special character such as the space between words. Each character written in ASCII code takes a byte to represent it, so 1,750 characters takes 1,750 bytes.

Dec	Char	Dec	Char	Dec	Char	Dec	Char	Dec	Char	Dec	Char	Dec	Char	Dec	Char
0	Null	32	Space	64	@	96	`	128	Ç	160	á	192	└	224	α
1	Start of heading	33	!	65	A	97	a	129	ü	161	í	193	┴	225	ß
2	Start of text	34	"	66	B	98	b	130	é	162	ó	194	┬	226	Γ
3	End of text	35	#	67	C	99	c	131	â	163	ú	195	├	227	π
4	End of transmit	36	$	68	D	100	d	132	ä	164	ñ	196	─	228	Σ
5	Enquiry	37	%	69	E	101	e	133	à	165	Ñ	197	┼	229	σ
6	Acknowledge	38	&	70	F	102	f	134	å	166	ª	198	╞	230	µ
7	Audible bell	39	'	71	G	103	g	135	ç	167	°	199	╟	231	τ
8	Backspace	40	(	72	H	104	h	136	ê	168	¿	200	╚	232	Φ
9	Horizontal tab	41	)	73	I	105	i	137	ë	169	⌐	201	╔	233	⊕
10	Line feed	42	*	74	J	106	j	138	è	170	¬	202	╩	234	Ω
11	Vertical tab	43	+	75	K	107	k	139	ï	171	½	203	╦	235	δ
12	Form feed	44	,	76	L	108	l	140	î	172	¼	204	╠	236	∞
13	Carriage return	45	-	77	M	109	m	141	ì	173	¡	205	═	237	ø
14	Shift out	46	.	78	N	110	n	142	Ä	174	«	206	╬	238	ε
15	Shift in	47	/	79	O	111	o	143	Å	175	»	207	╧	239	∩
16	Data link escape	48	0	80	P	112	p	144	É	176	░	208	╨	240	≡
17	Device control 1	49	1	81	Q	113	q	145	æ	177	▒	209	╤	241	±
18	Device control 2	50	2	82	R	114	r	146	Æ	178	▓	210	╥	242	≥
19	Device control 3	51	3	83	S	115	s	147	ô	179	│	211	╙	243	≤
20	Device control 4	52	4	84	T	116	t	148	ö	180	┤	212	╘	244	⌠
21	Neg. acknowledge	53	5	85	U	117	u	149	ò	181	╡	213	╒	245	⌡
22	Synchronous idle	54	6	86	V	118	v	150	û	182	╢	214	╓	246	÷
23	End trans. block	55	7	87	W	119	w	151	ù	183	╖	215	╫	247	≈
24	Cancel	56	8	88	X	120	x	152	ÿ	184	╕	216	╪	248	°
25	End of medium	57	9	89	Y	121	y	153	Ö	185	╣	217	┘	249	∙
26	Substitution	58	:	90	Z	122	z	154	Ü	186	║	218	┌	250	·
27	Escape	59	;	91	[	123	{	155	¢	187	╗	219	█	251	√
28	File separator	60	<	92	\	124	|	156	£	188	╝	220	▄	252	ⁿ
29	Group separator	61	=	93	]	125	}	157	¥	189	╜	221	▌	253	²
30	Record separator	62	>	94	^	126	~	158	₧	190	╛	222	▐	254	■
31	Unit separator	63	?	95	_	127	⌂	159	ƒ	191	┐	223	▀	255	□

The 256 characters (0 through 255) of the American Standard Code for Information Interchange

An ordinary home computer in use in the year 2003 could send or receive text from the Internet at about 56,000 bits a second. This is 7,000 bytes per second: 56,000 bits per second/ 8 bits per byte = 7,000 bytes per second. The computer could download from the Internet about four pages of text a second: Dividing 7,000 bytes/sec by 1750 bytes/page equals four pages.

The expression 7,000 bytes can also be written as 7 KB. The "K" stands for the prefix kilo and the "B" stands for bytes. The word kilo in the metric system is equal to 1,000. But in computer use, kilo means 1,024 because 1,024 is the nearest power of two to 1,000: 2^{10} = 1,024. The expression 7 KB is read as "seven kilobytes."

One megabyte, written 1 MB, has 2^{20} =1,048,576 bytes. A gigabyte, written 1 GB, is 2^{30} = 1,073,741,824 bytes.

Plain text can be sent over the Internet quickly. However, a picture or other graphic file takes far longer. An image is made of millions of individual pixels crowded closely together. The word pixels is a blending of the words "picture elements." A computer display puts 72 pixels to the inch. A person with ordinary eyesight can see the individual pixels by peering closely at the display.

At 100 pixels to the inch, the human eye cannot detect individual pixels. A row of 100 pixels an inch long forms what looks like a line without any gaps in it.

High quality graphics have pixels even closer together. Most photographs are converted to computer files with 300 pixels to the inch. A color photograph measuring only one inch on the side requires 90,000 pixels: 300 x 300 = 90,000. An 8 x 10-inch photograph needs more than seven million pixels: 8 in x 10 in x 90,000 pixels/sq in = 7,200,000 pixels.

Some people talk about pixels and bits as if one is equal to the other, but they are not equal. The number of bits in a pixel depends on whether the image is a line drawing, a black and white photograph, or a color image.

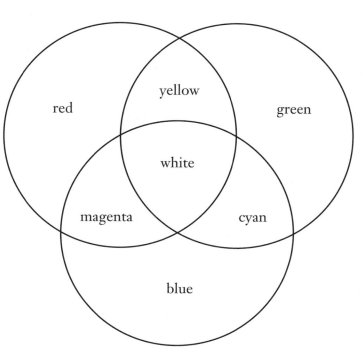

In terms of light, the three primary colors — red, green, and blue — can add together to give all the colors of the rainbow. When all three overlap, the result is white. Artists use pigments, so the colors produced are not the same as in the additive process of light.

A single bit can represent each pixel in a black and white line drawing. Either the bit is on (pure black) or it is off (pure white).

Black and white photographs have shades of gray. A single bit is not enough to show the different shades of gray that a pixel may have. Two bits will give four different shades for each pixel: 00 (pure white), 01 (light gray), 10 (darker gray), 11 (pure black). An entire byte of eight bits gives a choice from 256 different shades of gray for each pixel. Each pixel in a black and white photograph takes one byte. An 8x10-inch black and white photograph has 7,200,000 pixels and each one takes a byte. That is a little more than seven megabytes, 7 MB.

Color images need more bytes for each pixel than black and white photographs. James Clerk Maxwell, a mathematician from Scotland, investigated color vision. He proved that

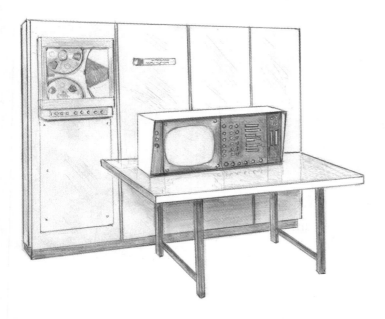

Early large scale computer

a full-color image could be created using only the colors red, green, and blue. In 1861, he combined red, green, and blue images to make a photograph with all colors of the rainbow.

Color computer screens and color printers use the same principle. Each pixel has three bytes — one for red, one for green, and one for blue. In other words, a color photograph takes as many bytes as three black and white photographs. An 8 x 10-inch color photograph has almost 22 megabytes: 7,200,000 pixels x 3 bytes / pixel = 21,600,000 bytes, about 22 MB.

Because they require more bytes, large files such as color photographs required lots of time to download. Today, however, text and graphic images can be sent faster because they are compressed. Compression makes files smaller so that they contain fewer bytes. Software packages, called compression routines, reduce the size of a file. One way that compression routines work is to transmit differences.

As an example, the list of ten words below has 67 characters. In binary code, each character takes a byte to represent it. The entire list takes 67 bytes.

run
runabout
runabouts
runaround
runaway
runaways
runback
rundown
rung
rungs

The information could be simplified by merely sending the first word, run, and then how each word differs from run. The new list contains the same information as the previous one. But it has 40 characters rather than 67.

run
about
abouts
around
away
aways
back
down
g
gs

Additional savings can be made by using a single byte to stand for common combinations of letters. The letters "th" are found in many different common words: the, that, them, then, they, this, thus, bath, math, with, and moth are only a few. A single byte can stand for the pair. As another example, any word in the English language that starts with the letter q will be followed by the letter u. The letters "qu" can be replaced with a single byte.

Keeping track of differences and combining similar pixels can reduce the number of bytes in a color photograph, too. If an image has a lot of blue sky, then one blue-sky pixel is pretty much like its neighbor. A whole string of blue-sky pixels will differ only slightly from each other or not at all. Compression routines can reduce a 22-MB image to a 5-MB image without any noticeable loss of quality.

Motion pictures are made of individual still images that are seen rapidly one after another. Theaters show 24 individual images per second. The images are called frames. Television video cameras display 30 frames per second. The total amount of data to record a two-hour movie and the stereo sound can be about five gigabytes, 5 GB.

A stream of video images can be compressed by transmitting only how one frame differs from the previous one. Suppose a reporter is standing still and talking. The scene behind him and most of his body do not move. A large part of the current image is exactly like the previous image. Only the difference from one frame to the next — such as changes in the position of the reporter's lips, eyes, and face muscles — need be transmitted.

Each year new inventions and better communication methods increase the speed at which files are sent from one computer to another. At the same time, compression routines get better. Every four to five years the speed increases by a factor of eight. Personal computers in the year 2004 could transmit

information eight times faster than a personal computer in the year 2000.

The increased speed illustrates Moore's law that computers double in power every 18 months. Gordon Moore was one of the founders of Intel Corporation, a maker of computer chips. In 1965, he noticed that his company's latest computer chip had twice the speed and power of one it replaced. The company released a new chip about every 18 months. Moore's law appears to be true because computers have been doubling in processing speed every 18 months for several decades.

During World II, Howard Aiken (1900–1973) at Harvard University built Mark I, the first large-scale computer. It was designed for the single purpose of calculating firing angles for Naval guns. Mark I had both mechanical and electrical parts. The computer was 51 feet long, 8 feet high, weighed 35 tons, and had 500 miles of wire with three million connections.

Electromagnets operated the relays. Each one of the millions of parts could fail. When a computer stopped working, it was often difficult finding the cause. Grace Hopper (1906–1992) was an American mathematician and a member of the navy. She worked on Mark II. The new computer replaced Howard Aiken's Mark I in 1947. Like Mark I, the newer computer had thousands of relays. Once, when it unexpectedly shut down, Grace Hopper traced the problem to an insect. A moth had flown through an open window and into one of the mechanical relays. It had gotten squished between the contacts and prevented the relay from closing.

Grace Hopper reported the incident and taped the bug into the computer logbook. Since then, whenever a computer does not work right, people say, "There is a bug in the system."

The first all-electronic computers used thousands of vacuum tubes. A vacuum tube was about the size of a small light bulb. Inside were electrical components that acted as off and on switches and also boosted the flow of electricity. Thousands of vacuum tubes were wired together and placed in cabinets. The first computers took up entire floors of buildings.

ENIAC was the first large-scale, general purpose, digital computer. ENIAC stands for Electronic Numerical Integrator and Computer. ENIAC, completed in 1945, contained more than 18,000 vacuum tubes. Larger models had as many as 30,000 vacuum tubes.

Like light bulbs, vacuum tubes burned out. Dozens of a computer's vacuum tubes burned out every day. Circuits were designed with extra tubes so that if one failed, the circuit would switch to another one to keep operating.

A workman was assigned to replacing vacuum tubes as his sole duty. The workman carried an egg basket filled with spare vacuum tubes. He walked around the dimly lit floor to replace vacuum tubes that no longer glowed.

Like glowing light bulbs, vacuum tubes generated heat. Large air conditioners and huge fans kept the computer room from overheating. The early vacuum tube computers had mechanical switches that opened and closed with a click. Information was printed out on a typewriter-like device known as a teletype. The roar of the air conditioning, hum of thousands of vacuum tubes, clicks of mechanical switches, and the clatter of teletypes made a computer room a deafening place to work.

By the late 1960s, transistors reduced computers to the size of cabinets that took up one wall of a room. By the end of the 1970s, the cabinet-sized calculating machines had become desktop computers. In 1985, an integrated circuit in a simple calculator contained as many as 50,000 parts. These fit on small silicon chips less than a millimeter square. Today, integrated circuits contain 100 million devices.

One reason computers can operate faster is because they are made smaller. Builders of computers

face a cosmic speed limit — the speed of light. Electricity travels at the same speed as light, which is fixed at 186,000 miles per second (300,000,000 m/sec) in a vacuum. It is even slower in solid substances such as a wire. As computers became faster, they were delayed by the time it took for electricity to go from one component to another.

In 2003, the fastest home computers could process an instruction in two billionths of a second. During the time a computer processed a single instruction, an electric signal traveled only about six inches. Should the components be farther apart than that, then the computer had to wait for the electric signal to go from one device to the other. Packing semiconductor devices close together improved a computer's speed.

In addition to numeric calculations, computers are used for a variety of other purposes. They can sort lists, find data that match, and answer true or false questions about data. Computer software can search a list of cities and towns and answer true or false to a statement such as "The states of Missouri and Illinois each have a town named Springfield." (The answer is true.)

Operations that involve sorting, comparing, and making a true or false decision is known as computer logic. Because there are only two possibilities — true or false — binary numbers can be used to represent logic statements in mathematics.

One interesting mechanical logic machine was built in the 1950s by students at MIT (Massachusetts Institute of Technology.) At that time, building elaborate model train railroads was a popular hobby among science-minded students. At MIT, students combined their train sets to make a large model railroad in the basement of the engineering building. Soon the vast array of switches, trains, and tracks were programmed to answer simple questions in computer science. The answers

Silicon computer chip

Model train and tracks

depended on whether a train could travel along tracks with switches set open or closed.

An open switch is one that does not let a train pass. An open switch makes a gap in the track. A closed switch connects the track and lets a train pass.

The students programmed the trains and switches to answer questions in logic. Suppose a track had two switches along its length. Both switches had to be closed for the train to go the entire length of the track. If a single switch were open, the train could not pass.

The case of a single track with two switches could be shown as the multiplication table for binary numbers. Let A and B represent the switches. An open switch prevented a train from finishing its journey and a closed switch let it pass. The train could not get through in any of the cases except for the last case where both switches were closed.

Switch A	Switch B	Train gets through?
open	open	no
open	closed	no
closed	open	no
closed	closed	yes

The same table can be written using 0 to stand for open and no and 1 for closed and yes. The table is the multiplication table for the binary digits.

Switch A		Switch B		Train gets through?
0	x	0	=	0
0	x	1	=	0
1	x	0	=	0
1	x	1	=	1

Next, the students set up a train with the choice of two different routes along two parallel tracks. Each track had a single switch, and each one could be open (train could not pass) or closed (train could pass). The train could get through on parallel tracks in every case except for the first case where both tracks had its switch open.

Switch A	Switch B	Train gets through?
open	open	no
open	closed	yes (send train on track B)
closed	open	yes (send train on track A)
closed	closed	yes (either track will do)

The same table can be written as the addition of binary numbers. The train can reach its destination provided a one is anywhere in the sum.

Switch A		Switch B		Train gets through?
0	+	0	=	0
0	+	1	=	1
1	+	0	=	1
1	+	1	=	10

In computer usage, the binary digit 0 always stands for false, no, off, or is not

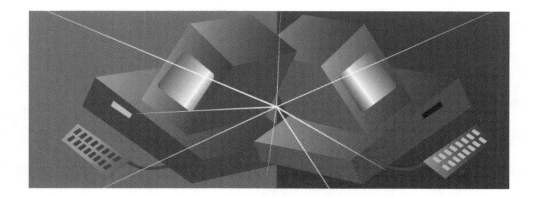

possible. The binary digit 1 stands for true, yes, on, or is possible.

The switches and tracks illustrate the mathematical meaning of the words OR and AND. The single track represented two switches connected by an AND. For a train on a single track to get through, switch A AND switch B had to be closed. For a train with a choice of two tracks, switch A OR switch B (or both) must be closed.

Many computers in libraries allow AND or OR searches for keywords in the titles of books. Suppose you want information about household pets. You could ask the computer to look for books about "dogs" OR "cats." A large library might have hundreds of books about pets. Some would be about dogs. Others would be about cats. And others might be about both dogs and cats. The query "dogs" OR "cats" might result in a listing of hundreds of books.

Each possible book is known as a citation. To reduce the number of citations, you change the query with an AND to make it more specific. A query for books about "dogs" AND "cats" would give only those books about both dogs and cats. The query would probably reduce the number of books to a few dozen at most. You could look through the book titles to find the ones you wanted.

But you could narrow the search even more with another AND term. Suppose you wanted to know if your favorite author had written about the two types of pets. Your query would be [author's name] AND "dogs" AND "cats." Now the query may reduce the number of citations to only one book — or none at all. A query can become so specific that it eliminates all possibilities.

The use of AND and OR can soon build to complicated queries. A query such as [author's name] AND ("dogs" OR "cats") will identify books about cats or dogs by your favorite author but not by any other author. The query can be tricky to write correctly. A query for [author's name] OR "dogs" OR "cats" will get a lot of books. It will include every book your favorite author has written on any subject, every book about dogs by any author, every book about cats by any author, and every book about both cats and dogs by any author.

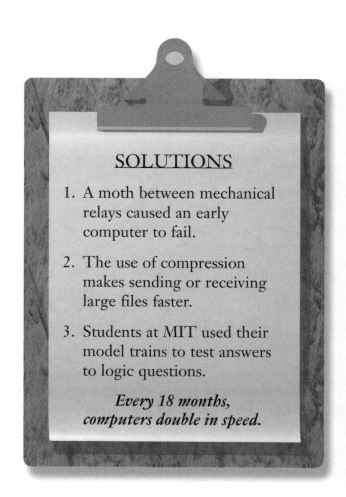

SOLUTIONS

1. A moth between mechanical relays caused an early computer to fail.

2. The use of compression makes sending or receiving large files faster.

3. Students at MIT used their model trains to test answers to logic questions.

Every 18 months, computers double in speed.

1. Base 10 uses the digits 0 through _____.

T F 2. Base 2 uses the digits 0, 1, and 2.

A B C D 3. In computer usage, a single position for a binary digit is called (A. bit B. byte C. kilo D. pixel).

A B C 4. A single bit can have (A. one B. two C. ten) different values.

A B C D 5. In personal computers, a byte of data is made of (A. one B. two C. eight D. 10) bits.

T F 6. Each character written in ASCII code takes a byte to represent it.

A B C 7. A pixel in a (A. black and white photograph B. color photograph C. line drawing) requires the greatest number of bytes.

A B C D 8. In 1861, James Clerk Maxwell made a color photograph using (A. computer enhancement B. color ink drops sprayed on paper C. polarized light D. the three colors of red, green, and blue).

T F 9. Text files cannot be compressed.

T F 10. A pixel is always equal to one bit.

A B C D 11. Video images can be compressed by (A. converting black and white images to color images B. having reporters avoid standing in front of a blue sky C. transmitting all pixels that are the same as the previous one D. transmitting only those pixels that are different from the previous one).

A B C D 12. Moore's law states that computers double in power every 18 (A. days B. months C. decades D. years).

A B C D 13. The bug that Grace Hopper found in the Mark II computer turned out to be (A. a hardware problem B. a moth caught between mechanical relays C. a software problem D. a problem caused by human error).

A B C D 14. A computer with components put farther apart will run more slowly because (A. electric signals can go no faster than the speed of light B. larger components must be made of less costly materials C. of resistance in the wires D. the electrons get lost).

A B C D 15. Engineering students at MIT in the 1950s answered simple questions in computer science with (A. mechanical calculators B. model cars C. model trains D. radio controlled airplane).

T F 16. The binary digit 1 stands for true, yes, on, or is possible.

A B 17. The query that is most likely to result in more citations is (A. an OR query B. an AND query).

Try Your Math:

18. The Constitution of the United States has 4,609 words and 26,747 characters. At the rate of 7,000 bytes per second, how long would it take a computer to download the Constitution of the United States as an uncompressed text file?

$$\tan\phi = \frac{X_c}{R}$$

$$E = \Delta mc^2$$

$$\sqrt{a^2 + b^2}$$

$$L = 2\pi f L$$

Math on Vacation

Numbers can amuse as well as instruct. Here is a good "arithmetrick" you can ask a friend. Let him secretly choose a number from one to ten. Then tell him to add six to the number, double the result, and divide his answer by four. Now direct him to subtract half of the original number he picked.

When your friend has finished, you say, "Your answer is three." You will be right, because the number he has left is always three!

Another fascinating number trick is found with the number 142,857. What is so special about 142,857? The number 142,857 gives interesting results when multiplied by 1 through 6:

1 x 142,857 = 142,857
2 x 142,857 = 285,714
3 x 142,857 = 428,571
4 x 142,857 = 571,428
5 x 142,857 = 714,285
6 x 142,857 = 857,142

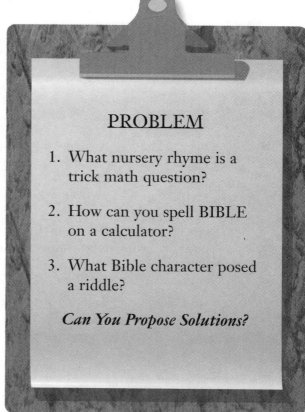

PROBLEM

1. What nursery rhyme is a trick math question?

2. How can you spell BIBLE on a calculator?

3. What Bible character posed a riddle?

Can You Propose Solutions?

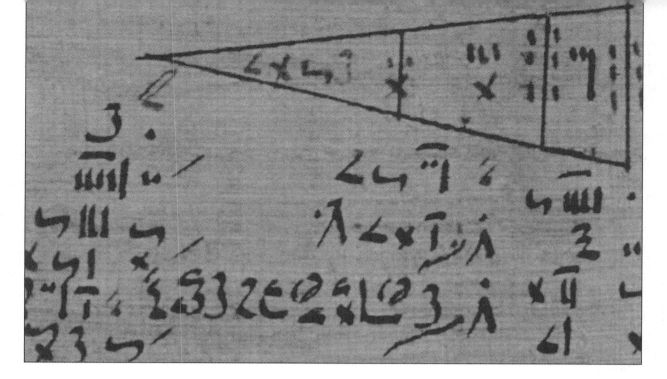

Detail of the Rhind Papyrus (Courtesy of the British Museum)

The digits in the answer cycle through the digits 142,857 in the same order. You might predict that the answer to 7 x 142,857 would have the same digits. Such a prediction would be wrong. Multiply 7 x 142,857 and see the surprising answer. See "Puzzle 1: Multiplying by Seven" at the back of this chapter to understand the reason for the unexpected result.

Some numbers are fun to play around with.

2 x 99 = 198
3 x 99 = 297
4 x 99 = 396
5 x 99 = 495
6 x 99 = 594
7 x 99 = 693
8 x 99 = 792
9 x 99 = 891

The left-most digit (the one in the 100s place) in the answer goes from 1 to 8 while the right-most digit (the one in the 1s place) goes from 8 to 1. Try to figure out the reason for the pattern. You can learn more by reading "Puzzle 2: Multiplying 99" at the back of the chapter.

Here is a puzzle that was in the oldest mathematics manuscript yet uncovered. It is problem 79 of the ancient Egyptian Rhind

papyrus written in 1650 B.C. by scribe Ahmes. A rich person had an estate with seven houses, each house had seven cats, each cat caught seven mice, each mouse ate seven heads of wheat, and each head of wheat would yield seven measures of grain. House, cats, mice,

For More Study:
Why the Arithmetrick Always Gives Three

You can discover why the answer to the puzzle on page 142 is always three, by using a letter, such as n, to stand for the starting number.

Add six to the number: $n + 6$
Double the result: $2(n + 6)$
Divide by 4: $2(n + 6)/4$
Subtract ½ of the original number:
   $2(n + 6)/4 - \frac{1}{2}n$
Distribute the 2 and 4: $2n/4 + 12\frac{4}{4} - \frac{1}{2}n$
Collect like terms and simplify:
   $\frac{1}{2}n - \frac{1}{2}n + 3$
Final answer: 3

$$\begin{array}{r} S\,E\,N\,D \\ +\,M\,O\,R\,E \\ \hline M\,O\,N\,E\,Y \end{array}$$

Here is an addition problem with letters taking the place of numbers. Solve the problem by replacing each letter with one of the digits 0 through 9. Use the same digit for the same letter throughout. In a puzzle like this, it is understood that zero is not allowed as the first letter in any of the words.

Hint: Start on the left side. M in MONEY must be 1 because even with a carry, the sum of S and M is less than 20. For the complete solution see "Puzzle 4: Send More Money" at the back of this chapter.

heads of wheat, measures of grain — how many of these in all did the rich man have?

Answer:

number of houses per estate = 7 houses

7 cats for each of 7 houses = 49 cats

7 mice for each of 49 cats = 343 mice

7 heads of wheat for each of 343 mice = 2,401 heads of wheat

7 measures of grain for each of 2,401 heads of wheat = 16,807 measures of grain

Total of all things on the rich man's estate = 19,607

Although you are adding unlike things, the final answer is 7 + 49 + 343 + 2401 + 16,807 = 19,607. Ahmes stated that he had copied the problem from a still older book, which proves that number puzzles were popular more than 5,000 years ago.

A very similar problem appeared in Fibonacci's *Book of Calculating* written in 1202: Seven women were on the road to Rome. Each woman had seven mules, and each mule carried seven sacks. Each sack contained seven loaves. With each loaf were seven knives that came with seven sheaths. Women, mules, sacks, loaves, knives, and sheaths, how many are there in all on the road to Rome? As in the Ahmes puzzle, each step is a power of 7, but in the Fibonacci puzzle there is the additional step of 117,649 sheaths, and the overall total is 137,256.

Later, the people on the road puzzle was turned into an English children's rhyme:

> As I was going to St. Ives
> I met a man with seven wives;
> Every wife had seven sacks;
> Every sack had seven cats;
> Every cat had seven kits [kittens];
> Kits, cats, sacks, and wives,
> How many were going to St. Ives?

Can you figure out the answer to the riddle? See "Puzzle 3: On the Road to St. Ives" at the back of this chapter.

Most people enjoy solving puzzles. The Bible contains many unexpected and delightful puzzles that increase the fun of reading the Scriptures.

Some of the psalms have an unusual design. Psalm 119 is especially elaborate. The first word in the first eight verses in the original Hebrew begins with *aleph,* the Hebrew letter A. The next eight verses begin with *beth,* the letter B. This continues through the alphabet to *tau,* the last letter.

Another number problem occurs in John 21:11 that tells of Jesus commanding Simon Peter to pull a net out of the Sea of Tiberias. The net held 153 fish.

Why 153 fish? What is so special about the number 153? To understand one possible answer, look at cube numbers.

A cube has length and width like a square, but it has a third dimension of height. A cube is like a block with all of the sides equal and all the angles right angles. Suppose you wanted to build a cube twice as big in each dimension using the smaller blocks. You would need four in the bottom layer and four in the top layer, a total of eight blocks.

Stacking three blocks along each side triples the size of the cube. How many blocks will be needed? The answer is 27. Each layer needs nine blocks, and there are three layers.

But you don't have to build the figure to count the number of blocks needed to make the cube. A cube with four blocks on each side would hold 64 blocks. This can be written as 4 cubed: $4^3 = 4 \times 4 \times 4 = 64$. Similarly, five cubed is $5^3 = 5 \times 5 \times 5 = 125$.

Look again at the number 153, the number of fish Simon Peter found in the net. This

Peter's catch of 153 fish

For More Study
The 3n + 1 Problem

Mathematicians often find a problem that is easy to state but difficult to prove. More than 2,000 years passed before mathematicians proved that the Greek problem of squaring the circle with straight edge and compass alone could not be done. Fermat's last theorem states that $x^n + y^n = z^n$ has solutions in whole numbers only for n = 2. However, proving the theorem resisted the best efforts of great mathematicians for almost 400 years.

Here is another easy-to-state problem that has not yet been proven. It is called the 3N + 1 Problem. Pick a number, divide by two if it is even. But if it is odd, then multiply by 3 and add one. Keep on doing this to see where it leads.

For instance, start with 6 (even)
Divide: $6 \div 2 = 3$ (odd)
Multiply by 3 and add 1: $3 \times 3 + 1 = 10$ (even)
Divide: $10 \div 2 = 5$ (odd)
Multiply by 3 and add 1: $3 \times 5 + 1 = 16$ (even)
Divide: $16 \div 2 = 8$ (even)
Divide: $8 \div 2 = 4$ (even)
Divide: $4 \div 2 = 2$ (even)
Divide: $2 \div 2 = 1$ (stop)

In every number that mathematicians have tried, the result is always one. However, no one has yet been able to supply a proof or find an example that does not end with one.

Try it with 18. See "Puzzle 5: For More Study — The 3N + 1 Problem" at the end of this chapter for the sequence of numbers.

number contains three digits: three, five, and one. Cube each digit. Three cubed is $3^3 = 3 \times 3 \times 3 = 27$. Five cubed is $5^3 = 5 \times 5 \times 5 = 125$. One cubed is $1^3 = 1 \times 1 \times 1 = 1$.

Now add the results: $27 + 125 + 1 = 153$! This interesting number relationship was hidden in the New Testament for centuries before anyone noticed it.

People of long ago had no television, newspaper or video games. They worked hard all day at their many chores such as tending sheep, collecting firewood, going for water, and harvesting crops. At night, they rested by exercising their minds. Sometimes a family member would pose a problem for the others to think about during the next day as they worked.

The Bible has puzzles such as Samson's riddle in Judges 14:14: He replied, "Out of the eater, something to eat; out of the strong, something sweet." You can find the answer in Judges 14:8, or read "Puzzle 6: Samson's Riddle" at the back of this chapter.

Some logic puzzles are intended more to be thought-provoking rather than having a real answer. For instance, suppose a village has but one barber. Some people cut their own hair. Others come to the barber to have their hair cut. The village passes a law that anyone who does not cut his own hair must come to the barber to have his hair cut. But if a person comes to the barber, then that person cannot cut his own hair. The question is this: "Who cuts the barber's hair?" Think about it and you will see the contradiction. If he cuts his own hair then he cannot cut his own hair!

Albrecht Dürer drew this portrait of himself at age 13.

Logic puzzles are still fun today. Here is one you can try. Because of an electrical power failure, a boy must get dressed in a dark bedroom. His sock drawer has ten blue socks and ten black socks, but in the darkness he cannot tell them apart. He dresses anyway. He reaches into the drawer to grab spare socks so he can change into matching colors later. How many should he take to be certain he has a matching pair? See "Puzzle 7: Sock Puzzle" at the back of this chapter for the answer.

Another logic puzzle is of the river crossing type. In this type of puzzle, a canoeist must cross a river with three things, but his canoe can hold only one thing at a time. How can the canoeist get a wolf, goat, and carrots across a river? If left alone, the wolf would eat the goat, and the goat would eat the carrots. See "Puzzle 8: River Crossing" at the end of this chapter for the solution.

Artists are attracted to the symmetry of math and the pleasing beauty of the golden ratio. They often hide mathematical symbols in their paintings. For example, Albrecht Dürer (DYOOR-er) grew up in Germany the late 1400s as Europe struggled out of the Dark Ages.

Dürer wanted to be an artist. However, his older brother died, and it became Albrecht's duty to learn the goldsmith's art from his father. After two years, Albrecht Dürer summoned enough courage to ask to study art. His father was unhappy, not because Dürer wanted to be an artist, but because his son had wasted two years in the goldsmith shop.

Dürer learned that his time had not been wasted. Delicate muscle control was needed to etch intricate designs in gold. He learned as an artist that making woodcuts required the same skill. The design was carved into the wood and dabbed with ink. Paper was pressed against the wood to pick up the ink. Several hundred identical designs could be printed from one wood block.

At age 19, Albrecht Dürer finished his art apprenticeship. Art at that time was usually of religious scenes to be put in churches or portraits of nobility to be hung in castles. Few artists drew nature scenes. Dürer was an exception. He painted watercolors of gentle valleys, cultivated fields, castles, and people going about their business. He drew hidden figures in his paintings to make them more interesting. He showed a mountain with a town at its base and a castle on its crest. He filled the scene with hidden faces.

Dürer worked for two years on 15 woodcuts that told the story of Revelation in the Bible. The final scene was one of triumph. It showed the apostle John looking at the Heavenly City while an angel locked Satan away.

One of Albrecht Dürer's most famous woodcuts is *Melancholia I.* Melancholia means loneliness and sadness. He did it shortly after his mother died. He filled it with artistic and mathematical symbols. A window in the background had four rows of four glass panes. In each pane, he placed a number from 1 to 16. The arrangement of numbers was unknown in Europe until Dürer showed it in his painting.

16	3	2	13
5	10	11	8
9	6	7	12
4	15	14	1

Dürer woodcut of the final scene of triumph from Revelation

The square has many unusual properties. Every row adds to 34. Every column adds to 34. The numbers along the diagonals add to give 34. Pick the four numbers at each corner (16 + 13 + 4 + 1), they also add to give 34. Pick the center four numbers (10 + 11 + 6 + 7), their total is also 34. Other combinations also give 34. How many can you find? The middle two numbers in the bottom row give the date, 1514, when Dürer made the drawing.

The squares are called "magic" squares, although there is nothing magic about them. Benjamin Franklin, the American printer, inventor, scientist, and statesman, was also an amateur mathematician. He became an expert at making magic squares. One of his had eight rows and eight columns. It had the same number of squares as on a chessboard and used the numbers from 1 to 64.

You can try your hand at making a number square by using the digits 1 through 9 in a three by three square. Each of the rows, columns, and diagonals should add to the same number. Eight different squares are possible. One solution is shown at the end of the chapter. See "Puzzle 9: Number Square."

The invention of the pocket calculator in the late 1960s opened an entirely new way of making puzzles. Several digits look like letters when the calculator display is held upside down. For example, type in the number .07734 in a calculator and turn the display upside down. The letters make the word HELLO. As another example, type in 37818 and then turn the display upside down. The letters make the word BIBLE.

Here is a problem to work on a calculator. The answer, when held upside down, shows the name of a four-legged animal that can change green grass into white milk. Find the product of the prime numbers 7, 17, and 23. Add to that answer the area in square feet of a field that is 201 feet on a side, the number of seconds in a day, and 186,000 miles per second (the speed of light). In adding these numbers, ignore the units. Now turn the calculator display around. What name do you see? See "Puzzle 10: Grass to Milk" at the end of this chapter for the answer.

Pythagoras teaching

Ten Greatest Mathematicians of All Time

In this book, we have looked at many great mathematicians. Who can resist making a list of the ten greatest mathematicians of all time?

The mathematicians on this list contributed to the progress of both mathematics and science.

Pythagoras (about 560–480 B.C.) was the Greek philosopher who studied the harmony produced by stringed instruments in music, proved the Pythagorean theorem, and discovered that π is an irrational number. In astronomy, he recognized that the bright morning star and bright evening star were in fact the same object — the planet Venus. He was the first to state that the earth was a sphere, although he believed the earth and not the sun was at the center of the planetary system.

Euclid (about 325–270 B.C.) was a Greek mathematician who wrote the *Elements of Geometry*. It became the standard textbook in geometry for 2,000 years, and thus became the most successful textbook ever written. He gave convincing proof that π is an irrational number, and he also proved that there is no largest prime number; that is, the number of prime numbers is infinite.

Archimedes (about 287–212 B.C.) was the greatest scientific mind of the ancient world. He discovered the law of buoyancy that stated an object in water loses weight equal to the weight of the water that it displaces. He figured the mechanical advantage of simple machines such as the lever. He calculated the value of π to an accuracy never before achieved.

Leonardo Fibonacci (about 1170–1240), an Italian, was the first great mathematician of modern times — the period after the Dark Ages. He is credited as helping to bring the revival of learning in Europe. He also wrote several books on mathematics, including *Book of Calculating*. He described the advantage of using place value and Arabic numerals for numerical calculations. He also stated the rabbit problem that gave the Fibonacci series: 1, 1, 2, 3, 5, 8, and so on.

Archimedes

Pierre de Fermat (1601–1665) was the French mathematician who worked on mathematical problems for his own enjoyment. He seldom published his results. He is also known for his irritating habit of only expressing his results in brief fashion without supplying the proof. One famous example is Fermat's last theorem in which he said that he'd found a truly wonderful proof but the margin of the book was too small to contain it. With Blaise Pascal, he developed modern number theory and the laws of probability.

Blaise Pascal (1623–1662) was the French mathematician who built a mechanical calculating machine. With Fermat he showed how to calculate permutations, combinations, and probability. He developed the arithmetic triangle called Pascal's triangle. He was a scientist, too. He showed that air pressure is less on top of a high mountain than at sea level. He developed the hydraulic press, a type of simple machine that used oil or other fluid to gain a mechanical advantage. In later life, he devoted himself entirely to his Christian beliefs. His books on religion are still studied today.

René Descartes (1596–1650) was a French philosopher and mathematician. He received a religious education and remained a devout Christian all of his life. In mathematics, he developed the Cartesian coordinate system that made it possible to express geometric graphs as algebraic equations and to plot algebraic equations as geometric curves. The combination of algebra and geometry became known as analytical geometry. It is considered one of the key developments in mathematics of the last 500 years.

Isaac Newton (1642–1727), English scientist and mathematician, is generally considered the greatest mathematician and scientist of all time. He invented the reflecting telescope, stated the three laws of motion, developed the law of gravity, and invented a powerful mathematical tool known as calculus. What is often not reported about him is that Isaac Newton spent more time studying the Bible than any other subject, and he wrote two books about the Bible. A short biography of his life is presented below.

Karl Friedrich Gauss (Courtesy of the Smithsonian)

Leonhard Euler (1707–1783) was a Swiss mathematician who spent most of his life in Russia and Germany. His father was a minister of the gospel and, in his early days, Euler thought about becoming a minister. He wrote more papers on mathematics than any other mathematician, an even more remarkable feat when you consider that he was totally blind for the last 17 years of his life. He invented many of the symbols used in mathematics, including using the Greek letter pi, π, to stand for the ratio of the circumference to the diameter of a circle. He was a devoted Christian family man who often had his grandchildren playing around his table while he worked.

Karl Friedrich Gauss (1777–1855) was a German mathematician and astronomer. Gauss developed a mathematical procedure known as the method of least squares. The method allowed scientists to predict the outcome of experiments even with incomplete or inaccurate data. Gauss invented the process when he was 20 years old. An astronomer had glimpsed Ceres, the first asteroid (minor planet), but lost the object when its orbit carried it into the glare of the sun. Using only a few observations and his method of least squares, Gauss predicted where Ceres would reappear. In mathematics, Gauss proved that every whole number can be represented as the product of primes in one and only one way. He developed a new type of geometry called non-Euclidean geometry. Gauss had an exceptional memory. Throughout his life he learned new languages to keep his mind active.

The above listing is by date of birth. It would be difficult to rank them in importance. However, the top spot belongs to the greatest mathematician of all time — Isaac Newton.

Isaac Newton is today remembered as the greatest scientific genius who ever lived. His discoveries about light, physics, and mathematics have changed the world.

Isaac Newton was born on a cold Christmas Day in 1642 outside the English town of Woolsthorpe. His father died before his birth. His mother was poor. She was afraid Isaac would not live through the harsh winter.

Newton did survive the first few days, and he grew into a healthy farm boy. He enjoyed making wooden models of clocks, wagons, and windmills. His models actually worked. At school, Newton made his best grades in Bible class. The Bible was his favorite book. He read it through time and again.

One morning in 1658, Isaac Newton awoke to a threatening sky. Dark, dangerous-looking clouds raced overhead. A few hours later, a powerful storm swept across England. Newton rushed outside to lead the animals into the barn and to bolt the doors. Lightning flashed and thunder rumbled. The wind howled and uprooted trees. Limbs flew through the air.

The vicious storm frightened most people, but not Newton. Its force fascinated him.

When Newton grew older, he attended Cambridge University. He paid for his room and board by doing chores for his professors. He polished shoes, delivered messages, ran errands into town, and served the professors their meals. Isaac studied theology and mathematics at Cambridge.

Isaac Newton and the famous apple

In 1665, the Black Death — bubonic plague — interrupted Isaac's schooling. The forced holiday gave him time to think deeply about the unsolved problems of science. In good weather, he worked at a study table in the apple orchard on his mother's farm.

Newton explored a dozen different subjects, including light, astronomy, mathematics, chemistry, and physics. When he tired of one subject, he switched to some other unsolved mystery of science.

For instance, scientists were puzzled by the fact that bodies on earth and bodies in the heavens appeared to follow different laws. Imagine a ball rolling across a perfectly smooth and level table. It rolls forward at a constant speed in a straight line. It only slows because of air resistance and the friction between it and the table. The moon, like a ball on a flat and perfectly smooth table, keeps moving year after year without slowing. However, the moon does not travel in a straight line. Instead, it circles the earth.

Why didn't the moon travel in a straight line?

Newton remembered the force of the wind. Although invisible, it turned his windmill. The force of the storm had uprooted trees. He concluded that a force acts upon the moon to bend its straight-line path into a closed orbit. What was the unknown force?

One day, an apple fell from the tree overhead and banged onto Newton's work table in

Newton's boyhood home

the orchard. He picked up the apple. As he held it, he noticed the moon, which had risen in the east.

Could it be, Isaac asked, that the moon and the apple are both subject to the same force of gravity?

Newton proved that gravity acts on both the apple and the moon. He showed that earth's gravity extends far out into space and controls the moon in its orbit.

Newton returned to Cambridge where he taught mathematics. Working off and on for the next 20 years, he proved that all objects attract each other according to a simple equation. The sun, moon, planets, even apples and grains of sand, are all subject to the law of gravity.

The law of gravity became Isaac Newton's best-known and most important discovery. Newton warned against using it to view the universe as only some machine like a great clock. He said, "Gravity explains the motions of the planets, but it cannot explain who set the planets in motion. God governs all things, and knows all that is or can be done."

Although Newton always looked for the easy way to solve a problem, he never let the difficulty of a task prevent him from tackling an idea. Sometimes he would go for days keeping a problem in his head. He would fill page after page with calculations.

He gave himself difficult tasks such as figuring the area under curves. On one occasion, he tried to measure the area of an arch-shaped doorway. Isaac replaced the area of the door with several rectangles that covered the shape of the arch. As Isaac divided the doorway into more and more rectangles, they became smaller and smaller.

Newton wondered if he could sum an infinite number of vanishingly small rectangles. Would the result give a meaningful answer? It seemed a contradiction. On the one hand, the number of rectangles increased without number. On the other hand, the size of the rectangles became so small their areas became

practically zero. His unusual solution to the problem did give an accurate answer.

Later, he developed the idea into a powerful mathematical tool that became known as calculus.

As the years passed, people came to understand the importance of his many discoveries. Newton received many honors. In 1705, Queen Anne knighted him, Sir Isaac Newton. It was the first knighthood for scientific discoveries rather than deeds on the battlefield or in government.

Despite his fame as a scientist, the Bible and not nature had been Isaac Newton's greatest passion. He devoted more time to the study of Scripture than to science. He said, "I have a fundamental belief in the Bible as the Word of God, written by those who were inspired. I study the Bible daily."

SOLUTION

1. The Road to St. Ives is a nursery rhyme with a trick answer.

2. Type in .37818 and turn the calculator upside down.

3. Samson proposed a lion and honey brain twister.

For more than 5,000 years people have found fun ways to enjoy mathematics.

Chapter 14 — Answers to Puzzles

PUZZLE 1: Multiplying by Seven. You discover that 7 x 142,857 = 999,999. The reason that the answer suddenly goes to all nines is surprising, but only because the source of the number 142,857 was not given. The number 100,000 divided by 7 is a repeating decimal: 1,000,000 ÷ 7 = 142,857.142857142857 . . . with the pattern 142857 repeating. Now 1,000,000 ÷ 7 x 7 = 1,000,000, so 7 x 142,857.142857142857 . . . would also be 1,000,000. However, if only the first group is used, then 7 x 142,857 = 999,999. The final one needed to roll the number up to one million is missing because the repeating part of the decimal fraction was not used.

PUZZLE 2: Multiplying by 99. The left-most digit (the one in the 100s place) in the answer goes from 1 to 8 while the right-most digit (the one in the 1s place) goes from 8 to 1. This result is easy to see once you think that the number 99 is 100 - 1. Multiplying by two gives 200 - 2 = 198; by three gives 300 - 3 = 297; by four gives 400 - 4 = 396 and so on.

PUZZLE 3: On the Road to St. Ives. Only one person is on the road to St. Ives. Instead of a large number, this is a trick question. The last line of the rhyme asks how many were going to St. Ives. The wives and the things they carried were going away from St. Ives. The narrator (the "I" person) is the one going to St. Ives.

PUZZLE 4: Send More Money.

$$S\ E\ N\ D$$
$$\underline{+\ M\ O\ R\ E}$$
$$M\ O\ N\ E\ Y$$

$$9\ 5\ 6\ 7$$
$$\underline{+\ 1\ 0\ 8\ 5}$$
$$1\ 0\ 6\ 5\ 2$$

M in MONEY must be 1 because even with a carry, the sum of S and M is less than 20. O must be zero because M is 1 and S must be 9 or 8 with a carry of 1. Either value for S forces O to be zero. Now that we know O is zero, S must be 9 because 8 is too small even with a carry of 1 to be ten.

The total of N and R must be greater than 10 to give a carry of 1; otherwise E plus zero and no carry would equal R, and two letters cannot have the same value. N is one more than E. Trying the remaining numbers in E + 0 = N and N + R = 10 + E shows that R is 8, N is 6 and E is 5. D = 7, E = 5, M = 1, N = 6, O = 0, R = 8, S = 9, Y = 2.

PUZZLE 5: For More Study — The 3N + 1 Problem. The sequences is 18, 9, 28, 14, 7, 22, 11, 34, 17, 52, 26, 13, 40, 20, 10, 5, 16, 8, 4, 2, 1.

PUZZLE 6: Samson's Riddle. Judges 14:14 tells how Samson came to think of the puzzle. He found a lion's carcass with a honeycomb from a beehive inside. Out of the eater (lion), something to eat, out of the strong, something sweet (honey).

PUZZLE 7: Sock Puzzle. One extra sock is enough. If the socks he is wearing match, he does not need the spare one. If his socks are not alike, then one will be the same color as the one he is carrying, giving him a matching pair.

PUZZLE 8: River Crossing. First, take the goat across and leave him on the far bank. The carrots will be safe left alone with the wolf. Return for the carrots and leave them on the far bank but pick up the goat and return with him to the near bank. Leave the goat and paddle the wolf across. Leave the wolf with the carrots and return for the goat.

PUZZLE 9: Dürer's Number Square. To get started, you should figure out the sum for each row, column, and diagonal. The numbers 1 through 9 sum to 45, and each row (and column and diagonal) must sum to 15 (45/3 = 15). One possible arrangement is:

8	1	6
3	5	7
4	9	2

The other seven solutions are merely rotations and mirror images of this solution.

PUZZLE 10: Grass to Milk. BESSIE is the cow's name.

Multiply prime numbers: 7 x 17 x 23 = 2,737.
Find area: A = L x W = 201 ft x 201 ft = 40,401 sq ft
Seconds in a day: 60 sec/min x 60 min/hr x 24 hr/day = 86,400 sec.
Speed of light 186,000 mi/sec.
Adding the numbers (ignore the units): 2,737 + 40,401 + 86,400 + 186,000 = 315538.

Bibliography

FOR FURTHER READING:

Adler, David A. *Roman Numerals*. New York: HarperCollins Publishers, 1977.

Caron, Lucille, and Philip M. St. Jacques. *Pre-Algebra and Algebra*. Berkeley Heights, NJ: Enslow Publishers, Inc., 2000.

Fekete, Irene, and Jasmine Denyer. *Mathematics*. New York: Facts on File Publications, 1984.

Howard, W.J. *Doing Simple Math in Your Head*. Chicago, IL: Chicago Review Press, Inc., 1992.

McSharry, Patric, editor. *Everyday Numbers*. New York: Random House Reference, 2002.

Rhodes, Bennie. *Calculator Word Games*, 2nd Edition. Milford, MI: Mott Media, 1981.

Schmandt-Besserat, Denise. *The History of Counting*. New York: Morrow Junior Books, 1999.

Vorderman, Carol. *How Math Works*. London: Dorling Kindersley Limited, 1996.

REFERENCE:

Asimov, Isaac. *Asimov's Biographical Encyclopedia of Science and Technology*, second revised edition. Garden City, NY: Doubleday & Company, Inc., 1982.

Hart, Michael H. *The 100: A Ranking of the Most Influential Persons in History*. Secaucus, NJ: Carol Publishing Group, 1993.

Kasner, Edward, and James Newman. *Mathematics and the Imagination*. New York: Simon and Schuster, Inc., 1940.

McKenzie, A.E.E. *The Major Achievements of Science*. New York: Simon and Schuster, 1960.

Morris, Henry M. *Men of Science, Men of God*. San Diego, CA: Creation-Life Publishers, 1982.

Ulam, Stanislaw. M. *Adventures of a Mathematician*. New York: Charles Scribner's Sons, 1976.

Illustrations/Photo Credits

Answers to Chapter Questions

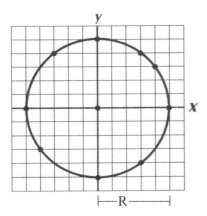

Chapter 1
1. F 2. F
3. So the calendar will match the seasons. Or, so the calendar year will be the same length as the solar year.
4. A 5. c 6. e 7. d 8. a 9. b
10. 969 years x 365 days per year = 353,685 days
11. 120 days, 72 days, 18 days, 6 days (divide 360 by 3, 5, 20, and 60)
12. divide the population by 1,461

Chapter 2
1. A 2. F 3. D 4. A 5. F 6. C 7. D 8. B 9. B 10. B
11. 6:30 A.M. The second watch began at 4:00 A.M. Each bell is ½ hour. Five bells are 2½ hours: 4:00 A.M. + 2 hr 30 min = 6:30 A.M.
12. Answer varies depending on actual heart rate. For 72 beats per min: 72 beats per min x 60 min per hr x 24 hr per day = 103,680 beats per day.
13. 8 hours. One way to solve the problem is to change to military time and subtract. 9:00 a.m. is 0900 and 5:00 p.m. is 1700: 1700 - 0900 = 0800 or 8 hours.
14. one hour later, 4:00 P.M. MST is 5:00 p.m. CST

Chapter 3
1. B 2. A 3. C 4. A 5. F 6. B
7. 5,280
8. pound
9. B 10. A 11. A 12. B 13. A
14. 60 inches, 5 feet. Multiplying 15 hands by 4 inches per hand gives 60 inches. Sixty inches is equal to five feet: 60 in ÷ 12 in per ft = 5 ft.
15. answer varies. Multiply weight in pounds by the conversion factor of 16 ounces per pound.
16. 5.499 miles or about 5.5 miles. Divide 29,035 feet by the conversion factor of 5,280 feet per mile.

Chapter 4
1. B 2. B 3. F 4. D. 5. T 6. B 7. B
8. B 9. A 10. D 11. D 12. F   13. C

Chapter 5
1. B 2. T 3. F 4. B   5. D 6. F   7. A
8. D 9. A 10. A 11. e   12. a   13. d
14. c   15. b   16. d   17. e   18. f
19. b   20. a   21. c
22. 140 tiles. The area of the room is 140 square feet, A = L x W = 14 ft x 10 ft = 140 sq ft, and each tile covers one square foot, so 140 tiles are needed.

Chapter 6
1. B 2. squares, square 3. A 4. D
5. A 6. e 7. d 8. c 9. a 10. b
11. b 12. d 13. a 14. c

Chapter 7
1. T 2. F 3. T 4. T 5. F
6. T 7. T 8. F 9. F 10. F
11. F 12. F 13. F

Chapter 8
1. B. 2. C. 3. A 4. A 5. A 6. C 7. B
8. A 9. B 10. F 11. T 12. B 13. C
14. 233 = 89 + 144
15. F 16. b 17. c 18. a 19. d 20. e

Chapter 9
1. B 2. B 3. T 4. T 5. F 6. T 7. D
8. C 9. B 10. A 11. A 12. F 13. B
14. D 15. a 16. g 17. b 18. e 19. c
20. f 21. d

Chapter 10
1. T 2. C 3. A 4. B 5. T 6. F 7. C
8. B 9. C 10. b 11. d 12. c 13. a
14. b 15. d 16. a 17. c

Chapter 11
1. A 2. A 3. C 4. B 5. B 6. C 7. B
8. F 9. e 10. b 11. a 12. d 13. c
14. 17,576,000 — Any one of 26 letters (A through Z) can be chosen to fill the first three positions. Any one of 10 digits (zero through nine) can be chosen to fill the second group of three positions: 26 x 26 x 26 x 10 x 10 x 10 = 17,576,000.

Chapter 12
1. B   2. F 3. T 4. F 5. T
6. three, ten, 0.477
7. D 8. B 9. T 10. B
11. central processing unit
12. A 13. h 14. c 15. d 16. f
17. g 18. a 19. e 20. b

Chapter 13
1. 9 2. F 3. A 4. B 5. C 6. T
7. B 8. D 9. F 10. F 11. D 12. B
13. B 14. A 15. C 16. T 17. A
18. About 3.8 seconds: 26,747 characters / 7,000 bytes (characters) per second = 3.821 seconds

Chapter 14
Answers to puzzles are on page 153.

Glossary

analog (AN-uh-log) — using moving parts to show changing information; the movement of one quantity measures another quantity, as the hands of a clock measure the passage of time.

calendar (KAL-uhn-dur) — a chart showing the length and divisions of a year, usually by days, weeks, months, and seasons.

celestial (suh-LESS-chuhl) — having to do with the sky or the heavens.

census (SEN-suhss) — an official count of the people living in a country, sometimes for the purpose of taxation.

citation (si-TA-shuhn) — a record of interest from information stored in a computer.

civilized (SIV-i-lized) — technically well-developed and organized; such as a society that lives under the rule of law.

digital (DIJ-uh-tuhl) — a display that uses digits such as 0 and 1 or 0 through 9 to show time, speed, or other quantity.

factorial (fak-TOR-ee-uhl) — the product of the numbers from one to a given number, symbolized by n!; 4! is equal to 4 x 3 x 2 x 1 = 24.

formula (FOR-myuh-luh) — a rule in mathematics that is written with numbers and symbols.

geometry (jee-OM-uh-tree) — the branch of mathematics that deals with the relations of points, lines, angles, shapes, surfaces, and solids.

mathematical operation (math-uh-MAT-i-kul op-uh-RAY-shuhn) — a process such as addition, subtraction, multiplication, division, raising numbers to powers or taking their roots, that follow exact rules.

nautical mile (NAW-tuh-kuhl mile) — a unit for measuring distance at sea or in the air; one nautical mile equals 6,076 feet.

number theory (NUHM-bur THIHR-ee) — the branch of mathematics that deals with the properties and relationships of numbers.

odometer (o-DOM-uh-tur) — An instrument that shows the distance a vehicle has traveled.

power (POU-ur) — in mathematics, the number of time to use a number as a factor in multiplication; two to the fifth power is $2^5 = 2$ x 2 x 2 x 2 x 2 = 32.

reciprocal (ri-SIP-ruh-kuhl) — a number related to another number in such a way that when multiplied together their product is 1; the reciprocal of ⅓ is 3 because ⅓ x 3 = 1.

semiconductor (sem-ee-kuhn-DUHK-tur) — a substance whose ability to conduct electricity is not as good as a conductor such as copper, but is better than an insulator, such as plastic; silicon is a semiconductor, and it is used in electronic devices including computers.

theorem (THIHR-uhm) — a statement that can be proved to be true, or a statement that is to be proven true on the basis of assumptions.

trigonometric function (TRIG-uh-nuh-met-rik FUHNGK-shuhn) — an equation that gives the relationships between the sides and the angles of triangles; a trigonometric function can be used to calculate information such as the flight of a rocket or the strength of a crosswind blowing across an airport runway.

Index

SURVEY OF SCIENCE HISTORY & CONCEPTS

Students will study four areas of mathematics, physics, biology, and chemistry, gaining an appreciation for how each subject has affected our lives, and the people God revealed wisdom to as they sought to understand creation.

978-0-89051-466-5

978-0-89051-552-5

978-1-68344-065-9

978-0-89051-412-2

978-0-89051-295-1

5 BOOK SET 978-0-89051-764-2

The Top-selling Exploring Series for Jr. High

by John Hudson Tiner and Gary Parker

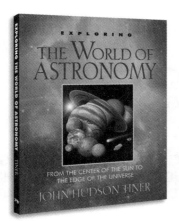

The World of Astronomy
ISBN-13: 978-0-89051-787-1

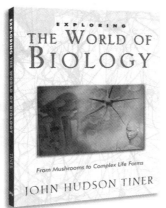

The World of Biology
ISBN-13: 978-0-89051-552-5

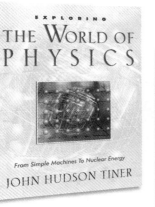

The World of Physics
ISBN-13: 978-0-89051-466-5

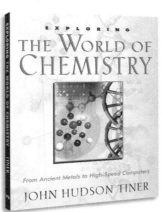

The World of Chemistry
ISBN-13: 978-0-89051-295-1

A great evolution-free resource tool!

This series provides a solid foundation of fact for each subject. Concise information, along with chapter questions, illustrations, and photos to emphasize the facts builds a strong foundation for understanding their respective topic from a Christian world view. Each book includes over 100 illustrations, charts, and photos along with key facts, terms, definitions, chapter review questions, and answer key.

- *Exploring Astronomy* investigates deep sky wonders and brings God's creation to life.
- *Exploring Biology* is a look at life, from the smallest proteins to complex life systems.
- *Exploring Planet Earth* uncovers the history of civilization, historical people, and places.
- *Exploring the History of Medicine* examines modern medicine from ancient Greeks to today.
- *Exploring the World Around You* tours the planet and its seven biomes.
- *Exploring the World of Mathematics* traces the history of mathematic principles and theories.
- *Exploring the World of Physics* captures the workings of simple machines to nuclear energy.
- *Exploring the World of Chemistry* investigates ancient metals to high-speed computers.

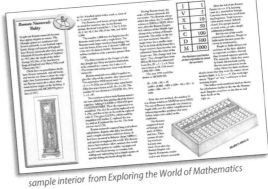

sample interior from Exploring the World of Mathematics

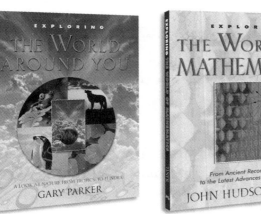

The World Around You
ISBN-13: 978-0-89051-377-4

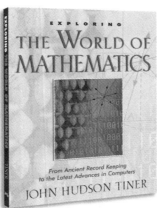

The World of Mathematics
ISBN-13: 978-0-89051-412-2

Planet Earth
ISBN-13: 978-0-89051-178-7

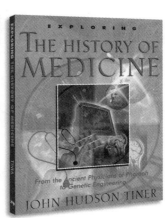

The History of Medicine
ISBN-13: 978-0-89051-248-7